Tracing the (Post)Apartheid Novel beyond 2000

Tracing the (Post)Apartheid Novel beyond 2000

Interviews with Selected Contemporary South African Authors

Danyela Dimakatso Demir and Olivier Moreillon

Routledge
Taylor & Francis Group

LONDON AND NEW YORK

UNIVERSITY OF KWAZULU-NATAL PRESS

First published 2024
by Routledge
4 Park Square, Milton Park, Abingdon, Oxon OX14 4RN

and by Routledge
605 Third Avenue, New York, NY 10158

Routledge is an imprint of the Taylor & Francis Group, an informa business

Print editions not for sale in Sub-Saharan Africa

British Library Cataloguing-in-Publication Data
A catalogue record for this book is available from the British Library

ISBN13: 9781032632193 (hbk)
ISBN13: 9781032632230 (pbk)
ISBN13: 9781032632247 (ebk)

DOI: 10.4324/9781032632247

Typeset in Sabon Ltd
by UKZN, South Africa

UNIVERSITY OF KWAZULU-NATAL PRESS

For uMama Lindiwe Stiebel and the 'four-leggeds' of the 'magic house' at the end of Pinsent Road. For your love, generosity, encouragement and warmth.

Contents

Acknowledgements

It would not have been possible to write this book without the support and generosity of many people across the disciplines. First and foremost, our gratitude and appreciation goes out to all the interviewees. We are grateful for the time they made for us despite their busy schedules. What started as a small project of a handful of interviews soon grew into a book project that we have been pursuing over the past five years, a time that fostered several friendships that have offered us so much more than what we had initially hoped for and imagined. Thank you for your wonderful contributions to South African literature. May it continue to grow!

Equally important were the guidance and reassurance shown to us by Professor Emeritus Lindy Stiebel from the University of KwaZulu-Natal. Her belief in this project from its very early stages has been a great source of motivation and her feedback on the initial book proposal and, later on, different parts of the manuscript have made the book all the better. Thank you for shelter, laughter and being a wonderful role model, both in academia and 'real' life.

Furthermore, our heartfelt thanks go to Jonathan Branch and Lena Schwarz, who transcribed the interviews for this volume. We know it was not always an easy task, what with the quality of the recordings not always being as good as you might have hoped for. Without you, the completion of this book would have taken even longer . . .

We would also like to thank many people from different publishing houses for establishing contact with various authors, many of whom we could not have connected with otherwise. Moreover, they were very generous in sharing review copies of several books that, at the time of our request, we had not had access to. We would like to particularly mention Fourie Botha (Umuzi), Ester Levinrad (Jacana), Colleen Higgs (Modjaji Books) and Adele Branch (University of KwaZulu-Natal Press).

And last but not least, a huge shout-out to the team at UKZN Press, in particular to Sally Hines, who despite the difficulties that the COVID-19 pandemic caused kept pushing forward and believing in this project so that it now, with more than a year's delay, gets to see the light of day at long last.

Reflecting on Anglophone (Post)Apartheid Literature beyond 2000
A World-Literary Perspective

Reconceptualising (post)apartheid literature beyond 2000
In a 2003 article, André Brink, commenting on the development of post-apartheid anglophone South African literature, asks: 'One question no South African writer can escape these days is: Is there anything left to write about after apartheid?'[1] Brink's answer – in stark contrast to the pessimism he harboured ten years earlier when he claimed that with the advent of South Africa's democracy, the country's authors had run dry of their main cause, that is, the anti-apartheid struggle (1993) – is a resounding 'yes' in two respects. On the one hand, he argues that, due to the disillusionment with the democratic government's endemic corruption, post-apartheid writers are not in danger of running out of issues to deal with any time soon. On the other hand, he posits that while the apartheid regime dominated the country's literary output both in its thematic and imaginary scope, in post-apartheid,

> the spectrum of choice has widened immeasurably. One of the first, and most obvious, discoveries made by the writers has been that apartheid, operating primarily as racial oppression, was never the only form of oppression the country knew. Other forms of domination and subjection were always operating in its shadows – the oppression of women, gays and all kinds of

---

1. See https://www.washingtonpost.com/archive/opinions/2003/12/07/imagination-after-apartheid/1e4b0891-ec53-4270-b576-8834856fb4b5/?utm_term=92dbf570f35 (accessed 16 April 2019).

minorities. And these territories are now being reclaimed with an incisiveness, a determination and often an exuberance that lends diversity to much of the new writing in South Africa.[2]

Brink corroborates his '(re-)assessment' by making reference to a number of texts from the late 1990s and early 2000s, such as his own novels *Imaginings of Sand* (1996) and *Devil's Valley* (1998), Zakes Mda's *Ways of Dying* (1995) and *Heart of Redness* (2000) and Diane Awerbuck's *Gardening at Night* (2003).

In a similar vein, Michael Chapman, in his and Margaret Lenta's essay collection *SA Lit: Beyond 2000*, argues that South African English literature after 2000 has, both quantitatively and qualitatively, departed from South Africa's literary output in the preceding decade (2011). To account for this shift, Chapman conceives of the label 'SA Lit beyond 2000' to describe 'South African literature in the transnational moment, "transnational" denoting the nation caught in movement – possibly transformational movement – "in-between" local and global demands' (2011: 1). He uses J.M. Coetzee's *Disgrace* (1999) as the 'jump-off point' for his proclamation of a new phase within post-apartheid anglophone literature, maintaining that *Disgrace* marks Coetzee's shift 'beyond his traumatised version of his home country' (2011: 1). Coetzee's works of the 2000s indeed move away from a predominantly South African focus to a more global range, both in terms of setting and theme. Nevertheless, Chapman rightly argues that despite its strong concern with innovation, South African anglophone literature beyond 2000 is still deeply invested in its connection to, and (continuation of) working through, the country's apartheid past (2011). While we second Chapman's delineation of a new phase within post-apartheid literature and focus on a fictional text in his theorisation, we would like to add the following works that have, in our view, significantly influenced South Africa's literary landscape after 2000: Phaswane Mpe's *Welcome to Our Hillbrow* (2001) as well as K. Sello Duiker's *Thirteen Cents* (2000) and *The Quiet Violence*

---

2. See https://www.washingtonpost.com/archive/opinions/2003/12/07/imagination-after-apartheid/1e4b0891-ec53-4270-b576-8834856fb4b5/ (accessed 16 April 2019).

of Dreams (2001). The influence of these two writers, particularly on younger black authors – such as Niq Mhlongo and Kgebetli Moele, who started publishing in the mid-2000s, and more recent 'newcomers', such as Perfect Hlongwane and Songeziwe Mahlangu, whose debuts, *Jozi: A Novel* and *Penumbra*, were published in 2013 and 2014 respectively – cannot be neglected.[3] If we consider Mpe's and Duiker's works in conjunction with the significance of *Disgrace*, the momentum of the shift within South African literature beyond 2000 thus becomes even more substantial.

In 'The End of "South African" Literary History? Judging "National" Fiction in a Transnational Era' (his contribution to Chapman and Lenta's book), Leon de Kock laments the decrease in 'detailed stocktaking' of more recent literary texts within South Africa's academia (in Chapman and Lenta 2011: 21).[4] The reason for this neglect, according to De Kock, is twofold. In accordance with Chapman, De Kock firstly highlights that the number of publications within South Africa's literary scene – and with it the number of new voices – has grown exponentially since 2000, making it increasingly difficult to keep abreast of the country's contemporary fiction. Secondly, he states that contemporary academics are more concerned with writing about particular themes, such as the importance of the city or the ocean, in post-apartheid literature. De Kock regards this trend of neglecting the larger bulk of texts in favour of a selected handful in order to feed the interest in, what he calls, 'sexy topics' as problematic (in Chapman and Lenta 2011: 20). According to him, this overlooks and marginalises texts that do not neatly fit into the thematic interests pursued by academia.

While Ronit Frenkel and Craig MacKenzie also acknowledge the rapid growth of post-apartheid literature, they do not share De Kock's

---

3. In Mzamane (2005), Mpe and Duiker's untimely deaths were commemorated, and their work celebrated, in a collection of interviews, tributes, essays and poems.

4. De Kock (2005) hints at this in his article 'Does South African Literature Still Exist? Or: South African Literature is Dead, Long Live Literature in South Africa', where he proclaims the death of a 'unified' (or singular form) of South African literature, as it was known under apartheid, in order to announce the birth of a more pluralistic form that reflects and acknowledges the country's diversity.

anxiety about the narrow focus of South Africa's academia. Instead, they celebrate the 'extraordinary range and diversity' of South African literature in what they call 'the post-2000 period' (Frenkel and MacKenzie 2010: 1). Frenkel and MacKenzie suggest the term 'post-transitional' as a theoretical framework to conceptualise the developments within South African literature from 2000 onwards. Conceiving of it as a temporal marker rather than an artistic movement (such as romanticism, realism, modernism, and so on), they describe 'post-transitional South African literature' as writing 'which is often unfettered to the past in the way that much apartheid writing was, but may still reconsider it in new ways. Equally it may ignore it all together. Other features include politically incorrect humour and incisive satire, and the mixing of genres with zest and freedom' (2010: 2). Frenkel and MacKenzie emphasise that while these characteristics are not, in any way, all-encompassing, they mark a distinct departure from apartheid writing, which they see as typically tied to resistance, realism, moral seriousness, race and expectedness (that is, in terms of plot). What Frenkel and MacKenzie label as post-transitional literature may, as Olivier Moreillon argues elsewhere (2019), display a broader range of both form and content. The realist mode, however, is still prevalent, despite the growing body of speculative fiction, and thus far from being obsolete. The work of Lauren Beukes, Charlie Human and Fred Strydom, for example, should be seen as a valuable counterpoint to the realist genre in that they offer alternative modes of writing and reading rather than being a competing genre outstripping the realist mode. South African literature beyond 2000 is, furthermore, by no means devoid of moral seriousness. While sexuality and sex, as well as moral dubiousness more generally, for instance, may have become more visible in literary texts, such as in Nthikeng Mohlele's *Rusty Bell* (2014) and *Pleasure* (2016), Niq Mhlongo's *Way Back Home* (2013) or Charlie Human's *Apocalypse Now Now* (2013), they serve to expose socio-cultural and socio-economic shortcomings within South Africa's new dispensation; the continuing importance of race, which Frenkel and MacKenzie see as sidelined, being one of them. Humour and satire are predominant features of South African literature beyond 2000. Yet, many authors whose early work is characterised by its humorous stance can be said to have 'sobered up' in their later writing. Zukiswa Wanner's *London, Cape Town, Joburg* (2014), Imraan

Coovadia's *High Low In-Between* (2009) and *Tales of the Metric System* (2014) and Niq Mhlongo's *Way Back Home* (2013) are indicative of this point.[5]

Even though the post-transitional is local in nature, Frenkel and MacKenzie ask for the concept to be understood within a more global framework. Based on Ashraf Jamal's contribution to their special issue, 'Bullet through the Church: South African Literature in English and the Future-Anterior' (2010), they suggest the post-transitional to be 'a zone of activity' and argue:

> As such, post-transitionality is Janus-faced, as one transitional experience is already present in another in some form but, as a signifier, it can be situated in, rather than bounded by, a timeframe. As a zone of activity and a discourse, it points to a broadening of thought and form that is context-bound but global in orientation as it attempts to frame South Africa in the present, as well as in terms of the transnational relations that connect it to the globe (Frenkel and MacKenzie 2010: 4).

Frenkel and MacKenzie see South Africa's growing visibility after the demise of apartheid within the global context as inextricably linked to the Truth and Reconciliation Commission (TRC). According to them, 'the spectacle of the TRC' faded fifteen years into the country's democracy, a development they use as a catalyst for their re-conceptualisation of post-apartheid South African literature (2010: 4). While we agree with Frenkel and MacKenzie that the importance of the TRC, with regard to South Africa's (re-)emergence within the 'global consciousness', cannot be emphasised enough and that with the end of the TRC hearings, 'the spectacle' and international media presence that came with them have indeed 'worn out', they fail to specify what this means on a more local scale, both with regard to South African politics and literary and/or cultural production. With the benefit of hindsight and with a focus on the country's literary output (paying attention to fictional texts), the

---

5. See Demir (2019) for a similar argument with regards to this shift away from humour and satire.

TRC has been both in the public eye and visible within literature far beyond the hearings, the Commission's reports, and the media attention that surrounded them, that is, far beyond what Frenkel and MacKenzie call 'the TRC spectacle'. Pivotal literary examples are Ishtiyaq Shukri's *The Silent Minaret* (2005), Zoë Wicomb's *Playing in the Light* (2006), Imraan Coovadia's *Tales of the Metric System* (2014) and – even if more implicitly – C.A. Davids' *The Blacks of Cape Town* (2013), Niq Mhlongo's *Way Back Home* (2013), Mongane Wally Serote's *Rumours* (2013) and Mandla Langa's *The Texture of Shadows* (2014). These texts speak to the continuing importance of the TRC as they all, in one way or another, confront issues such as the African National Congress's detention camps (Mhlongo and Langa),[6] betrayal within the liberation movement (Davids, Mhlongo and Langa) or the intrusion of the TRC hearings into people's quotidian lives (Wicomb, Serote and Coovadia). Such topics were sidelined during the TRC proceedings as they did not fit the overarching grand narrative of South Africa as the 'rainbow nation'. We thus concur with Aghogho Akpome, who criticises Frenkel and MacKenzie's conceptualisation of the post-transitional as a combination of both a fruitful discursive marker and, at the same time, a mere temporal marker along an overarching timeline of South African history. Akpome argues for the impossibility 'to separate post-transitionality from the discursive idea of "the transition" as little more than a set of discrete fleeting past events. Such an understanding consequently renders the post-transitional as a short-lived moment on a linear historical timeline . . .' (2016: 48).

In addition, we suggest that Frenkel and MacKenzie's conceptualisation tries to unify the country's 'entangled' socio-economic realities (both past and present), to borrow Sarah Nuttall's concept (2009),[7] in an overly simplistic temporal marker, which is an aporia. Such a

---

6. See, for example, Cleveland (2005).
7. Nuttall defines 'entanglement' as 'a condition of being twisted together or entwined, involved with; it speaks of an intimacy gained, even if it was resisted, or ignored or uninvited. It is a term which may gesture towards a relationship or set of social relationships that is complicated, ensnaring, in a tangle, but which also implies a human foldedness. It works with difference and sameness but also with their limits, their predicaments, their moments of complication' (2009: 1).

simplistic concept of time is surprising, considering that Frenkel and MacKenzie do position South Africa within the broader postcolonial context by means of Achille Mbembe's postcolonial theory. What they disregard, however, is that with the 'time of entanglement', Mbembe convincingly argues for the need for a multi-linear concept of time in the theorisation of postcolonial subjectivity in order to avoid overarching grand narratives and, instead, to account for the many nuances of co-existing (hi)stories within the postcolonial world (Mbembe 2001).[8]

Consequently, it is not unexpected that, in response to Frenkel and MacKenzie, Chris Thurman cautions against the use of the post-transitional. Firstly, he argues that the innovations of the country's more recent literary output are not significant enough to distinguish post-apartheid literature from what came before (Thurman 2010). Secondly, and more relevant to our argument, he poignantly remarks:

> How can there be such a thing as 'post-transitional literature' (which would imply that we have completed a transition)? Aren't we still in a process of transition from apartheid to something else? What is that something else? We have done away with legally enforced segregation, but we certainly cannot claim to be 'beyond' apartheid. Ongoing social, racial and economic divisions are evidence that even terms such as 'post-apartheid South Africa' are problematic (Thurman 2010: 91).

In contrast to Thurman, we see, alongside Lenta (2011), significant genre-related and topic-related changes in more recent South African literature. We agree, however, with Thurman's second premise. We think there is good reason for the claim to be sceptical of post-apartheid as a term in itself due to the country's ongoing socio-economic disparities (see, for example, Bundy 2014), but we would argue that the end of apartheid

---

8. While we fully support Akpome's critique of Frenkel and MacKenzie's concept at large, we find his alternative of a 'post-TRC literature' instead of a 'post-transitional literature' equally problematic as we ask ourselves whether Akpome's term, which he borrows from Shane Graham (2009) without elaborating on the basis and supposed usage, does not hold the same pitfalls for which he reproaches Frenkel and MacKenzie.

marks such a momentous event in the country's history that there is no way around 'post-apartheid' as a term, just as one cannot avoid the 'post' in the 'post-independence' of formerly colonised countries, 'post-Second World War' or, more recently, 'post-9/11'. Especially if embedded within a more global context, we contend that in the long run, the term post-apartheid will supersede any term attempting a categorisation on a smaller scale, which is what Frenkel and MacKenzie attempt with their concept. We therefore share Meg Samuelson's concerns about 'over-categorizing what remains an emergent, amorphous body of work' (2010: 113)[9] and David Medalie's (2010) hesitation to endorse the post-transitional, or any other concept for that matter, other than the broad category of 'post-apartheid literature', at least for the time being. This is why we also align ourselves with the usage of the purely temporal marker 'beyond 2000' as suggested by Chapman and Lenta (2011).

The continuing importance of the apartheid past in the post-apartheid present has been theorised at length by Derek Hook in *(Post) Apartheid Conditions*, where he posits: '[E]veryday South African experience is characterised by historical dissonance, by the continuous juxtaposition of forward- and backward-looking temporalities' (2013: 5). Basing his argument on Sigmund Freud, Hook calls this affliction of South Africa's post-apartheid present with its apartheid past 'apartheid *nachträglichkeit*' (2013: 185; original emphasis). In essence, apartheid *nachträglichkeit* implies a deferral of the apartheid past's impact on the present. Since the present is thus under a constant threat of the past, it is always a precarious one at best. Nevertheless, this precarious situation offers the possibility of a temporal oscillation between past and present, as the past can be (re-)visited and (re-)gauged. However, this prospect of the past's (re-)evaluation bears both risks and chances, as it might become a 'future past' (Hook 2013: 186–7). In its undesired form, such a future past will, for example, manifest in the form of restorative

---

9. Samuelson, even though not with the direct intention to theorise a new term, sees the 'post-transitional' as a new moment within post-apartheid South Africa when '"rainbow nationalism" increasingly drops its variegated visage in order to reveal its deathly xenophobic face' and a new place where '[t]he discomfiture or sense of stasis entailed in inhabiting the transitional margin is met by a desire to move on – to enter into a post-transitional state in which to create new structures of intimacy' (2008: 133, 134).

nostalgia, in other words, a form of nostalgia seeking a return to a lost home and the wish of its re-creation (Boym 2001).[10]

Using the term '(post)apartheid literature beyond 2000' is thus a compromise. On the one hand, we feel that it is paramount to acknowledge the qualitative and quantitative shift within South Africa's literary landscape since 2000. Hence the temporal marker 'beyond 2000' (Chapman and Lenta 2011), the strength of which lies in its 'contextual neutrality', that is, the fact that it is not linked to a particular historical event in potential need of later re-evaluation. On the other hand, the usage of the term '(post)apartheid' – and we follow Hook in putting the 'post' in brackets to account for apartheid *nachträglichkeit* – emerges out of our interest in a (more) 'distant reading' (Moretti 2000, 2013) of more current South African literature. In doing so, we follow the recent interest in Transnational Studies within South African academia, even if our analysis is carried out within the framework of 'world-literature',[11] and thus under slightly different auspices. Within the field of (South African) Transnational Studies, the work of various scholars comes to mind, such as Isabel Hofmeyr (2010), Isabel Hofmeyr, Preben Kaarsholm and Bodil Folke Frederiksen (2011), Lindy Stiebel (2016), Rachel Matteau Matsha and Lindy Stiebel (2017) and Stefan Helgesson (2009).[12] The consolidation of various attempts at tracing the developments within South Africa's more recent literary production and our suggestion to apply the term (post)apartheid literature beyond 2000 is, however, only one of two aspects that we would like to raise.

---

10. Boym understands restorative nostalgia as opposed to a reflective (or more critical) form thereof. While restorative nostalgia is tradition-oriented, totalitarian and nationalist in its tendencies, reflective nostalgia realises and accepts the imperfections in the act of remembrance and consequently is both of a more flexible and individual character and can be critical, ironic or humorous (2001).
11. We have to mention Jane Poyner's *The Worlding of the South African Novel: Spaces of Transition* (2020) here, which was published after the completion of our manuscript. Despite the similarities between the theoretic frameworks in Poyner's and our own work – we both draw on the Warwick Research Collective's conceptualisation of world-literature – we could not engage with her arguments here in detail, but intend to do so in a subsequent publication.
12. Although *Afropolitan Literature as World Literature* (2020) does not specifically focus on South African writing, this book might be of interest in the framework of world-literature and African literature within a global(ised) context.

In a next step, we propose a way of reading (post)apartheid literature that is a combination of the classic 'close reading' with a (more) 'distant reading', thus heeding De Kock's call for a literary stocktaking of (post)apartheid literature (2011: 21).

In favour of a 'distant close reading' of (post)apartheid literature beyond 2000

As mentioned above, De Kock criticises the lack of a broader engagement by academics working within the context of South African literature with a larger corpus of texts. In the concluding remarks to his essay 'The End of "South African" Literary History?', De Kock asks the somewhat sarcastic and rhetorical question as to who, apart from the judges of the country's literary prizes, 'is conducting a critical audit of everything written by South African writers in every given year and rating/evaluating it as well as making notes on it' (2011: 36). Besides the fact that the judges' notes are generally not accessible to the public, which De Kock identifies as an essential issue, there are, in our opinion, two further concerns here. We would argue that there are certain publications that are not entered for any of the country's literary prizes and therefore not considered, either because they are not submitted by the respective publishers or, more often than not, because there is an increasing number of self-published and independently published texts. This in itself already undermines De Kock's rather grand claim of an all-encompassing literary stocktaking. (Nonetheless, the literary prizes and their long lists and short lists offer a broad range of literary texts to newcomers and established academics working within the field.) Furthermore, we question the extent to which the judges have the capacity to critically engage with each and every entry and take extensive notes on them. We do, however, support De Kock's call for a need to review the methodological engagement with literary texts within the global/globalised context. He states: 'What we increasingly have, I suggest, is a "problem" rather than a "literature" and that problem remains, how do we best read the writing by and among South Africans, wherever they are, in the context of, and in relation to, the much larger world to which we have become integral?' (2011: 36–7). De Kock does not offer further theorisation on the matter, which, to be fair, is not his primary concern in the article. Nevertheless, the fact that he outlines this need as a 'problem' is an entry point to reformulating De Kock's concerns within the theoretical frame of 'world-literature'.

'World-literature' has become a thriving field over the last twenty years. The coinage of the term can be traced back to Johann Wolfgang von Goethe and is mentioned by Karl Marx and Friedrich Engels in their *Communist Manifesto* (1848).[13] With the world's increasing globalisation, particularly during the twentieth century, the access to, and interest in, literatures from nations further afield grew significantly. 'World-literature' became a field of study of its own in the late 1990s and early 2000s. According to the Warwick Research Collective (WReC), the interest in 'world-literature' grew out of the crisis of the Humanities in general, and literary studies in particular, and their respective veins of (periodic) 'disciplinary rethinking and reorientation', with both fields sharing a fundamental concern regarding the effect and relevance of 'globalisation' on cultural developments and production (WReC 2015: 4).[14] 'World literature', for the research collective, can thus be seen as *'the remaking of comparative literature after the multicultural debates and the disciplinary critique of Eurocentrism'* (2015: 4; original emphasis). Leading scholars within the field, besides the WReC, include Manfred Schmeling (1995), Franco Moretti (1998, 2000, 2005, 2013), David Damrosch (2003, 2009), John Pizer (2000, 2006), Christoph Prendergast (2004), Pascale Casanova (2007) and Emily Apter (2013).

Moretti, in his seminal but controversial essay, 'Conjectures on World Literature',[15] defines '(world) literature' as a problem, rather

---

13. For a concise overview of the concept's genealogy see Pizer (2000, 2006) for a more detailed account.

14. The WReC self-ironically states: '[A]cademics are rather given to pronouncing the fields or sub-fields in which they themselves work as moribund or in crisis' (2015: 3).

15. Chapman, in his article 'Introduction: Conjectures on South African Literature' (the introduction to the special issue for the 21st anniversary of *Current Writing* – the issue that was, in its revised version, to become the 2011 book *SA Lit: Beyond 2000*), makes a brief reference to Moretti to acknowledge the provenance of his article's title and a brief comment on the fact that Moretti's approach serves as a starting point for the special issue (2009). However, Chapman does not, as one might expect, further elaborate on the concept of 'world-literature' in relation to Moretti's 'Conjectures on World Literature' (2000), but instead opts for positioning (post)apartheid literature within the rhetoric of transnationalism.

than an object, in search of new methodological approaches to reading literary texts (2000: 54–5). According to Moretti, we need 'a little pact with the devil ... Distant reading: where distant ... is *a condition of knowledge*: it allows you to focus on units that are much smaller or much larger than the text: devices, themes, tropes – or genres and systems' (2000: 57; original emphasis). Moretti prompts scholars to abandon 'close reading' in favour of 'zooming out' of a single text and, instead, adopting a (more) 'panoptic view' of literature. He is well aware that this implies a loss in scholarly appreciation for an individual text in order to look at 'the bigger picture' (2000: 57–8). This requires a careful outline of what exactly 'close reading' and 'distant reading' entail.

In an attempt to define close reading, Jonathan Culler provocatively states: 'We don't really seem to have an antonym for *close reading*, which may be part of the problem. The most obvious might be Franco Moretti's "distant reading," but this is scarcely reading at all' (2010: 20; original emphasis). Since Moretti's approach disregards the individual text in favour of identifying larger patterns, such as the development of the novel as a genre across Europe or marriage patterns in Jane Austen's *oeuvre*, Culler further argues that seeing distant reading as the opposite of close reading 'would turn any sort of attention to an individual text into close reading' (2010: 20). Culler's comment on Moretti's approach should not be taken entirely at face value as it is used for dramatic effect in constructing his argument in favour of 'close reading'. Reaching a working definition of 'close reading' as paying particular 'attention to how meaning is produced or conveyed' in a text, which therefore 'involves poetics as much as hermeneutics', Culler then moves on to suggest a tentative typology of various forms of close reading, which, as the article's title suggests, displays different degrees of 'closeness' (2010: 22).

Moretti's 'distant reading', in contrast, certainly is a radical suggestion, one that could be considered to have been carried to extremes if one, for example, looks at his book *Graphs, Maps, Trees: Abstract Models for a Literary History* (2005) that seems to be reducing literature to statistical data. De Kock comments on Moretti's work as follows:

> Moretti's controversial advocacy of *not actually reading writers*, but taking a distant, conceptual-theoretical-historical view of them as part of a trendline (because there are too many of them to read in the quest to describe the arc of 'world literature') represents the acme of Readerly authority over writers. Of course, Moretti belongs to the Academy. He gets paid to put writers in their place, literally. It pays him to consign writers to categories, or in his fabulously disdainful book title, to *Graphs, Maps, Trees*, where 'distant reading' means writers become micro-points somewhere on a graph, a map or a conceptual tree (De Kock 2010: 111; original emphasis).

In De Kock's defence, he immediately relativises what, out of context, may seem an overly pointed critique of Moretti's suggested method. De Kock is aware that in an increasingly globalised world the growing abstraction, also within literary studies, is (in the long run) an inevitable development.

The approach has since been further developed, particularly with the advent of 'literary big data' and computational criticism in places such as the Stanford Literary Lab, which Moretti, together with Matthew Jockers, founded in 2010,[16] and within the field of Digital Humanities at large (Jänicke et al. 2015). Yet, we would argue that it is not a prerequisite to retain such a great distance for a reading to fall into the category of a distant reading. The usefulness of Moretti's approach, in our opinion, lies in the vertical axis that opens up through his proposed method. As Moretti's quote above suggests, it is the thematic focus of a particular study that will influence the degree of distance involved. We furthermore agree with Julia Flanders and Matthew L. Jockers in that rather than seeing close and distant reading as two incommensurable methods, they are two sides of the same coin, and distant reading is just as 'interested in the careful and sustained explication of detail', only on a different level.[17] Moretti and other scholars working within the field are hence invested in what we call different forms of 'close distant reading'.

---

16. See https://litlab.stanford.edu (accessed 16 April 2019).
17. See https://digitalcommons.unl.edu/cgi/viewcontent.cgi?article=1106&context=englishfacpubs (accessed 16 April 2019).

A statistical analysis of (post)apartheid literature beyond 2000 is, however, not our aim. In contrast to a close distant reading, we opt for a (more) 'distant close reading', where the 'distant', as suggested by Moretti, involves the engagement with, or reading of, a greater number of texts under the auspices of various thematic and, to a certain extent, formal aspects, as we show in the final section of this introductory chapter, though without compromising appreciation for the individual text and thereby maintaining a certain closeness in our reading of the texts in question. In order to do so, we follow the WReC in its theorisation of 'world-literature' as *the literature of the world-system – of the modern capitalist world-system*' and the concept's hyphenation in analogy to the term 'world-system' (2015: 8, original emphasis). The starting point for the WReC is, as for many scholars working within the field of world-literature, Moretti's landmark essay. Following Immanuel Wallerstein's world-system theory (1974, 1980, 1989, 2011), Moretti defines world-literature as anchored in the world-system and thus as:

> . . . simultaneously *one* and *unequal*, with a core and a periphery (and a semi-periphery) that are bound together in a relationship of growing inequality. One, and unequal: *one* literature (*Weltliteratur*, singular, as in Goethe and Marx), or perhaps, better, one world literary system (of inter-related literatures); but a system which is different from what Goethe and Marx had hoped for, because it's profoundly unequal (2000: 56; original emphasis).

The WReC appropriately reminds us of the fact that any description of the world-literary system 'as one, and unequal' leads back to the theory of 'combined and uneven development', such as championed by Friedrich Engels, Vladimir Lenin and, in particular, Leon Trotsky. The latter's work is based on his analysis of the socio-economic and socio-political situation in Russia at the beginning of the twentieth century and that of China in the mid-1920s. According to the WReC: 'The theory of "combined and uneven development" was therefore devised to describe a situation in which capitalist forms and relations exist alongside "archaic forms of economic life" and pre-existing social and class relations' (2015: 11). This, consequently, allows us to conceive of the world as consisting of many sub-systems within the larger 'world-system', all of which change simultaneously but not necessarily at the same pace.

It is a direct consequence of the WReC's inclusion of 'combined and uneven development' in their conceptualisation of world-literature that leads to their following Fredric Jameson's understanding of modernity as a singular and (globally) simultaneous event (2015: 12). In doing so, the WReC highlights:

> Modernity is neither a chronological nor a geographical category. It is not something that happens – or even that happens *first* – in 'the west' and to which others can subsequently gain access; or that happens in cities rather than in the countryside; or that, on the basis of a deep-set sexual division of labour, men tend to exemplify in their social practice rather than women. Capitalist modernisation entails development, yes – but this 'development' takes the forms also of the development of underdevelopment, of maldevelopment and dependent development. If urbanisation, for instance, is clearly part of the story, what happens in the countryside as a result is equally so (2015: 13; original emphasis).

There are, hence, three pillars to the WReC's world-literary theory, which they themselves succinctly summarise as follows: 'A single but radically uneven world-system; a singular modernity, combined and uneven; and a literature that variously registers this combined unevenness in both its form and its content to reveal itself as, properly speaking, world-literature' (2015: 49).

In contrast to the vertical component of Moretti's distant reading, the WReC's theorisation provides an additional horizontal flexibility, as their approach opens up avenues for investigating different (literary) centres and their (semi-)peripheries as well as their positions within the world-literary system at large. South Africa, for example, can be regarded as a centre as well as (semi-)peripheral. If one looks at southern Africa, one could argue that South Africa might be regarded as one of its literary centres due to its size and current global 'visibility'. Angola and Mozambique, for example, could be seen as further centres, but of the lusophone literary landscape.[18] On a more global scale, however, South Africa is more likely to be seen as a (semi-)periphery of anglophone literature since it 'competes' with centres such as England, the United States, Canada, Australia and New Zealand. This becomes particularly evident if one considers the origins of anglophone South African literature that lie in the late nineteenth century, with Olive Schreiner's *The Story of an African Farm* (1883) often considered to be the founding text (see, for example, Heywood 2004). Thus, anglophone South African literature begins some 80 years after what the WReC considers to be the starting point of world-literature at large, which they regard as the literary production of the last 200 years, taking the nineteenth century as its starting point. The research collective sees the advent of world-literature coinciding with what they argue to be the beginning of modern capitalism, without, however, failing to acknowledge its foundations around 1500 (2015: 15).

The WReC sees the novel as a fruitful entry point to assess the representation of, engagement with and reaction to (both positive and negative) the realities of the capitalist world-system. They maintain:

> [W]e will treat the novel paradigmatically, not exemplarily, as a literary form in which combined and uneven development is manifested with particular salience, due in no small part to its fundamental association with the rise of capitalism and its status in peripheral and semi-peripheral societies as an import . . . The peculiar plasticity and hybridity of the novel form enables it to incorporate not only multiple literary levels, genres and modes, but also other non-literary and archaic cultural forms – so that, for example, realist elements might be mixed with more experimental modes of narration, or older literary devices might be reactivated in juxtaposition with more contemporary frames, in order to register a bifurcated or ruptured sensorium of the space-time of the (semi-)periphery (2015: 16).

---

18. Stefan Helgesson remarks: 'English being the dominant language . . . anglophone literature tends to be absorbed into other linguistic communities, whereas the relatively weaker Portuguese has a much harder time being transferred to the anglophone world' (2009: 11).

In their view, it is the novel, as the archetypal literary form of modernism, that allows the formulation of tentative '(semi-)peripheral aesthetics' (2015: 72), which the WReC see as characterised by 'irrealism', a term they borrow from Michael Löwy (2007), as its most distinct feature. Irrealism, here, signifies the b(l)ending of 'ideal-type' realism, that is, the characteristics generally associated with the 'canonical' Anglo-American texts of the nineteenth century, and 'residual forms' from the (semi-)periphery, such as narrative fragmentation, the inclusion of frame narratives, or folklore, oral traditions and local dialects. Such irrealist components in texts from within the (semi-)periphery reflect the state of precarious experiences of postcolonial subjects in the postcolony (WReC 2015: 72, 76). Put differently, these irrealist modes become a form of textual resistance to the colonial centre.

This resistance to the colonial centre, the WReC argues, is particularly pronounced in literary texts from urban writers. According to the collective: 'Literature originating from (semi-)peripheral nations is very frequently produced by metropolitan writers who inhabit a "core" relative to a "periphery" within the (semi-)periphery itself' (2015: 55). This certainly holds true for the South African context in general and the (post)apartheid context in particular. Apartheid consisted of an entanglement of laws that had an all-encompassing reach from the national to the more local (particularly urban) and interpersonal. The apartheid regime, as Ivan Turok argues, aimed 'to fracture the physical form of [South Africa's] cities and disrupt the lives of black residents through forcing them to the periphery' (2012: 1). Considering the South African city's importance within the scheme of implementing the apartheid machinery, it is not surprising that the city, urban life and its influence on the individual subject continue to be major topics in (post)apartheid literature.

Despite the importance of (urban) centres with regard to the WReC's analytical endeavours, they caution:

[T]he face of modernity is not worn exclusively by the 'futuristic' skyline of the Pudong District in Shanghai or the Shard and Gherkin buildings in London; just as emblematic of modernity as these are the favelas of Rocinha and Jacarezinho in Rio and the slums of Dharavi in Bombay and Makoko in Lagos, the ship graveyards of Nouadhibou and the Aral Sea, the vast, deindustrialised wastelands north, east, south and west, and the impoverished and exhausted rural hinterlands (2015: 12–13).

Within the South African context, certainly for apartheid and the post-1994 era, we do not put our heads above the parapet by saying that while the rural is significant for the South African literary imaginary, the bulk of the literary output focuses on urban spaces. However, this is where our particular interest in the representation of the metropolis in (post)apartheid literature and its positioning within the global context is rooted. We are not the first scholars with this interest, though, as our discussion of Chapman and De Kock's work on this topic in the previous section shows.

Although not within a world-literary theoretical framework, Lenta, in 'Expanding "South Africanness": Debut Novels' (2011), is similarly concerned with modes of innovation, even if predominantly on a thematic rather than a formal level and within the (post)apartheid context, where the formal and thematic b(l)ending are concerned with a breaking away from the apartheid past, more than a resistance to a colonial centre. The underlying principle, however, is similar. In her article, Lenta discusses a whole range of South African debut novels beyond 2000 along the following six themes: (1) 'previously silenced communities'; (2) 'sex and gender'; (3) the 'mixture of languages', which Lenta sees as a distinct characteristic of works by young(er) black South African writers; (4) a 'writing back' to earlier works by local authors; (5) the *roman à thèse*, the focus of which is on a particular theme such that the text 'becomes a fictionalised argument'; and (6) an element of 'fusion' which Lenta understands as 'the fact that people of different ethnic communities are now free to know each other outside their work and to form what ties they wish' (2011: 53). All of these themes are concerned with the question of what makes a particular (post)apartheid literary text South African and thus deal with world-literary issues in the broadest sense. But themes (3), (4) and (5), in particular, are concerned with more formal aspects in an attempt to register a break away from previous writing that, in line with the WReC, might be labelled irrealist modes of (post)apartheid writing.

What renders Lenta's approach so fruitful is the flexibility between categories that allows for multiple thematic overlaps in a single literary text. Futhi Ntshingila's *Shameless* (2008), for example, can be regarded as both a rewriting of the Jim Comes to Joburg trope and engaging with Lenta's category of 'sex and gender'. With the novel's protagonists Zonke and Thandiwe moving from KwaZulu-Natal to Johannesburg, the novel reimagines the Jim Comes to Joburg trope from a female perspective. Once in Johannesburg, the two women pursue very different routes. While Zonke studies at the university, Thandiwe becomes a sex worker. The novel thus unveils two extremes of potential life paths of black women in the (post)apartheid metropolis. Another example is Charlie Human's *Apocalypse Now Now* (2013), which can be seen as a *roman à thèse* propagating the embrace and 'fusion' of different cultural heritages within South Africa's new dispensation. When Baxter, the novel's protagonist, begins to search for his missing girlfriend, he comes into contact with Cape Town's magical underworld where he learns about his mixed, magical heritage, and, in order to save both his girlfriend and the city of Cape Town, he has to reconcile the two conflicting magical lineages.[19]

Further 'expanding South Africanness'

As a continuation and expansion of Lenta's work, we suggest the following thematic fields: (a) the 'retelling' of particular parts of South African history; (b) nostalgia; (c) aspects of 'movement' in an exploration of newly found freedoms as well as confrontations with residues of past restrictions; and (d) aspects of dis-ease as an expression of dis-enchantment with the status quo. We will illustrate the importance of these themes in some of the novels by the authors interviewed for this book as well as other authors' works. Our suggested additional themes, together with the examples given, however, are by no means exhaustive.

The retelling of South African history

A first example of what we call retelling is Charlie Human's Baxter saga. Human's novels, introduced above, confront lesser-known aspects of the Second South African War (1899–1902), such as the legend of the Boer

---

19. See Moreillon and Muller (2016) for a discussion of both of Human's novels (2013, 2014), which uses Sarah Nuttall's concept of entanglement in connection with Melissa Steyn's observations of South African whiteness to illustrate how Human's novels renegotiate South African whiteness by endowing it with a distinctly (southern) African inflection.

prophet Niklaas van Rensburg, whose story is linked to Baxter's family history. The saga (re-)imagines or (re-)writes the legend and history within its speculative framework in that Baxter inherits the gift of clairvoyance from the Van Rensburg family. The possession of Baxter's gift is mixed with further magical and fantastical aspects. It is Baxter's hybridised status that poses moral and psychological challenges for him throughout the saga. Ultimately, Baxter's clairvoyance can be seen as a metaphor for the sought-after ideal of an inclusionary new South Africa, which, due to the novel's speculative character, seems to be depicted as more of a utopian desire than a realistic possibility.

Another example is Fred Khumalo's *Dancing the Death Drill* (2017), which retells the story of the sinking of the SS *Mendi* from the perspective of a young Coloured soldier called Pitso Motaung. It focuses on the experiences of the black soldiers aboard the SS *Mendi* (Pitso is the only mixed-race soldier the reader knows of), who were sent to France to support the British troops in the First World War. The novel presents the various characters' reasons for joining a war that was not 'theirs to fight' and the harsh treatment and racism that is meted out to them during their time in Europe. With this retelling, Khumalo's novel foregrounds another lesser-known event within South African history, re-embedding it into public discourse and thus commemorating the South African soldiers' struggles.

Lauren Beukes' *Moxyland* (2008) and its partial retelling of the history of Cape Town's District Six, Niq Mhlongo's *Way Back Home* (2013) and its retelling of the urban legend of Vera the Ghost, Imraan Coovadia's *Tales of the Metric System* (2014) and its retelling of various pockets of apartheid and (post)apartheid history, Fred Strydom's *The Raft* (2015), which can be seen as a retelling of human history at large, and Mohale Mashigo's *Intruders* (2018), which is a retelling of various South African township myths and legends, all fall within this theme.

Nostalgia

A first example of the theme of nostalgia in (post)apartheid literature beyond 2000 is Fred Khumalo's *Bitches' Brew* (2006), which nostalgically evokes Durban's township life of the 1960s and 1970s through the love story of its protagonists Lettie and Zakes. Aspects of nostalgia become particularly poignant in the portrayal of the shebeen and the figure of the shebeen queen, which conjure up the vibrancy and creativity of a bygone era, also famously depicted in the works of the so-called 'Sophiatown' and 'District Six' writers, such as Bloke Modisane, Nat Nakasa, Richard Rive and Alex La Guma. Lettie and Zakes' letters to each other, which are filled with (reflectively) nostalgic reminiscences, serve as the bedrock for keeping traditions of storytelling, among other things, alive to the present day.

C.A. Davids' *The Blacks of Cape Town* (2013) similarly sees its main character, Zara, reimagine District Six, its inhabitants and her father's role in the anti-apartheid struggle. However, while nostalgia functions as a stabilising element in Khumalo's novel, it has the opposite function in *The Blacks of Cape Town* and comes with an element of distrust, maintaining a facade of pretences and lies. As Zara digs deeper into her family history and her father's involvement in the anti-apartheid struggle, she is constantly forced to readjust her personal memories as well as her image of the people closest to her.

Further texts that deal with the theme of nostalgia are Imraan Coovadia's *The Wedding* (2001) and Mariam Akabor's *Flat 9* (2006), both of which engage with notions of nostalgia in relation to Durban's Grey Street community, and Rozena Maart's *Rosa's District Six* (2004) and Nadia Davids' *An Imperfect Blessing* (2014), which both focus on nostalgia in relation to Cape Town's District Six. The importance of nostalgia in (post)apartheid literature has previously been argued for by David Medalie, who reasons for a 'literature of nostalgia' (2010: 36), Nedine Moonsamy (2014), who speaks about 'Nostalgia of Contretemps' with reference to a number of texts published between 2002 and 2006, and Olivier Moreillon, who discusses notions of nostalgia in relation to aspects of place (and space) and 'shifting post-apartheid subjectivities' (2019: 31) in Maart's *Rosa's District Six* (2004) and Akabor's *Flat 9* (2006). The topic of nostalgia in (post)apartheid literature, however, has not yet been approached from a world-literary perspective, that is, on the basis of a large(r) body of texts and a comparative approach that maps out a specifically South African form of nostalgia, in contrast to other notions of nostalgia held around the globe. This approach also includes the analysis of more formal aspects, such as the texts' confessional mode, fragmentation, multi-perspectivity and non-linearity.

Movement

Two examples of texts dealing with the theme of 'movement' are Imraan Coovadia's *Green-Eyed Thieves* (2006) and *High Low In-Between* (2009). Both novels deal with the flow of criminal capital and goods within South Africa as well as on a global level. In *High Low In-Between*, for example, the confluence of the local and the global is particularly striking. The restricted range of movement of the novel's protagonist Nafisa is forcefully widened after her husband's mysterious and sudden death. Her subsequent investigation into the alleged murder leads to her discovery of an organ-trafficking ring and her own illicit past actions also resurface, with Nafisa then being investigated for tax fraud. Ultimately, the convergence of the local and the global threaten Nafisa's very existence and are thus exemplary for the global (as well as more local) threats on the (post)apartheid subject more generally.

Further possible texts that engage with this theme of 'movement' are Coovadia's *Tales of the Metric System* (2014), which can be considered a fictionalised 'walk through' apartheid and (post)apartheid history, his *A Spy in Time* (2018), a time-travelling tale that breaks all boundaries of the space-time continuum, and Fred Strydom's *The Raft* (2015) and *The Inside-Out Man* (2017), the former dealing with different forms of escaping restrictions in movement and the latter with self-restricted forms thereof.

Dis-ease

Notions of dis-ease can be found in Yewande Omotoso's *Bom Boy* (2011). The novel tells the story of Leke, who, when his adoptive mother dies from cancer, falls into a state of dispiritedness. He starts to aimlessly walk and drive around Cape Town, soon developing the habit of stalking people, stealing little things and visiting doctors under all sorts of pretexts. Amid his emotional turmoil, Leke finds himself prompted to read his biological father's letters to him, through which he finds out about a curse on his family. Confronted with his own multi-layered identity and his family's complex history, Leke is forced to confront the 'cancerous' past in order to free himself both from the family curse and his personal ailments. The theme of 'dis-ease' not only serves to unearth some of the innermost socio-historical complexities of (post)apartheid subjectivities, but also the spatio-temporal intricacies of the (post)apartheid city.[20]

---

20. Andrew van der Vlies (2017) similarly claims that there is a sense of disappointment discernible in more recent South African writing, focusing on texts by J.M. Coetzee, Nadine Gordimer, Marlene van Niekerk, Ivan Vladislavić, Ingrid Winterbach, Zoë Wicomb, Songeziwe Mahlangu and Masande Ntshanga.

Johan van Wyk's novella *Man Bitch* (2006), in turn, is an unapologetic chronicle of the sexual encounters and failing and failed relationships between the first-person narrator and seven black prostitutes. The narrative, as Moreillon argues (2019), leads the reader through an increasingly erratic succession of snapshots of the narrator's self-imposed exile in Durban's red-light district. The further the narrative progresses, the more the protagonist's surreal perception of the neighbourhood clashes with the fictional(ised) reality. All interracial relationships the protagonist has fail, not least due to his abandonment neurosis, which can be seen as the protagonist's attempt to find his place within post-apartheid South Africa and a manifestation of white anxiety. Overall, the increasing eroticisation and fetishisation of the black women reflect the protagonist's (and by implication the country's) inability (to want) to see the continuing role of race and white privilege.[21]

Further texts that fall within this theme are Nthikeng Mohlele's *The Scent of Bliss* (2008), *Small Things* (2013), *Rusty Bell* (2014) and *Pleasure* (2016); Lauren Beukes' *The Shining Girls* (2013) and *Broken Monsters* (2014); Mohale Mashigo's *The Yearning* (2016); and Yewande Omotoso's *The Woman Next Door* (2016).

Consolidating theme and form

This is, of course, but a 'fractional stocktaking' of (post)apartheid literature beyond 2000 and one that primarily focuses on thematic features. In line with the WReC, we would like to think through theme in conjunction with form. Many of the listed themes so far, both Lenta's as well as our own, lend themselves to an intersectional analysis of theme and form. Such a cross-sectional approach is not new and has previously been adopted by other scholars within South African academia, even without the aim of a literary inventory or a specifically world-literary approach – the representation and function of trauma in (post)apartheid literature being one prominent example. Here, Pumla Gobodo-Madikizela and Chris van der Merwe's *Memory, Narrative and Forgiveness: Perspectives on the Unfinished Journeys of the Past* (2009), Shane Graham's *South African Literature after the*

---

21. See Visagie (2005), McNulty (2005), Nkosi (2001) and Stiebel and Steffen (2014) for a somewhat more optimistic reading of the novella.

Truth Commission: Mapping Loss (2009) as well as Rajendra Chetty and Jaspal K. Singh's *Trauma, Resistance, Reconstruction in Post–1994 South African Writing* (2010) come to mind. Further thematic fields with a crossover between form and theme are life-writing, crime fiction and Indian Ocean Studies.

We will demonstrate the possibility of dis-ease as a theme in connection to form on the basis of Perfect Hlongwane's *Jozi: A Novel* (2013) and Niq Mhlongo's *Way Back Home* (2013). In doing so, we will consider two different aspects that many (post)apartheid novels beyond 2000 share: (a) a fragmented, non-linear narrative structure (often from multiple perspectives); and (b) the collapse of space and time (often occurring in the form of dream sequences or surreal intrusions).

As we have argued elsewhere (Demir, Moreillon and Muller 2015), the protagonist Frank's mental instability in Hlongwane's novel, *Jozi*, is mirrored in the book's fragmented and at times disparate and incoherent narrative structure. Frank's story is told from three different perspectives. At the outset of the novel, Frank is the first-person narrator. This changes during the novel when the narrative voice shifts from first to third person, with Frank as the 'focaliser'. The third perspective is somewhat more complicated. In a narrative largely reflecting Frank's vantage point, readers follow the story of Frank's 'opposite [twin] of his messed-up self' (Hlongwane 2010: 51). Frank's twin personality is his 'friend the poet' (2010: 1), who seems to be an entirely different person in the beginning of the novel. However, it becomes clear that the poet is, in fact, Frank's alter ego. These multiple narrative perspectives reflect not only the protagonist's unstable subjectivity and his mental health, but also the precariousness of a life spent within South Africa's new dispensation. This precariousness, on another level, finds expression in the text's b(l)ending of elements of a classic five-act play with prose elements. On the one hand, the novel consists of five chapters following the classic dramatic structure. On the other hand, the novel is written in prose and, besides its conventional novelistic style, also includes diary reflections and social commentary in the form of article drafts that Frank/the poet writes. The text's genre b(l)ending, similar to the narrative multi-perspectivity, demonstrates the protagonist's dis-eased state of mind and perhaps also the shifts and changes in (post)apartheid Johannesburg itself. Frank is ultimately unable to adapt to the fast-paced capitalist lifestyle in the city and falls victim to its criminal underbelly.

The narrative, however, gives no answer to the question as to whether it is the 'Janus-faced' Johannesburg that makes Frank/the poet ill or whether it is his dis-eased state of mind that makes it impossible for him to fit into a globalised (post)apartheid Johannesburg.

Mhlongo's *Way Back Home* (2013), on the other hand, tells the story of Kimathi, a former uMkhonto we Sizwe (MK) soldier, who was born in exile. During his time at a camp in Angola, Kimathi falls in love with Senami, one of his female comrades. Unwilling to accept Senami's refusal of his sexual advances, he tortures, rapes and kills her. After the end of apartheid, Kimathi returns to South Africa and becomes a successful businessperson, but his past catches up with him. The interconnectedness between the past and the present is also reflected on a narratological level. The novel's main narrative strand, predominantly set in Johannesburg in 2007, is frequently interrupted by a second narrative strand that focuses on Kimathi and Senami's MK past in Angola. This second narrative often disrupts Kimathi's present in the form of dreamlike sequences, which highlight Kimathi's post-traumatic stress and the resulting bipolar disorder. From the very beginning, readers are thus faced with a space/time overlap of past and present. As Kimathi's mental health deteriorates, the unrest of Senami's dead soul becomes ever more acute. Senami's ghost appears to Kimathi in various forms and instances, leading to his repeated hospitalisation. Since Western medicine does not alleviate Kimathi's illness, he seeks help from a sangoma. The initial space/time overlap ultimately culminates in a space/time collapse. On the sangoma's recommendation, Kimathi and Senami's parents travel to Angola, where Senami's body is believed to be buried, in order to put her spirit to rest. On the way to Angola, the past haunts Kimathi in ever-more erratic dream sequences (reflected in the decreasing length of chapters), revealing the terrible deeds he has committed both in the present and the past. It is in Angola that the two narrative strands collapse and it is with this spatio-temporal breakdown that Senami's spirit can be freed and that her parent's process of mourning can be initiated. At the same time, this spatio-temporal collapse symbolises Kimathi's ultimate mental breakdown, which leads to his suicide. The novel's narrative complexity, in connection with Kimathi's ill health and suicide, reflects the resurfacing of buried and repressed parts of the armed anti-apartheid struggle and the toll they took, and continue to take, on (post)apartheid subjects as well as the dis-enchantment with the struggle movement.

While we started out by considering dis-ease as an expression of dis-enchantment and a feeling of a deeply ingrained stagnation, hopelessness and the end of a (better) future, the matter proves to be more complex. The two brief examples we have given, particularly the idea of a collapse of space and time, show that the boundaries between illness and healing are more fluid than we had anticipated.

Here we would like to return to the WReC's observations on irrealism and state that these two texts can be considered as irrealist texts from an urban centre within the South African (semi-)periphery. They both describe how the protagonists, for different reasons, find themselves on the margins. The irrealist form is thereby a reflection of their resistance to any easy assimilation and categorisation within the (post)apartheid status quo in particular and in relation to (post)apartheid subjectivities' positioning within the capitalist world-system more generally. Hlongwane and Mhlongo's novels – and many others, such as K. Sello Duiker's *Thirteen Cents* (2000) and *The Quiet Violence of Dreams* (2001), Nthikeng Mohlele's *Pleasure* (2016), Songeziwe Mahlangu's *Penumbra* (2014), Nakhane Touré's *Piggy Boy's Blues* (2015), Mishka Hoosen's *Call It a Difficult Night* (2015) and Mohale Mashigo's *The Yearning* (2016) – show how the collapse of space and time and representations of dis-ease are linked and how they seem to induce a (literary) catharsis that becomes prominent in (post)apartheid literature beyond 2000.

Structure of the book

It is against the backdrop of our discussion of the qualitative and quantitative shifts within (post)apartheid literature beyond 2000 and our attempt to thematically and, to a certain extent, formally cluster the country's vast literary production, as outlined above, that we step beyond pure literary theory and analysis by allowing a selection of authors to speak and assess the literary landscape of which they form a part and which they co-create.

The book consists of fourteen interviews that were conducted between January 2015 and February 2019. Each interview is preceded by a short author portrait detailing the circumstances surrounding our meeting with the writers as well as a short insight into both their educational background and private life. We hope that these vignettes might provide a glimpse 'behind the scenes' and bring the person behind the books a little closer, something that might be of particular interest to a wider readership. The final section of the portrait is dedicated to a listing and summary of each individual author's works.

The interviews themselves are comprised of five standard questions:

- How important is the representation of place in your work?
- Which aspects of home, belonging and community do you engage with in your fiction?
- Although South Africa is recognised as having one of the most liberal constitutions in the world, its society is still largely conservative. What taboos do you think have yet to find their way into contemporary South African literature?
- In your opinion, what might be some of the new voices or perspectives we can see developing in South African literature?
- Which different genres do you see becoming more prominent as an attempt to break away from realist conventions?

The remaining questions focus more specifically on the individual author's *oeuvre*. There will, however, be certain overlapping questions, for example, for the writers working within the genre of speculative fiction, whom we asked about their reasons for choosing to work within this genre, or with authors whose work shows certain thematic overlaps, such as identity, memory, history, movement and music.

Although some of the selected authors have published short stories, the focus of our interest lies in the (post)apartheid novel and on authors whose debut novels were published in or since 2000. This is in line with the WReC, which sees the novel as the paradigmatic literary form of the capitalist world-system and, as such, a productive entry point into a discussion of various literary centres and their (semi-)peripheries as well as their development from a world-literary perspective, as we argued in detail in the previous section. Due to the continuing interest in the city, both with regard to the country's literary production as well as South Africa's academia, we have opted for novels set in Johannesburg, Cape Town and Durban, South Africa's three biggest metropolitan centres. As Stiebel asserts: 'Johannesburg is the economic powerhouse, an urban edgy metropolis; Cape Town is the tourist destination, a geographically beautiful city with a cosmopolitan, even "European" feel; Durban is the Cinderella city – subtropical, slower, spread out' (2013: 227).

In an attempt to create a representative sample, we have selected both established authors (those with three or more publications) as well as newer voices (writers with one or two publications). All but three of the chosen authors have also either been shortlisted for, or have won, one or more local or international literary awards. Those three authors who do not meet this particular criterion have been chosen due to their work's intrinsic interest. In contrast to Johannesburg and Cape Town, which have served as settings for numerous literary works in (post)apartheid literature, the number of authors opting for Durban and its surrounds as a backdrop for their works of fiction is considerably smaller. Futhi Ntshingila and Mariam Akabor are two authors whose works focus on Durban. While Ntshingila's work may not have been shortlisted for any literary prizes, her second novel, *Do Not Go Gentle* (2014), was longlisted for the 2015 Barry Ronge Fiction Prize. Furthermore, it was translated into Portuguese in 2016 and was released in North America by Catalyst Press in 2018, which points to her work's growing significance both in South Africa and abroad. Mariam Akabor, in contrast, has neither won any literary prizes nor has she yet been longlisted or shortlisted. However, she is one of the so-called Grey Street writers who are important for Durban's literary history. These writers' works offer a documentation (both fictional and non-fictional) of the (former) hub of South Africa's Indian population (McNulty and Stiebel 2017).[22] Alongside Imraan Coovadia, Akabor is one of two younger authors who engage with this specific area and history of Durban. It is particularly her shift towards the younger generation of Indian South Africans, her critical stance regarding their needs within post-apartheid society and the intergenerational conflicts within the community that warrant her inclusion in this volume. As with Akabor, Charlie Human has not received any formal literary accolades. Yet, his work forms an integral part of South Africa's growing body of speculative fiction. His novels can be seen as a re-negotiation of white subjectivity within South Africa's new dispensation (Moreillon and Muller 2016). It is the specifically local tone and setting of his novels that contribute to ongoing conversations about critical whiteness within the South African context. The optioning of his first novel, *Apocalypse Now Now* (2013), for film and the translation of his novels into Afrikaans, Italian, Czech,

---

22. See also http://www.literarytourism.co.za/index.php?option=com_content& view=article&id=68:grey-street-writers-trail&catid=16:trails&Itemid=30 (accessed 16 April 2019).

Turkish, German and Japanese further illustrate the success of Human's work, both locally and internationally

Besides our five core questions listed above, which we discuss in detail in our conclusion, we refrain from commenting on the interviews as we would like the authors to speak for themselves and, indirectly, to each other as, time and again, different authors make reference to other writers who were interviewed for this book as well as other authors who were not included in our volume. Unavoidably, our selection is far from comprehensive and, despite the criteria we have outlined, necessarily always guided by our academic interest and personal taste. We hope this book will reach academics and students as well as all those interested in (post)apartheid literature beyond 2000, both locally and internationally.

References

Akabor, Mariam. 2006. *Flat 9*. Durban: umSinsi Press

Akpome, Aghogho. 2016. 'Towards a Reconceptualization of "(Post)Transitional" South African Cultural Expression'. *English in Africa* 43(2): 39–62.

Apter, Emily. 2013. *Against World Literature: On the Politics of Untranslatability*. London: Verso.

Awerbuck, Diane. 2003. *Gardening at Night*. Cape Town: Umuzi.

Beukes, Lauren. 2008. *Moxyland*. Johannesburg: Jacana Media.

———. 2013. *The Shining Girls*. Cape Town: Umuzi.

———. 2014. *Broken Monsters*. Cape Town: Umuzi.

Boym, Svetlana. 2001. *The Future of Nostalgia*. New York: Basic Books.

Brink, André. 1993. 'To Re-Imagine Our History'. *Weekly Mail Review/Books*, 24–30 September.

———. 1996. *Imaginings of Sand*. London: Secker & Warburg.

———. 1998. *Devil's Valley*. San Diego: Harcourt Brace and Company.

Bundy, Colin. 2014. *Short-Changed? South Africa since Apartheid*. Johannesburg: Jacana Media.

Casanova, Pascale. 2007. *The World Republic of Letters*. Cambridge, MA: Harvard University Press.

Chapman, Michael. 2009. 'Introduction: Conjectures on South African Literature'. *Current Writing: Text and Reception in Southern Africa* 21(1–2): 1–23.

———. 2011. 'Introduction: SA Lit beyond 2000?', in *SA Lit: Beyond 2000*, edited by Michael Chapman and Margaret Lenta, 1–18. Pietermaritzburg: University of KwaZulu-Natal Press.

Chapman, Michael and Margaret Lenta (eds). 2011. *SA Lit: Beyond 2000*. Pietermaritzburg: University of KwaZulu-Natal Press.

Chetty, Rajendra and Jaspal K. Singh (eds). 2010. *Trauma, Resistance, Reconstruction in Post–1994 South African Writing*. New York: Peter Lang.

Cleveland, Todd. 2005. '"We Still Want the Truth": The ANC's Angolan Detention Camps and Post-Apartheid Memory'. *Comparative Studies of South Asia, Africa and the Middle East* 25(1): 63–78.

Coetzee, J.M. 1999. *Disgrace*. London: Secker & Warburg.

Coovadia, Imraan. 2001. *The Wedding*. New York: Picador.

———. 2006. *Green-Eyed Thieves*. Cape Town: Umuzi.

———. 2009. *High Low In-Between*. Cape Town: Umuzi.

———. 2014. *Tales of the Metric System*. Cape Town: Umuzi.

———. 2018. *A Spy in Time*. Cape Town: Umuzi.

Culler, Jonathan. 2010. 'The Closeness of Close Reading'. *ADE Bulletin* 149: 20–5.

Damrosch, David. 2003. *What is World Literature?* Princeton, NJ: Princeton University Press.

———. 2009. *How to Read World Literature*. Oxford: Wiley-Blackwell.

Davids, C.A. 2013. *The Blacks of Cape Town*. Cape Town: Modjaji Books.

Davids, Nadia. 2014. *An Imperfect Blessing*. Cape Town: Umuzi.

De Kock, Leon. 2005. 'Does South African Literature Still Exist? Or: South African Literature is Dead, Long Live Literature in South Africa'. *English in Africa* 32(2): 69–83.

———. 2010. 'Notes on the Construction of "South African English Writing"'. *English Studies in Africa* 53(1): 108–12.

———. 2011. 'The End of "South African" Literary History? Judging "National" Fiction in a Transnational Era', in *SA Lit: Beyond 2000*, edited by Michael Chapman and Margaret Lenta, 19–49. Pietermaritzburg: University of KwaZulu-Natal Press.

Demir, Danyela. 2019. *Reading Loss: Post-Apartheid Melancholia in Contemporary South African Novels*. Berlin: Logos Verlag.

Demir, Danyela, Olivier Moreillon and Alan Muller. 2015. 'In Search of a "Rock Star": Commemorating Kabelo Sello Duiker's Life and Work Ten Years on'. *Current Writing: Text and Reception in Southern Africa* 27(1): 26–37.

Duiker, K. Sello. 2000. *Thirteen Cents*. Cape Town: David Philip.

———. 2001. *The Quiet Violence of Dreams*. Cape Town: Kwela Books.

Frenkel, Ronit and Craig MacKenzie. 2010. 'Conceptualizing "Post-Transitional" South African Literature in English'. *English Studies in Africa* 53(1): 1–10.

Gobodo-Madikizela, Pumla and Chris van der Merwe (eds). 2009. *Memory, Narrative and Forgiveness: Perspectives on the Unfinished Journeys of the Past*. Newcastle upon Tyne: Cambridge Scholars Publishing.

Graham, Shane. 2009. *South African Literature after the Truth Commission: Mapping Loss*. New York: Palgrave Macmillan.

Helgesson, Stefan. 2009. *Transnationalism in Southern African Literature: Modernists, Realists, and the Inequality of Print Culture*. New York: Routledge.

Heywood, Christopher. 2004. *A History of South African Literature*. Cambridge: Cambridge University Press.

Hlongwane, Perfect. 2013. *Jozi: A Novel*. Pietermaritzburg: University of KwaZulu-Natal Press.

Hodapp, James (ed.). 2020. *Afropolitan Literature as World Literature*. New York: Bloomsbury Academic.

Hofmeyr, Isabel. 2010. 'Universalizing the Indian Ocean'. *PMLA* 125(3): 721–9.

Hofmeyr, Isabel, Preben Kaarsholm and Bodil Folke Frederiksen. 2011. 'Print Cultures, Nationalisms and Publics of the Indian Ocean'. *Africa* 81(1): 1–22.

Hook, Derek. 2013. *(Post)Apartheid Conditions: Psychoanalysis and Social Formation* (Studies in the Psychosocial). London: Palgrave Macmillan.

Hoosen, Mishka. 2015. *Call It a Difficult Night*. Grahamstown: Deep South Publishing.

Human, Charlie. 2013. *Apocalypse Now Now*. Cape Town: Umuzi.

———. 2014. *Kill Baxter*. Cape Town: Umuzi.

Jamal, Ashraf. 2010. 'Bullet through the Church: South African Literature in English and the Future-Anterior'. *English Studies in Africa* 53(1): 11–20.

Jänicke, Stefan, Greta Franzini, Muhammad Faisal Cheema and Gerik Scheuermann. 2015. 'On Close and Distant Reading in Digital Humanities: A Survey and Future Challenges'. Eurographics Conference on Visualization, 2015. https://pdfs.semanticscholar.org/20cd/40f3f17dc7d8f49d368c2efbc2e27b0f2b33.pdf (accessed 16 April 2019).

Khumalo, Fred. 2006. *Bitches' Brew*. Johannesburg: Jacana Media.

———. 2017. *Dancing the Death Drill*. Cape Town: Umuzi.

Langa, Mandla. 2014. *The Texture of Shadows*. Johannesburg: Pan Macmillan.

Lenta, Margaret. 2011. 'Expanding "South Africanness": Debut Novels', in *SA Lit: Beyond 2000*, edited by Michael Chapman and Margaret Lenta, 50–68. Pietermaritzburg: University of KwaZulu-Natal Press.

Löwy, Michael. 2007. 'The Current of Critical Realism: A Moonlit-Enchanted Night', in *Adventures in Realism*, edited by Matthew Beaumont, 193–206. Oxford: Blackwell.

Maart, Rozena. 2004. *Rosa's District Six*. Toronto: Tsar Publications.

Mahlangu, Songeziwe. 2014. *Penumbra*. Cape Town: Kwela Books.

Marx, Karl and Friedrich Engels. [1848] 2014. *The Communist Manifesto*. New York: International Publishers.

Mashigo, Mohale. 2016. *The Yearning*. Johannesburg: Pan Macmillan.

———. 2018. *Intruders*. Johannesburg: Pan Macmillan.

Matteau Matsha, Rachel and Lindy Stiebel. 2017. 'Deep Sea Writing: Recent Conversations with Lindsey Collen, Writer and Activist from Mauritius'. *Journal of the Indian Ocean Region* 13(3): 326–34.

Mbembe, Achille. 2001. *On the Postcolony*. Oakland, CA: University of California Press.

McNulty, Niall. 2005. 'Reading the City: Analysing Literary Space in Selected Postapartheid Urban Narratives'. MA thesis, University of KwaZulu-Natal.

McNulty, Niall and Lindy Stiebel. 2017. *A Literary Guide to KwaZulu-Natal*. Pietermaritzburg: University of KwaZulu-Natal Press.

Mda, Zakes. 1995. *Ways of Dying*. London: Picador.

———. 2000. *Heart of Redness*. New York: Farrar, Straus & Giroux.

Medalie, David. 2010. 'The Uses of Nostalgia'. *English Studies in Africa* 53(1): 35–44.

Mhlongo, Niq. 2013. *Way Back Home*. Cape Town: Kwela Books.

Mohlele, Nthikeng. 2008. *The Scent of Bliss*. Cape Town: Kwela Books.

———. 2013. *Small Things*. Pietermaritzburg: University of KwaZulu-Natal Press.

———. 2014. *Rusty Bell*. Pietermaritzburg: University of KwaZulu-Natal Press.

———. 2016. *Pleasure*. Johannesburg: Pan Macmillan.

Moonsamy, Nedine. 2014. 'Nostalgia Contretemps: A Theory of Contemporary South African Literature'. PhD thesis, University of the Witwatersrand.

Moreillon, Olivier. 2019. *Reading the Post-Apartheid City: Durbanite and Capetonian Literary Topographies in Selected Texts beyond 2000*. Berlin: Logos Verlag.

Moreillon, Olivier and Alan Muller. 2016. 'Half 'n Half: Mytho-Historical and Spatial Entanglements in Charlie Humans's *Apocalypse Now Now* and *Kill Baxter*'. *Journal of Literary Studies* 32(3): 77–97.

Moretti, Franco. 1998. *Atlas of the European Novel, 1800–1900*. London: Verso.

———. 2000. 'Conjectures on World Literature'. *New Left Review* 1: 54–68.

———. 2005. *Graphs, Maps, Trees: Abstract Models for a Literary History*. London: Verso.

———. 2013. *Distant Reading*. London: Verso.

Mpe, Phaswane. 2001. *Welcome to Our Hillbrow*. Pietermaritzburg: University of Natal Press.

Mzamane, Mbulelo Vizikhungo (ed.). 2005. *Words Gone Two Soon: A Tribute to Phaswane Mpe and K. Sello Duiker*. Pretoria: Umgangatho Media & Communications.

Nkosi, Lewis. 2001. 'The World of Johan van Wyk'. Unpublished.

Ntshingila, Futhi. 2008. *Shameless*. Pietermaritzburg: University of KwaZulu-Natal Press.

———. 2014. *Do Not Go Gentle*. Cape Town: Modjaji Books.

Nuttall, Sarah. 2009. *Entanglement: Literary and Cultural Reflections on Post-Apartheid*. Johannesburg: Wits University Press.

Omotoso, Yewande. 2011. *Bom Boy*. Cape Town: Modjaji Books.

———. 2016. *The Woman Next Door*. London: Chatto & Windus.

Pizer, John. 2000. 'Goethe's "World Literature" Paradigm and Contemporary Cultural Globalization'. *Comparative Literature* 52(3): 213–27.

———. 2006. *The Idea of World Literature: History and Pedagogical Practice*. Baton Rouge: Louisiana State University Press.

Poyner, Jane. 2020. *The Worlding of the South African Novel: Spaces of Transition*. London: Palgrave Macmillan.

Prendergast, Christopher (ed.). 2004. *Debating World Literature*. London: Verso.

Samuelson, Meg. 2008. 'Walking through the Door and Inhabiting the House: South African Literary Culture and Criticism after the Transition'. *English Studies in Africa* 51(1): 130–7.

———. 2010. 'Scripting Connections: Reflections cn the "Post-Transitional"'. *English Studies in Africa* 53(1): 113–17.

Schmeling, Manfred. 1995. *Weltliteratur Heute: Konzepte und Perspektiven.* Würzburg: Königshausen & Neumann.

Schreiner, Olive. 1883. *The Story of an African Farm.* London: Chapman & Hall.

Serote, Mongane Wally. 2013. *Rumours.* Johannesburg: Jacana Media.

Shukri, Ishtiyaq. 2005. *The Silent Minaret.* Johannesburg: Jacana Media.

Stiebel, Lindy. 2013. 'Lewis Nkosi's Durban: An Indian Ocean City in Flux'. *Journal of the Indian Ocean Region* 9(2): 227–37.

———. 2016. 'Sugar-Coated Stories? Plantation Literature by Selected South African Indian Writers'. *English Academy Review* 33(1): 7–23.

Stiebel, Lindy and Therese Steffen (eds). 2014. *Letters to My Native Soil: Lewis Nkosi Writes Home (2001–2009).* Berlin: LIT Verlag.

Strydom, Fred. 2015. *The Raft.* Cape Town: Umuzi.

———. 2017. *The Inside-Out Man.* Cape Town: Umuzi.

Thurman, Chris. 2010. 'Places Elsewhere, Then and Now: Allegory "Before" and "After" South Africa's Transition'. *English Studies in Africa* 53(1): 91–103.

Touré, Nakhane. 2015. *Piggy Boy's Blues.* Johannesburg: Blackbird Books.

Turok, Ivan. 2012. 'Urbanisation and Development in South Africa: Economic Imperatives, Spatial Distortions and Strategic Responses'. Working paper, International Institute for Environment and Development. http://pubs.iied.org/10621IIED.html (accessed 10 March 2020).

Van der Vlies, Andrew. 2017. *Present Imperfect: Contemporary South African Writing.* Oxford: Oxford University Press.

Van Wyk, Johan. [2001] 2006. *Man Bitch.* Self-published.

Visagie, Andries. 2005. 'Wit Mans, Swart Vroue: Johan van Wyk se Man-Bitch (2001) en Kleinboer se Kontrei (2003) as Seksuele Outobiografieë'. *Tydskrif vir Nederlands & Afrikaans* 12(2): 225–53.

Wallerstein, Immanuel. 1974. *The Modern World-System I: Capitalist Agriculture and the Origins of the European World-Economy in the Sixteenth Century.* New York: Academic Press.

———. 1980. *The Modern World-System II: Mercantilism and the Consolidation of the European World-Economy, 1600–1750.* New York: Academic Press.

———. 1989. *The Modern World-System III: The Second Era of Great Expansion of the Capitalist World-Economy, 1730s–1840s.* New York: Academic Press.

———. 2011. *The Modern World-System IV: Centrist Liberalism Triumphant, 1789–1914.* Oakland, CA: University of California Press.

Wanner, Zukiswa. 2014. *London, Cape Town, Joburg.* Cape Town: Kwela Books.

Wicomb, Zoë. 2006. *Playing in the Light.* New York: The New Press.

WRec (Warwick Research Collective). 2015. *Combined and Uneven Development: Towards a New Theory of World Literature.* Liverpool: Liverpool University Press.

'I'm hoping that through fiction I can raise awareness of problems within the Indian community.'

Mariam Akabor (photo: Olivier Moreillon)

Danyela Demir, Olivier Moreillon and Alan Muller

In Conversation with Mariam Akabor
(b. 1984)

We met Mariam Akabor, her husband, Mohammed, and her son, Zayd, at Nino's Café, which is situated at Durban's Moses Mabhida Stadium. Mariam Akabor is the author of the short story collection *Flat 9* (2006) and an unpublished novel titled 'The Muezzin's Daughter' (2009).

She is part of a group of South African Indian writers, the so-called 'Grey Street writers', whose work forms the basis of the KwaZulu-Natal Grey Street Literary Trail.[1] Among the authors represented in the trail are a number of non-fiction writers, such as Phyllis Naidoo, Dr Goonam, Fatima Meer and Ravi Govender, and writers of fiction, such as Aziz Hassim, Imraan Coovadia and, of course, Mariam Akabor. Tourists can visit a number of landmarks that feature in these author's works (Stiebel 2010; McNulty and Stiebel 2017).

After graduating with a degree in English and Media and Communication from the former University of Natal, Mariam went on to study Creative Writing at the University of KwaZulu-Natal, in Durban, under the supervision of Michael Cawood Green.[2] Dialogue is what fascinates her most about fiction writing. 'I like writing dialogues,' Mariam says, 'and not knowing what the character's going to say next.'

---

1. See http://www.literarytourism.co.za/index.php?option=com_content&view =article&id=68:grey-street-writers-trail&catid=16:trails&Itemid=30 (accessed 25 April 2018).
2. Michael Cawood Green is the author of *Sinking: A Verse Novella* (1997), shortlisted for both the Sanlam Award for unpublished fiction and winner of the University of Natal Book Prize in 1998, and *For the Sake of Silence* (2008). See http://www.literarytourism.co.za/index.php?option=com_content&view=%20 article&id=108 :michael-cawood-green&catid=13:authors&Itemid=28 (accessed 25 April 2018).

She was born and raised in Merebank, a suburb in the south of Durban. After getting married, she lived in the Grey Street area for two-and-a-half years before moving to Vryheid, a mining and farming town in northern KwaZulu-Natal, about three hours from Durban. Presently, Mariam and her family live on Durban's Bluff, the southern natural enclosure of Durban's harbour. She works as a practice manager at her husband's doctor's surgery and does freelance writing and editing.

Besides her work of fiction, Mariam has written various research articles for *Living and Loving*, a South African parenting magazine, for which she worked for about three years. She says that she 'thoroughly enjoyed' the work and acknowledges: 'My writing has changed since I became a mother. So has my reading. I'm reading more parenting and childhood development books.' More recently, she has begun blogging and editing and, whenever the family travels, she writes travel articles.

Mariam reads 'anything and everything. The only thing I don't read is science fiction, it's not my thing. But I have read *Lord of the Rings* . . . and I absolutely loved it. I didn't expect to like it so much but I really did.'

Her favourite spots in Durban are the Moses Mabhida Stadium – 'because my son likes it here', as Mariam explains laughingly – but also Grey Street, her former home, and the beach.

ॐ

Works

———. 2006. *Flat 9* (umSinsi Press)
Flat 9 follows the tenants of AK Mansions, a five-storeyed, dilapidated building situated in Durban's Grey Street. The collection focuses on the changes the neighbourhood has undergone since the end of apartheid.

———. 2009. 'The Muezzin's Daughter' (MA thesis, University of KwaZulu-Natal, Durban)
The novel tells the story of Imraan, an Indian Muslim, who falls in love with Salma, the daughter of a respected muezzin. Salma is, however, a black Muslim. The interracial romance presents a number of delicate problems, for both Imraan and Salma as well as their relatives and friends.

ॐ

What different aspects of home and/or coming home does your collection, *Flat 9*, deal with?

I think the concept of home is very important in my collection. Everyone wants to be a part of a warm, comfortable and cosy home. It gives one a sense of belonging. It is the same with the characters in the collection. Even though the building is dilapidated, the characters are content to call it their home. Their parents and grandparents lived there, so it's only fitting that they continue to live there.

It seems then that the idea of home is linked closely to a particular place. How important is place in your writing?

Place is very important in my writing, especially in *Flat 9*. The building, AK Mansions, where all the characters live, is in itself a 'character' if I may put it like that. I started writing this collection during my Honours year and my supervisor, Professor Michael Green, a very distinguished writer himself, read about three of my stories and it was his idea that I continue to write more short stories and create a collection that would use AK Mansions as the focal point. Personally, I feel that place contributes to the ambience of any writer's work. I got married while I was still an undergraduate and lived in Grey Street with my husband and his family. Three decades earlier, my father lived in the street parallel to where my new home was, so I grew up listening to his childhood stories of living in a block of flats. It was only when I moved to Grey Street that I truly understood and appreciated his stories, for I saw a different world in my new home: neighbours who are sometimes too close for comfort, but very helpful and supportive; the influx of foreigners in neighbouring buildings and generally the atmosphere of living in a communal type of set-up. Incidentally, after moving out of the building in Grey Street, I moved to a small town in northern KwaZulu-Natal where I lived for eighteen months. It was there that I was inspired to write my first novel for my Master's degree, which was set in a fictional small town in KZN.

Flat 9 opens with the story of the temperamental Rashida, Latif's mother, whose hopes for her son's return are answered on the Saturday morning that the collection's story begins. In what ways does *Flat 9* engage with the theme of a conflict between generations?

Conflict between generations exists in almost all societies. I think that with the introduction of newer technologies, globalisation via the Internet in a way, and with social media usage on the rise, there are going to be newer problems that societies will face. The conflict between parents and children always makes for interesting reading as it is universally identifiable. In *Flat 9*, the characters are mainly of South African Indian origin. Within the Indian culture, there is a tacit rule of obeying your parents unconditionally, and when this conflicts with the younger generations' own aspirations and dreams and even religion, there are bound to be problems. Problems with regard to the family members. Conflicts between the generations that affect the family life. Parents or children may be upset with one another and their relationship will no longer be cordial. I think the reason it came up in my collection is because it is very common among Indian families.

The female characters, particularly the ones from the younger generation, seem to be marked by a double if not triple marginalisation: (1) Indian culture; (2) their age; and (3) their gender. To what extent is *Flat 9* concerned with revealing gender inequalities?

Gender inequality is a sore point among the Indian community. It is no secret that even today, in India, male children are preferred over female children. The same can be found among South African Indians. I think that my stories reveal the situation that a lot of females in our society find themselves in, particularly of the older generation who did not complete their schooling and almost always had to rely on their husbands or sons or other male family members for everything. A lot of my characters are Muslim, so there is also conflict between religion and culture. Particularly for Muslim Indian women, there seems to be conflict. A lot of Muslim Indian women are expected to live with their parents-in-law and serve them and care for them, almost as if that is their duty, whereas in Islam, there is no such obligation. This has changed for the younger generation because we have religious leaders who are making Muslim women aware of their rights.

Religion is commonly associated with tradition. How important is tradition in *Flat 9*?

Very important. The Indian culture is replete with customs relating to almost every aspect of life – weddings, newborn babies, motherhood, cooking and so on – and these are evident in the stories in the collection. These traditions are the source of certain conflicts in the stories. The conflict of power, control, the manner in which things have to be done because this is what the elders in the family did, as compared to making educated decisions based on new research, for example, about childbirth and parenting.

In what ways does *Flat 9* break away from traditional gender roles, in particular, and tradition, more generally?
I don't think it actually breaks away. It just portrays things as they are in our Indian community: that women are expected to do so much, especially in the sphere of marriage and family, and that they have a lot of responsibility. When I wrote it, I just portrayed things as they are happening and the problems that we're facing at the moment. We're a patriarchal society. The woman has to be in the kitchen and she has to take care of the family. I hear stories from other people, or friends, or family members, and they've always got the same stories over and over again, and who actually listens to these women?

But then *Flat 9* does, in a sense, break away. Okay, maybe break away is the wrong expression. It criticises . . .
Yes, it does. It does criticise. And that's what I was saying, to make our community more aware. You can't just go and tell them: 'Oh, you know what, you're being like this.' If they read it in story form, they're more inclined to think: 'You know what, this actually doesn't look so good.'

To what extent does *Flat 9* write either back or against a Grey Street that is perhaps no longer there?
Maybe because it's just changed so much in the past five years. The building I lived in in Grey Street, now Dr Yusuf Dadoo Street, is a family building. My husband's auntie still stays there. There used to be a lot of people milling about at the bottom and now, every time we go and visit his auntie, I see more foreigners. The place now looks dirtier. Maybe a bit more dangerous? I don't know. Because his uncle and auntie have said there's much more pickpocketing and whatnot towards where you see the racecourse – that end of Grey Street.

I think a lot of people have been moving out and, just two months ago, they sold the entire building, so people will be moving out soon. I think they're going to convert it into a hostel or into some residence for students. That was what they heard through the grapevine. It's a bit of a sad thing that it's not going to be a residential type of area any more.

Nostalgia and tradition are often associated with conservatism. Do you see them as necessarily conservative?

I think they are conservative in a way. I think that new traditions can be created within the new South Africa and it has been happening in small ways since 1994. Each culture, with its distinct characteristics, combines to include parts of other cultures – almost like a fusion, be it in food, music, art and so on. I think this is crucial to overcome the issues of racism and to create different mindsets in the younger generation of South Africans.

In your opinion, what contribution can nostalgia and tradition make to the ongoing political debate in South Africa?

I think tradition can be attributed to the sense of identity of a particular people – the manner in which they do certain things in their lives. For a rainbow nation like South Africa, these customs and traditions contribute to the country's rich cultural heritage.

You have mentioned tradition. What possible contribution might nostalgia be able to make?

I don't think that nostalgia or sentimentality about the past, especially if, like me, you were not a born-free, has any place in today's South Africa. While I personally have wonderful childhood memories, which are restricted to my interactions with family and friends, I didn't quite fully understand until I was older just how disadvantaged the 'non-whites' in the country were. And I had to hear from my own parents and extended family members how difficult it was to live under apartheid laws, and how it impacted their daily lives and careers too.

Food and cooking seem to be underlying themes in *Flat 9*. They seem to be even more prominent in your unpublished novel, 'The Muezzin's Daughter'. What meanings do preparing and eating food have for your fictional characters?

Food is so important to Indian people. I think that's why it features so much in my writing. We were constantly being told when we were young that, when you get married, the way to a man's heart is through his stomach. My granny constantly told us that, and: 'You have to learn how to cook. Your in-laws will look down at you if you don't cook.' When there's a daughter in an Indian family, that's what she learns. And food is part of our culture, so I suppose that's why I feature it so much in my writing. I think in Farida's case, in 'The Muezzin's Daughter', cooking is her forte. She doesn't have any sort of career or any other thing that she can do, but she has control over food. That is her way to do something for her husband, and that's her way of being mean [*laughs*], and he, as most Indian men would, would get upset. Men get upset if they don't get their food because they've been brought up that way by their mothers. Indian boys especially get what they want. It puts a lot of pressure on Indian wives to be able to match their mother-in-law's cooking, but I don't do that for my husband [*laughter*]!

In Islam, when you get married, you have to look after your parents. The responsibility falls on the husband if it's his parents, and on the wife if it's her parents. But in our society, if the daughter-in-law doesn't serve the in-laws, it's a huge thing. But that's not Islamic; they're mixing up cultures. I know that in the Hindu culture the woman is supposed to serve her in-laws, so obviously there's a lot of confusion there. It's highly commendable for a Muslim wife to care for her husband's family, but it's not her obligation and she should never be treated like a slave. So, I think that's another factor in my writing. I'm hoping to show the difference through characters and their stories, what's actually allowed and what's not, because it's not easy to tell the older people.

Considering the critical tone of your writing, how has your work been received by those closest to you, such as your friends and family?
Oh, they absolutely loved it. Only my one sister was a bit concerned about why I had used the term 'kaffir' in my work. She thought maybe it was too strong, but then I told her that it is the truth. My sisters and my husband read my novel as I was writing it. I would email them chapters, so I always got their support. And a few of my very good friends too. Everybody absolutely loved it and they can't understand why I haven't revisited it and haven't had it published yet.

Moving now to South African fiction more generally: it is mostly with the younger generation of South African authors that formerly taboo topics, such as interracial or same-sex relationships, drug abuse and corruption, have been addressed in literary texts. In your opinion, what are further taboos that still have to find their way into contemporary South African literature?

I think that racism, especially within the new South Africa, is yet to be displayed in contemporary South African literature. The existing racism and ill-feeling in situations in the workplace, with the introduction of BEE [Black Economic Empowerment] positions, has yet to be explored.

What topics do you feel you cannot write about (yet)?
I don't really feel there are any topics I cannot write about.

What are some of the new voices or angles we might see developing in South African literature? What predictions do you have about this?
I think it would be interesting to see the perspective from the newer, younger generation of South African writers in the next few years, the 'born-frees'. Those born before 1994, like myself, were born while apartheid still existed. We might not have experienced the effects directly like our parents or grandparents did, but we knew of it and its indirect consequences. I think that the topics they choose to write about will not necessarily include topics such as apartheid because they did not really experience it. I may not have experienced apartheid directly in the way my parents did, but I did attend a school that had 99 per cent Indian pupils. The born-free writers were more likely to attend schools that were multi-racial. Basically, I think that when the new democratic South Africa was formed in 1994, a lot of things did change and these changes would be evident in South African literature.

The majority of contemporary (post)apartheid literature could perhaps be categorised as realist fiction. Which different genres do you see becoming more prominent as an attempt to break away from some of the tendencies of the realist genre?
There is Henrietta Rose-Innes as an example of speculative fiction and John van de Ruit as a humorous writer. I think these examples of writing genres just add to the country's rainbow literature. Our country has such a rich history and unfortunately has a lot of problems too – high HIV rates, violent crime, poverty and so on – and I think that contemporary writers will continue to be creative and produce literature that is realistic, funny, even tragic, perhaps motivated by the circumstances South Africans find themselves in.

What are you doing next?

I completed my first novel, 'The Muezzin's Daughter', a few years ago, which formed my dissertation for my Master's degree in English. I have yet to revisit that work and tweak it until I think it is ready for publication.

છ

References

Green, Michael Cawood. 1997. *Sinking: A Verse Novella*. Johannesburg: Penguin.

———. 2008. *For the Sake of Silence*. Cape Town: Umuzi.

McNulty, Niall and Lindy Stiebel. 2017. *A Literary Guide to KwaZulu-Natal*. Pietermaritzburg: University of KwaZulu-Natal Press.

Stiebel, Lindy. 2010. 'Last Stop "Little Gujarat": Tracking South African Indian Writers on the Grey Street Writers' Trail in Durban'. *Current Writing: Text and Reception in Southern Africa* 22(1): 1–20.

'People deserve a second chance.'

Sifiso Mzobe (photo: Olivier Moreillon)

Danyela Demir, Olivier Moreillon and Alan Muller

In Conversation with Sifiso Mzobe
(b. 1978)

We met Sifiso Mzobe in Durban's CBD on a scorching Monday afternoon. Sifiso is the author of *Young Blood* (2010), for which he won the 2011 Herman Charles Bosman Award, the 2011 Sunday Times Fiction Prize,[1] the 2011 South African Literary Award for a First-Time Published Author and the 2012 Wole Soyinka Prize for Literature in Africa. The novel was translated into German in 2015 by Peter Hammer Verlag, a prominent independent German publisher. Sifiso's short story collection *Searching for Simphiwe* was published in 2020.

Sifiso was born in Umlazi, a township situated south-west of Durban. After graduating from high school at St Francis College, he went on to study Journalism at Damelin College, a private university in Durban's CBD. He works as a freelance journalist, novelist and translator. He translates from English into *isiZulu* for the FunDza Literary Trust. Sifiso explains: 'They publish mobi-fiction, which is short fiction published on mobile phones. I do translations and sometimes write short stories for them.'[2]

Sifiso says about himself that he is 'a slow writer'. He dislikes the time-consuming aspects of writing fiction, commenting that it is difficult because sometimes he doesn't see the finishing line. About the manuscript for his second novel, 'Durban December', Sifiso says: 'It's been on and off, it's been a love/hate relationship . . . but the idea for it came immediately. I think it was in 2009 when I actually signed the contracts for *Young Blood*.' What he loves about writing, however, is its creative component, which allows him to shape stories.

---

1. The name of the prize was changed to the Barry Ronge Fiction Prize in 2015.
2. The project can be found at https://live.fundza.mobi (accessed 12 May 2018).

The most recent book Sifiso had finished reading before our conversation was Salman Rushdie's *Midnight's Children* (1981), which he particularly enjoyed because of its magical realist touch. About the book, he says: 'I like the way Rushdie writes. That guy's a bit crazy, a bit wild! It's almost folklore-ish.'

One of his favourite spots in Durban is Moyo's at the pier, which he finds a 'nice place to relax'. In Umlazi, he likes Eyadini Lounge, 'where you can chill and braai your meat'. Having lived there for a few months, Sifiso also loves Amanzimtoti, a coastal town just south of Durban.

⤙

Works

————. 2010. *Young Blood* (Kwela Books)
Young Blood is the story of seventeen-year-old Sipho from Umlazi, who drops out of high school and gets into a life of car theft and racing. The book, which has many characteristics of a *bildungsroman*, traces a year in Sipho's life, which sees him nearly 'drown' in the criminal web of Durban's gang life before a series of tragic events sees him reconsider his choices.

————. 2020. *Searching for Simphiwe* (Kwela Books)
This collection of short stories, as its title suggests, covers different facets of searching, both on a literal and philosophical level. One of the recurring characters is Detective Zandile Cele, who appears in several of the stories. The stories cover a range of topics, many of them related to crime, such as drug abuse, abduction, corruption and blackmail.

⤙

Young Blood, in a way, could be described as a version of *Gone in 60 Seconds* set in a township, minus the strong leading lady [*Sifiso laughs*]. To what extent would you agree or disagree with this observation?
It's a little bit like that. When people classify it they say it's crime fiction, but I think it's more of a coming-of-age story that happens to take place in a criminal environment. So you can say [*laughing*] it's *Gone in 60 Seconds*, a township version of it!

What about the bit minus the strong leading lady? Because obviously it circles all around . . .

. . . around guys, ja, you can say that, but I think in 'Durban December',[3] my next book, there is a very strong leading lady. But I think in time, I will write a family saga kind of thing. So, when I eventually get to that, I guess it will be more from the points of view of different women.

Umlazi is the main setting of *Young Blood*. How much has Umlazi influenced your identity, both as a person and as a writer?

I think it has influenced me a lot because when I was growing up it was all that I knew. It was all that was around me. So, you can say that Umlazi, the city I grew up in, has influenced the way that I put the story down. And being around these guys as well, it was so easy for me to get into the inner circle because I'm from around there. So, my township played a big part in writing this book.

So you got glimpses into the inner circles of . . .

. . . these car thieves and hijackers. It was so easy though.

Did you do that as research, or was that before you were even thinking of writing the book?

It was when I was doing the research, but you have to understand as well that it's not so hard to get information. I grew up with these people. They live maybe three houses down in my street. There's a guy that I went to school with, and our paths diverged because I stayed in school but he chose this life. So, the story was right at my fingertips.

In comparison to Johannesburg and Cape Town, Durban is far less often optioned as the setting for South African novels. How important is the representation of Durban as a place in your writing?

It's very important, I think. In the book, I tried to make the city and the townships almost a character as well. So, it was important for me to represent Durban because I think our stories are just as interesting, if not more, than the ones from other cities. We have the scenery, we have the beautiful weather, and it has to be put down there in the book.

---

3. See Wakatama Allfrey (2014) where an excerpt of the novel has been published under the title 'By the Tracks'.

Since a particular location, namely Durban, is so important in your writing, what aspects of home, belonging and community do you engage with in your fiction?
I try to put it in my work as much as I can [*laughs*]. It's very important that when a person reads it, they feel the city, they feel the culture of what I'm talking about. So, I try to put everything together as I go along, sometimes not even consciously. It happens when you finish reading it that you pick up those things.

Early on in the novel, Sipho makes the following statement: 'Both my maternal and paternal grandparents were of the last generation that lived in the same place for their whole lives. Times changed fast. Even I, bush mechanic that I was, vowed not to die in a township, let alone in my father's house' (54). The same seems true of the parents of both Sipho and Vusi, who could be described as both passive and static throughout the novel. In contrast, the novel's younger characters seem to be in states of perpetual motion. How important are different aspects of movement in your work?
It is important because the generation that I was talking about is today's generation. They want financial independence, sometimes by any means necessary. In *Young Blood*, the story was about car thieves, so I had to keep everything moving. It had to depict the life that they live as accurately as possible. That's why everything was so much in motion in *Young Blood*. And I think it's different in my other work, my new manuscript is not as fast as *Young Blood*.

So, 'Durban December' shifts in a different direction?
Yes. It moves in a different direction because I'm telling it from the side of the police. The main character is older. So, he's not as restless as a seventeen-year-old character. He's a bit more mature. He has a family, so he has that stability of a family unit, and though the story happens during December, a season that is a bit hectic, I tried to concentrate on certain moments.

The ending of *Young Blood* seems to have a moral lesson. In what way is your novel meant to be educational?
I have a saying that I don't like to be preached to. So, I tried not to be too preachy, but I think you have that responsibility, especially in

telling a story like this. It happens in a world of crime where you have these exciting moments. But you have to be responsible as well, so that a young person who reads the book – I'm not only talking about the spoils and everything, the high life – they must understand that this life has consequences.

But *Young Blood* does have a rather happy ending, what with Sipho staying together with Nana, making a living and going to a technical college in order to become a mechanic. Then again, if you look at the characters around Sipho, both Vusi and Musa die. So everyone who mattered to Sipho throughout the book is gone, or has been arrested by the police. That's not that much of a happy ending.
Ja, it's not that much of a happy ending, but I had to give Sipho a happy ending because the book is also about second chances. People deserve a second chance. So, for the main character, I decided that I should give him a second chance, but a lot of people still think it's a very grisly end to the book.

Was there a moment while you were writing *Young Blood* when you thought that Sipho doesn't deserve a second chance? I'm just wondering.
[*Laughter*] No! No, there wasn't. As I was writing the book, I liked the guy [*laughter*]. Seriously, I began to really like the guy. To make a character believable, you have to plan the good and the bad because a person is made of both. And in that life, I couldn't make him an angel because the truth is, these guys, they really womanise like crazy! So, I had to put that in the book as well.

In comparison with contemporary South African writers, such as Phaswane Mpe, K. Sello Duiker, Niq Mhlongo or Kgebetli Moele, among many others, there is no slang or code-switching in your work. To what extend was this a conscious effort on your part and if so why?
I think it was a conscious effort because I didn't want to exclude people. Sometimes as a writer, if you want, you can use slang because it adds that personality to the book. But I wanted the person who reads it, maybe in Germany, not to be excluded, not to have things that they don't understand. Plus, I like prose to be clean. If it's English, let it be English.

Despite the fact that there is no slang and code-switching in your novel, you are often, along with Niq Mhlongo and Kgebetli Moele, labelled as forming part of the Kwaito generation of South African writers. What is your response to this categorisation?

Kwaito is a South African genre of music – full of life, township and current. I don't have a problem with being labelled as 'full of life, township and current'. And I am happy to be grouped with Niq and Kgebetli because they are damn good writers.

If you read Niq Mhlongo and Kgebetli Moele's earlier work, there's a lot of Kwaito in there. *Young Blood*, however, seems to be different. Would you say that Durban-related writing, especially your writing, differs from Kwaito writing, in a way? If there is such a thing.

During the time that Niq and Kgebetli's books were written, the music that was consumed was mostly Kwaito, but here in Durban it's more House music. In Durban it's different. I put it in the book because at the time, in the era that I was trying to reflect on, there was a really big House explosion, especially here in Durban.

Although South Africa is recognised as having one of the most liberal constitutions in the world, its society is still largely conservative. What taboos do you think have yet to find their way into contemporary South African literature? And are there any topics you feel you can't write about yet?

Personally, I cannot write about things like child pornography or paedophilia, but there's a lot that is happening in the country. I think a writer can write about anything if he's tactful enough. A writer will write about a certain subject matter if it appeals to them. I just think that at the moment, writers are not interested in writing about certain things, but I think they'll write about anything.

What might be some of the new voices or perspectives that we can see developing in South African literature at the moment?

I think the younger generation, the 'born-frees', will write about things that are totally different to what we're writing about because they grew up in a different South Africa. I was born in 1978, but when I started seeing things in the late eighties, early nineties, it was a totally different country. So, I think future writers will write about stuff that is happening to them.

Are there any authors you would say one must watch out for because they're doing something at this very moment that is new or exciting?
There's Thando Mgqolozana. He's a very good writer and he's a fresh voice. Now, there's a guy who wrote about a taboo, because male circumcision is a secretive thing. When you're coming from there, you do not tell anyone what happens there, and he put everything in the book. And we have Lauren Beukes as well, who is doing wonderful things! There's a lot of writers coming up. I think there are too many to mention.

Which different genres do you see becoming more prominent in South African fiction as an attempt to break away from the realist convention?
I think speculative fiction, like what Lauren is writing, and more genre fiction, like proper crime fiction. I think crime fiction will emerge and South African crime fiction is quite popular in Europe. Mike Nicol and Deon Meyer are proper crime fiction writers who are widely read internationally.

We've heard about your current project, 'Durban December'. What future projects do you have in mind? What can we expect from you?
I want my next book to be speculative fiction. And then I would love to write a family saga as well, like a long family saga, something that covers maybe three generations? I'd love to write something like that.

References
Rushdie, Salman. 1981. *Midnight's Children*. London: Jonathan Cape.
Wakatama Allfrey, Ellah (ed.). 2014. *Africa 39: New Writing from Africa South of the Sahara*. New York: Bloomsbury.

'You want to celebrate that which has been destroyed by time; that which has disappeared.'

Fred Khumalo (photo: Olivier Moreillon)

Danyela Demir, Olivier Moreillon and Alan Muller

In Conversation with Fred Khumalo
(b. 1966)

We were warmly welcomed at the Sandton home of journalist and author, Fred Khumalo. He is the author of *Bitches' Brew* (2006); *Touch My Blood: The Early Years* (2006); *Seven Steps to Heaven* (2007); *Zulu Boy Gone Crazy: Hilarious Tales post Polokwane* (2010); *The Lighter Side of Robben Island: Banter, Past Times and Boyish Tricks* (2012), co-authored with Gugu Kunene and Paddy Harper; *#Zuptas Must Fall and Other Rants* (2016); *Dancing the Death Drill* (2017); *The Longest March* (2019); *Talk of the Town* (2019); and *A Coat of Many Colours* (2021). He was a runner-up for both the Nadine Gordimer Short Story Award in 1991 and the Bertrams V.O. Literature of Africa Award in 1996. In 2004, the manuscript for his novel, 'The Oneness of Two in Three',[1] received an honourable mention at the inaugural European Union Literary Awards. The following year, his novel *Bitches' Brew* was joint winner of the same award with Gerald Kraak's *Ice in the Lungs* (2006). Fred's autobiography, *Touch My Blood: The Early Years* was shortlisted for the Sunday Times Literary Award in 2007. In 2019, he won the National Institute of Humanities and Social Sciences Fiction Award for *Dancing the Death Drill* and in 2020 he was the recipient of the Nadine Gordimer Short Story Award. From 2011 to 2012 he was a Nieman Fellow at Harvard University.

After high school, he went on to obtain a diploma in journalism from the Natal Technikon in Durban. Over the last 30 years, he has held numerous journalistic positions. Among other things, he worked as the Insight and Opinion editor at the *Sunday Times*, for which he also wrote a weekly socio-political column. Fred comments that while journalism

---

1. This manuscript was published as *Bitches' Brew*.

has taught him discipline (in terms of sticking to deadlines and writing to a required length and tone), his fictional writing has 'taken a knock somewhat'. He continues: 'In journalism you get trained to write in a certain way. The assumption is that . . . our readers do not have time to think. That has a long-term effect on one as a creative writer. Your fiction starts to read like a piece of journalism. Negotiating the two worlds is one of the most challenging aspects of being both a journalist and writer of fiction.' Nevertheless, the freedom associated with fiction is what keeps him writing.

Most recently he has read Monica Ali's *Brick Lane* (2003) and M.G. Vassanji's *The In-Between World of Vikram Lall* (2003). He reread both novels as research for one of his works in progress that is concerned with the theme of displacement. Besides being extremely well read, Fred is also a great lover of music in general and jazz in particular. Not surprisingly, Miles Davis, who he says 'is a muse to him', and John Coltrane are constantly featured on his playlist.

Fred lives in Sandton with his wife and three children. His favourite place in Johannesburg is Yeoville, of which he says: 'That's the first place that became my anchor, my home, when I got to Joburg in 1995.' Even though the Yeoville of the mid- to late nineties is no longer there, Fred finds it 'very inspirational in the sense that it is one of the melting pots in Johannesburg, a cultural melting pot. You get Zimbabweans, you get Congolese people, Nigerians, Ghanaians. All these people from the diaspora and you just observe as an artist, as a writer, as a journalist. I'm always driven to places that are not predictable.' In addition, he cites the township of his childhood, Mpumalanga, near Hammarsdale in the Natal Midlands, as being one of his favourite places. Whenever he goes to Durban, he makes a point of finding time to 'go and visit his township' in order to 'see his old friends, or just to enjoy the neighbourhood'.

∻

Works

———. 2006. *Bitches' Brew* (Jacana Media)

Fred's epistolary debut novel focuses on the love story between Lettie and Zakes. It is set mainly in the Durban of the sixties and seventies and evokes the township of Cato Manor and the lives of those who lived there.

————. 2006. *Touch My Blood: The Early Years* (Umuzi)
Touch My Blood is Fred's memoir of his childhood and formative years as a young writer and journalist. It documents his friendship with renowned author Mafika Gwala,[2] as well as Fred's experiences during the height of apartheid.

————. 2007. *Seven Steps to Heaven* (Jacana Media)
Seven Steps to Heaven, Fred's second novel, tells the story of two childhood friends, Sizwe and Thulani. The largely autobiographical story, which shares many parallels with *Touch My Blood*, engages with the young protagonist's journey to become an established journalist and writer of fiction.

————. 2010. *Zulu Boy Gone Crazy: Hilarious Tales post Polokwane* (KMM Review Publishers)
Zulu Boy Gone Crazy is a collection of selected columns that Fred wrote for the *Sunday Times*.

————. 2012. *The Lighter Side of Robben Island: Banter, Past Times and Boyish Tricks* (Makana Investment Corporation)
The Lighter Side of Robben Island focuses on the quotidian lives of former political prisoners. It attempts to shed light on previously unexplored aspects of prison life on Robben Island, such as music, sport and love.

————. 2016. *#Zuptas Must Fall and Other Rants* (Penguin Random House)
In *#Zuptas Must Fall and Other Rants*, Fred comments and passes criticism on a wide range of current affairs and celebrity stories, looking back and ahead to position South Africa within a global context.

---

2. Mafika Pascal Gwala (1946–2014) was a South African poet and literary critic, who grew up in Verulam, north of Durban, and spent most of his life in Mpumalanga township in KwaZulu-Natal. He is the author of two collections of poetry: *Jol'iinkomo* (1977) and *No More Lullabies* (1982).

———. 2017. *Dancing the Death Drill* (Umuzi)
Dancing the Death Drill focuses on the sinking of the steamship
SS *Mendi*. On a broader political scale, the novel tells the story of black
South African soldiers who left the country to fight in the First World
War. On a more personal level, the book traces Pitso Motaung's life
prior to, during and after the sinking of the SS *Mendi*.

———. 2019. *Talk of the Town* (Kwela Books)
Talk of the Town is a short story collection that unites various aspects
of living in South Africa and abroad, both past and present. The topics
covered in the collection are eclectic and engage with themes such as
xenophobia, exile in Angola during apartheid and life in the township.

———. 2019. *The Longest March* (Umuzi)
The Longest March explores a lesser-known part of South African history.
It tells the story of Philippa and Nduku, who, together with some 7 000
mineworkers and their families, walked from Johannesburg to Natal as
the city's mines were closed down in 1899 due to the war between the
South African Republic and the British Empire. Against this historical
backdrop, the novel follows Philippa and Nduku's relationship, which
is put to the test.

——— (with Xoliswa Ndungeni-Ngema). 2020. *Heart of a Strong
Woman: From Daveyton to* Sarafina! *My Story of Triumph – A Memoir*
(Kwela Books)
Heart of a Strong Woman tells the story of managing producer Xoliswa
Nduneni-Ngema. The book spans from her career in the world of
theatre, her abusive marriage to Mbongeni Ngema, to their divorce and
her life thereafter.

———. 2021. *A Coat of Many Colours: Short Stories* (Kwela Books)
A Coat of Many Colours offers, as the title suggests, a 'potpourri' of
nine short stories. The collection is broad both in terms of genre as well
as the range of topics and characters that it portrays.

≈

**Besides being a novelist, you're also a journalist. To what extent do you
consider yourself to be more of one than the other?**

To be honest, I think my entry into journalism was supposed to be a shortcut to the literary world. But, it seems I've been stuck in this shortcut; in this rut. For what [*laughter*]? Twenty-six years, 27 years or something. So much so that I have enjoyed my life as a journalist. It has opened doors that wouldn't have opened, doors that don't open for an ordinary person. So I've enjoyed my status as a journalist but also the writing itself. Sometimes it's very fulfilling when you get an immediate response to what you've written, be it a column that is considered funny or a hard-hitting editorial opinion or an exposé. Let me just say that I straddle these two worlds equally. I'm happy in both but, at my age, I feel I want to be more in the creative environment, focusing on novels. Unfortunately, it's very difficult right now to earn a living as a novelist. So, one has to play this balancing act for quite a while until maybe one's book gets published overseas or maybe one gets a respectable advance. That's the reality.

Do your journalism and creative writing influence each other?
Yes, I think they do. You read the newspaper, you see a short report, a crime report, and it triggers something: either a short story, or it becomes a scene or a chapter in a bigger book that you're working on. Being a creative writer, it's always possible to steal, to appropriate stuff from the real world. You embellish it, you dress it in new clothes and you accommodate it into your mansion, the creative writing mansion. So the two do complement each other and also, when I'm writing my column, I try to be as creative as possible; not to be straight ahead, just reportage, I try to take the turn of phrase that I would use in a novel or a short story and employ it in a newspaper column. I find that readers love that! 'Wow! It reads like a short story but it's a column!' It's entertaining and they're getting their money's worth, I hope. As writers we're driven by ego so, when you get a Facebook response to your column, it does a world of good to your ego [*laughter*]. So ja, the two do complement each other very well. I'm happy with the balance.

You said that you've been a journalist for 27 years now, which is a very long time. How have both the job and the medium of journalism changed within the South African context in that time?
It has changed. When I started, we were using typewriters. That's just a basic thing. At my first job, I was a sports reporter and I hated it! But

it was the only job available [*laughter*], so I took it. I had to take it. Now we have the Internet, we have Facebook, we have Twitter, we have everything. In those days we were very particular. We were taught how to take notes; I took shorthand. At that time, let's say you had written a story that turned out to be defamatory about a person and that person took you to court, you delivered evidence. Your notebook could form part of the evidence. A tape-recorded interview, on the other hand, was not admissible in court back then. The medium itself: the circulation of newspapers was much higher than it is now. People have gone online. That has had an impact on the profession itself. A lot of newspapers have been retrenching, retrenching and retrenching. So they've got rid of the most senior guys in preference to younger guys who can be exploited. They can get away with that. Senior guys are more expensive, so you get a person straight from university as long as they can type on the computer, they can go on Twitter and they can go on Facebook. You throw them into the field and they get stories, they put them online, but the problem with that is the mistakes that we see in the newspapers. It's embarrassing. I'm not talking about the language, I'm talking about the facts. But, of course, the newspaper owners are interested in profits, profits, profits. Training is not considered a priority, quality control is almost not there, so newspapers have lost that gravitas, that level of credibility and I'm talking about just the newspapers. And then you've got online publications where there is no editing whatsoever. That's even worse. There's no gatekeeper, there's no editor, anything can go wrong. You see something, you put it online, and then you regret it. You might have seen people fighting, you just put it online, but you haven't checked what the fight was all about. Maybe it wasn't even a fight. And I've seen crazy, crazy things. People report at 12 o'clock that something happened. At quarter past 12 they are correcting themselves. But by then, the first dispatch has gone viral. The lack of quality control has even filtered into the newsrooms themselves. People were sitting at the Oscar Pistorius trial.[3] Instead of sitting down and waiting for the day's proceedings to end, they are tweeting every comment. By the end of the day you don't understand what happened during the course of the day. You then go to your Twitter account and you follow the tweets. They don't make sense

---

3. See https://www.theguardian.com/world/2014/oct/21/oscar-pistorius-trial-full-story-reeva-steenkamp (accessed 11 March 2015).

at all because there's no coherent thread. Many of those tweets were by reporters themselves. They then get to the newsroom, but they've forgotten what the story is, so they just regurgitate the tweets. It has had that unfortunate, debilitating effect on our reporting and on our journalism. The Web is a powerful tool, but unfortunately it has fallen into the wrong hands in many instances.

There have been various attempts to label (post)apartheid writing, such as transitional writing or post-transitional writing or the voices of the Kwaito generation. Where would you, as an author, position yourself within the broader field of South African literature?
I cannot presume to speak on behalf of South African writers who are writing at the present moment. There are so many. I know Niq Mhlongo is called a Kwaito-generation writer, and there is Sifiso Mzobe . . . and Niq loves that label. Maybe he came up with it, I don't know [*laughter*].[4] It would be really presumptuous as well for me to say I fit within this mould of writing. I just write what comes naturally to me. What I can say is, post-1994, many of us took this great sigh of relief that we're no longer writing under the shadow of apartheid. We are no longer obligated to use our art as a weapon of struggle. We can tell our stories without feeling guilty. Because in the eighties, especially as a black writer, if you had some education, you had a platform and you had skills, which is the writing itself. Therefore, you felt you could be the voice of the voiceless. You had to espouse the aspirations of the black majority, who were downtrodden, who were victims of the system. You felt it was your responsibility to expose the ills of the system, to report to the world what was happening at ground level. Now, post-1994, you feel this yoke of apartheid is finally removed. Now I can pursue my art without feeling guilty. I can write a love story without

---

4. Niq Mhlongo talks about a new generation of authors who started writing after the demise of apartheid, where he makes the following statement: 'The end of apartheid gave rise to this new, youthful and energetic generation that expresses itself through Kwaito, Afro-pop and rap music as well as through poetry – hence I refer to it as the Kwaito generation. This is the new national, hybrid generation that is united in a new kind of struggle: against Aids, poverty, xenophobia, unemployment, crime etc.' See https://www.oulitnet.co.za/young writers/niq_mhlongo.asp (accessed 15 March 2015).

feeling guilty. I can celebrate my music through my writing without feeling guilty. There's no longer that obligation to tell the story of the struggle or to expose the evils of the time. So the demise of apartheid was a liberation to us as writers, I think. It certainly was to me. Even though I do go back to the seventies, to the sixties, I'm now celebrating those lives that were overshadowed by apartheid. Now that the shadow is gone, we can go back and celebrate that which was hidden by this shadow and I think that's hopefully what I did through *Bitches' Brew* and my autobiography. Now, what I've written recently is post-post-. . . it's recent stuff. The novel that's being looked at by the publishers at the moment, for example, is about xenophobia. It is about what is happening now in this country. It's a reality that we will live with.[5] I go to Yeoville quite often. I have seen pockets of xenophobic incidents, not on this grand scale as we've seen more recently,[6] but almost every time I go there, you see people insult each other. It could be a South African insulting a Congolese, it could be a Nigerian insulting a Ghanaian, that kind of thing.

Pitso, the protagonist of *Dancing the Death Drill*, seems to be assuming different identities both within South Africa and, later on, in France. What is the significance of shifting identities for the story?
I deliberately made Pitso's identity fluid. Officially, he would have been classified as Coloured, as people of mixed parentage were called. His father is white and his mother a Mosotho woman. However, Pitso, in the face of the many privileges he would have enjoyed had he settled for the Coloured identity, decided he wanted to throw in his lot with his mother's people; this as an act of rebellion against his father. But I also decided to make Pitso's identity fluid for the simple reason that it offers us as readers a glimpse into many possibilities about the future in a country that has always seen things in black and white. The fluidity of his identity is, in a way, a subversive act.

---

5. The novel Khumalo refers to here was later published as a short story, titled 'Beds Are Burning', in *Talk of the Town* (2019).
6. See http://mg.co.za/article/2015-01-22-two-dead-foreign-owned-shop-burnt-in-soweto; http://mg.co.za/article/2015-01-26-foreign-owned-spaza-shop-torched-in-alexandra (accessed 11 March 2015).

More generally, how important is the representation of space and place in your writing?

It's very, very important. My initial instinct was to set *Bitches' Brew* in urban Johannesburg, but then I felt: 'No, Johannesburg has been done to death. Why don't we celebrate other spaces?' So I took the reader to Durban. I evoked the township of Cato Manor as it was at the time. It no longer exists, but through the pages of *Bitches' Brew* I evoked it. I evoked the township of Clermont, which is still there, and, of course, Durban as it was in the sixties and so on. So space is very, very important because it speaks through language. It speaks through language in the sense that in Durban, which is a very urbanised place, people sound different from their fellow South Africans elsewhere in the country. The kind of language that people use is different and, by locating or setting your piece of work in a particular place or space, you are saying to the reader: 'This is the language that is evocative of that place.'

What different aspects of home, belonging and community do you engage with in your fiction?

In *Seven Steps*, you will notice that the two young men are great buddies to the extent that Sizwe sometimes thinks that he's Thulani. They are so intimate in their brotherhood; so there is that sense of belonging, that sense of community in that story. And it stems from the neighbourhood that spawned them and the neighbourhood that they grew up in. In a way they are one person, but in many manifestations. They are one person, but one who views life from different perspectives.

You've been living in Johannesburg for quite a while now, but still your novels do focus on Durban and its surrounding townships. To what extent do you feel yourself writing back to a Durban that is maybe no longer there?

It stems from a sense of nostalgia, I suppose. You want to celebrate that past. You want to reach back to that enchanting past that is no longer there. You want to celebrate that which has been destroyed by time; that which has disappeared. So there's that sense of childhood memory. You want to be a child again because being an adult is such a challenging notion. You want to celebrate missed opportunities through your writing. You want to resuscitate that which can't be resuscitated – maybe in a way to redeem yourself as a writer, as a human being –

because I do believe that through my writing I'm not just writing to tell stories. It's part of celebrating who I am or redeeming myself to myself, not to other people. I could have been a criminal, but I was too cowardly to go through with it. So let me create this character who is a criminal, who lives out the fantasies I might have had as a young man. I could have been a political activist, but I couldn't do that, I couldn't go into exile, so let me celebrate it through the medium of art.

Cato Manor was destroyed long before I was born. My mother was born there. She used to tell me stories about growing up there, which, in a way, I saved in my memory bank and then I excavated those memories as I began writing *Bitches' Brew*. There are some beautiful moments that my mother used to describe growing up in Cato Manor and I had to resuscitate those through my writing.

Would you then consider your novels a rewriting of the Jim Comes to Joburg genre? For example, *Bitches' Brew* seems to be a particularly striking example if you consider the female protagonist.
Yes, yes, yes. There is that trope. My father, for example, was a typical case of a Jim Comes to Durban, in his case, because he was born in Ixopo, which is very rural, and he went to Durban to find work. That was during the height of apartheid. There was influx control, so the stories that he would relate to us as children would point to the challenges of a young black man moving from a very rural space to an urbanised kind of setting. It would always come back to me as I was growing up. This is the transition that my father and his generation had to make. So, when I was starting to tell stories, I would look at the characters and ask: 'Where does he come from? What gives him what he has now? What is his backstory? Bra Zakes, where does he come from? Sis Lettie, where does she come from? What makes her the person she is once she gets to Durban?' All these things . . . The person who is born in the city will obviously respond differently to it as opposed to the person who was born in a rural area and had to make the transition. I used to get that from my cousins, who were born in rural areas while I was born in the city. We are the same age; we have some education – all of us – but how we respond to contemporary issues is different.

Music plays an important role in your fiction. To what extent would you agree or even disagree with the statement that music can work as a signifier of a specific space and time in connection to your writing?

Ja, it is certainly a signifier because the minute I mention Miles Davis, I evoke a certain era: musically, aesthetically and artistically. I'm already prompting my reader to think in a certain kind of direction: this is urbanised, this is the fifties or sixties. That is the immediate reaction you get when you're reading, when there's mention in the text of Miles Davis or John Coltrane. You think of that era and, therefore, you would associate the character with that kind of era, with that kind of mindset, because people of the fifties had their own fashion sense, which has disappeared. So, when I wrote *Bitches' Brew*, I wanted to evoke that era through music; so it is a signifier, not only of the space and era, but also of the mindset. A person who would listen, typically, to Miles Davis would think of himself or herself as urbanised, streetwise, avant-garde, forward-looking, stylish, breaking with tradition. Those are the labels that you would pin to that person who listens to Miles Davis, especially of that era. It's pace, it's language, it's attitude, all those things.

So, it would be ideology and all the baggage that comes along?
Yes, yes. Ideology as well. The funny thing is, as I said, my musical tastes are very eclectic. When I was a kid, I was a Reggae person because of the message in the music. But, as I was growing up, people like Mafika Gwala exposed me to the jazz aesthetic. I latched onto that because it was more sophisticated; the abstract aspect of jazz is open-ended. It challenges the listener to think at a much higher level than Reggae. Reggae gives you the message as it is. It is there in writing, so to speak, whereas jazz is abstract. In its abstraction, it challenges you to think. Like good poetry, it encourages you to look at it from different angles, to interpret it as you would at different times, because one song today might sound different tomorrow. The same song of jazz would evoke totally different emotions when you listen to it the following day or in a different kind of setting. That is the beauty of jazz.

You mention that jazz, as opposed to Reggae, carries with it a specific kind of aesthetic, something that makes you engage more with the artistry that goes into performing a piece of really good jazz. Has listening to jazz impacted on the manner in which you craft your fiction, perhaps striving not only to convey a message but also to add artistry to your work?

Certainly. With *Bitches' Brew* that happened a lot. I used to irritate my wife. It took me a long time to think about headphones [*laughter*]. At that time, my office was adjacent to our bedroom, so I would lock myself into my office and play music. Obviously, the music would reach the bedroom [*laughter*]. So, it used to irritate her a lot, but she understood. I used to play a lot of music while writing *Bitches' Brew* and hopefully it translated into the structure of the sentences themselves. Certainly, some people thought it was very musical. So, yes, it does have that influence on my writing, certainly with *Bitches' Brew*. I'm not sure about the other things that I have written.

Moving on, away from music now: in *Seven Steps to Heaven*, you touch on same-sex relationships, a topic that has mainly found its entry into South African literature after the demise of apartheid. In hindsight, where do you see yourself having broken taboos in your fiction?
No, I don't think I've really broken new ground. What I think I have done, but maybe it's not breaking new ground . . . It's not often that male writers write their books solely from a woman's point of view. I did that with *Bitches' Brew*; very, very, very consciously so. Initially, I thought Zakes could be the focus of this story, but then I felt: 'No, what if I use Lettie as the focal point, as the voice of the novel?' Obviously, it was challenging. I'm not a woman. I had to listen more to my sisters when they discussed their problems, their issues with men, that kind of thing. It was an interesting exercise. So I did that, but let me not say I was breaking new ground.

Although South Africa is recognised as having one of the most liberal constitutions in the world, its society is still largely conservative. What taboos do you think have yet to find their way into contemporary South African literature, or are there topics you feel you cannot write about yet?
I don't think there's anything that I cannot write about. In the novel that I alluded to earlier, which is currently with the publishers, I look at virginity testing. I am not aware of any South African writer at the moment writing about virginity testing. And I've written about polygamy. Polygamy has been dealt with by many writers, but I've combined the two in this novel. What issues are South African writers not writing about? Or taboos? Um, no, I can't think of anything right now because

the topic of same-sex relationships has been dealt with in many texts to this day, racism obviously, xenophobia; those bigger themes, bigger issues, have been dealt with.

In your opinion, what might be some of the new voices or perspectives that we can see developing within South African literature?

I think it would go back to Njabulo Ndebele's exhortation to rediscover the ordinary;[7] just telling ordinary stories of how people live because we've been consumed by the spectacular, as he calls it. Yes, the spectacular needed to be captured, it needed to be reflected upon, but there are many other, ordinary stories that people tell at shebeens, on the train, in buses. One of the guys who's doing that is Imraan Coovadia. Imraan Coovadia is just brilliant. He tells ordinary stories, but very brilliantly, and the fact that he is funny helps a lot because for a long time, we have taken ourselves too seriously as South African writers. So, I could easily say he's one of the voices that you're going to have to watch. Humour is one major thing that we will be seeing and I'm happy there's a flourishing of crime fiction. This country is infested with crime, but reading our fiction, you wouldn't think it. Mike Nicol has been giving us some beautiful crime novels. There's also Margie Orford and Wessel Ebersohn. He used to write more political books in the seventies and eighties. Now he's writing crime. So, I'm reading his *The Top Prisoner of C-Max* (2012). It's entertaining, but it shows the reader where we are as a country. He melds crime and politics because they are inseparable. Our criminal justice system leaves a lot to be desired and he reflects that. Our policemen are being bribed. So, the kind of fiction that I think we should be producing should be reflecting those realities that we are grappling with and, thankfully, we have got writers such as Margie Orford, Wessel Ebersohn and others reflecting on those realities. Mike Nicol has been writing a lot about the *perlemoen* (abalone) scandals in Cape Town.[8] It reflects the kind of society we've become. Especially in Johannesburg, we are a very cosmopolitan city, but we don't understand our neighbours. Who are these Nigerians? We need their story to be told.

---

7. See Ndebele (1986, 1994).
8. See http://www.news24.com/Green/News/Perlemoen-poaching-hits-283-tons-20130527 (accessed 11 March 2015).

We don't know them. We don't really understand them. The Nigerians are here in huge numbers. The Congolese are doing great business in this country. I won't even mention the Zimbabweans because they are here, they are a part of us, but we don't understand them. Those are the challenges that our writers should be grappling with.

You've mentioned the flourishing of crime fiction. What other genres do you see becoming more prominent in an attempt to break away from the realist conventions when we have become so used to social commentary? I've seen Lauren Beukes and her books. I envy her; she has just signed a movie deal. Based on her success, I would suspect that this is the way contemporary writing will be going in the future. The publishers would be encouraging it because it sells. Younger writers will think: 'Okay, this is the way to go.' You are doing two things: you're breaking the mould, but also you are feeding the beast. The beast is saying: 'We need something new.' So, you're supplying what the market is demanding. I was doing this creative writing class at Wits in 2014. In my class of twelve of us, the majority of the class was doing speculative fiction. Their texts are set in the future, but in South Africa. So they deal with political problems, but in a future South Africa. Very entertaining stuff, I might say. Until then, I wasn't a reader of science fiction. Of course, being part of the workshop, you had to read what others wrote, which encouraged me beyond the class to read science fiction for the first time.

In closing, what can we expect from you?
I have just submitted a new manuscript to my publishers, Umuzi. The working title is *A Love Supreme* [published in 2019 as *The Longest March*]. Also a historical novel, like *Dancing the Death Drill*, this new work is set in Johannesburg and Zululand during the Anglo-Boer War. I am also overseeing the production of a stage adaptation of my novel *Dancing the Death Drill*. The adaptation is going to premiere in Southampton in July 2018.[9]

---

9. This did, in fact, go ahead. See https://www.theguardian.com/stage/2018/jul/06/ss-mendi-dancing-the-death-drill-review.

References

Ali, Monica. 2003. *Brick Lane*. London: Doubleday.

Ebersohn, Wessel. 2012. *The Top Prisoner of C-Max*. Cape Town: Umuzi.

Gwala, Mafika Pascal. 1977. *Jol'iinkomo*. Johannesburg: Ad Donker.

———. 1982. *No More Lullabies*. Johannesburg: Ravan Press.

Kraak, Gerald. 2006. *Ice in the Lungs*. Johannesburg: Jacana Media.

Ndebele, Njabulo S. 1986. 'The Rediscovery of the Ordinary: Some New Writings in South Africa'. *Journal of Southern African Studies* 12(2): 143–57.

———. 1994. *South African Literature and Culture: Rediscovery of the Ordinary*. Manchester: Manchester University Press.

Vassanji, Moyez G. 2003. *The In-Between World of Vikram Lall*. Toronto: Doubleday.

'We are like memory fighting to remember, or fighting to keep away from forgetting. So if in a small way my writing triggers something in someone who reads it, I'm hoping that it can do something for them.'

Futhi Ntshingila (photo: Olivier Moreillon)

Danyela Demir and Olivier Moreillon

In Conversation with Futhi Ntshingila
(b. 1974)

During the eighteenth Time of the Writer Festival in 2015, hosted by the University of KwaZulu-Natal (UKZN), we met Futhi Ntshingila. Futhi welcomed us to her hotel room on the seventh floor, which had a majestic view of the beachfront and from which we could hear the shushing of the sea during our chat.

Futhi has written two novels: *Shameless* (2008) and *Do Not Go Gentle* (2014). Besides having been longlisted for the Barry Ronge Fiction Prize 2015, the latter title was also translated into Portuguese as *Sem Gentileza* in 2016 and was released in North America as *We Kiss Them with Rain*, by Catalyst Press, in 2018. Futhi herself translated *Do Not Go Gentle* into *isiZulu*, which she found an enjoyable task.

Born in Pietermaritzburg, Futhi holds a BA Honours in English and theology from UKZN, a postgraduate diploma in Journalism from Rhodes University and an MA in Conflict Resolution and Peace Studies from UKZN.

The last book that Futhi had read at the time of our interview was *The Texture of Shadows* (2014) by Mandla Langa, which she 'could identify with because it is set in an area that I know and it takes place in the eighties, a time that was very violent in our country'.

Whereas Futhi enjoys writing when the story 'is flowing', she gets frustrated at times when she has trouble connecting the dots. But what she dislikes the most about writing comes after the actual process of constructing a story: 'When you have to sell the manuscript to the publishers. That is something I don't enjoy.'

Asked about her favourite spots to visit in Durban and Johannesburg, she told us that she loves Moyo's, situated at the Durban beachfront. While Durban seems to have a special place in Futhi's heart, she states passionately that she doesn't like Johannesburg at all because 'it's too hectic'. She prefers Pretoria to Johannesburg and particularly enjoys the city's botanical gardens.

Works

————. 2008. *Shameless* (University of KwaZulu-Natal Press)

Shameless focuses on the lives of Zonke and Thandiwe and their childhood experiences in the Pietermaritzburg of the 1980s and on the character Kwena, who films Thandiwe's life as a prostitute in Johannesburg in post-apartheid South Africa. Kwena soon realises that there are a few uncomfortable parallels between the job of a sex worker and a black journalist who is doomed to be a protégée of middle-aged white men.

————. 2014. *Do Not Go Gentle* (Modjaji Books)

————. 2018. *We Kiss Them with Rain* (second [American] edition, Catalyst Press)

Do Not Go Gentle tells the story of Zola and her daughter Mvelo, who live on the outskirts of Cato Manor. After Zola dies, Mvelo becomes pregnant and abandons her baby because she sees no way out of her precarious situation. The child is taken in by a white couple who cannot have their own children. Soon regretting her decision, Mvelo seeks a way of finding her lost child.

We see Kwena in *Shameless* and Nonceba in *Do Not Go Gentle*, although in different ways and for different reasons, try to come to terms with their identity. Also, during their first encounter, Nonceba is repulsed by Cetswayo's attempt at mimicking the American lifestyle. How important is the issue of (black) identity in post-apartheid South Africa within your novels?

I think it's very important. It's one of the key issues. People sense my voice when they read my book. I don't even try to act as if it's not there. It's there. And on the issues of, say, recolonisation, that's how I see it with the soft culture of America. I mean, there was a time in this country when you wondered if every other person was from America because they were putting on these accents. I know we were all at that point trying to come to terms with our identity. We had just come out of apartheid. We'd just been exposed to exciting cultures that we saw on TV, and it was what we aspired to. In that process, we've lost something and it's still happening. You find that kids now are going to English-medium schools and they can't speak indigenous languages. They can't speak Zulu, they can't speak Xhosa, or anything else because it's like speaking English is sophisticated. This worries me because I think it's killing something. So, besides just writing, I feel like it's a mission. We are like memory fighting to remember, or fighting to keep away from forgetting. So if in a small way my writing triggers something in someone who reads it, I'm hoping that it can do something for them.

I have a follow-up question about this because you raise the issue of language that I also find very important in memory and culture. In what kind of struggle is Kwena, the journalist in *Shameless*, involved?
Well, you steal from your life to make art! A little bit of background about *Shameless*: I started working around the early 2000s and I was observing what was happening to newly graduated black people going into a work environment and I was mad at what I was seeing. It felt like you would be an intern for years before you actually got to be taken seriously as a professional. So for me, Kwena was a tool to talk about these issues of what was happening to black graduates in the working environment. I mean, I would do stories with accountants who are qualified, who've got degrees, but when they get into the office, they would have to just do the basics: 'Photocopy this, scan this, do that', you know, but not the actual work that they're qualified for. With Kwena, I was trying to make the point that there's something wrong. That was my thing with her. Not so much the issue of identity, but to find her place, her proper place, in the work environment. I'm sure it's changing now, but at that time it was maddening.

What different aspects of home, belonging and community do you engage with in your fiction?
I see it in different ways. There's the micro and the macro way of seeing it. In a macro way, I'm seeing belonging as having a South African identity, owning it, feeling proud of it and working towards making it better

because we're developing. We're developing our state. My imagination and my wish is to see young people, who are up and coming, actually owning the country, feeling like they can have something to contribute. And then there's the micro level in the family since there's a bit of a breakdown there as well. I'm not sure if you've been following the phenomenon of fatherless children and of single mothers. For me, both levels are very important. It starts with the micro level, I guess, because if you come from a broken family, it's going to take some struggle to become a healthy, contributing citizen on a macro level. So both those themes are very important to me. I wish that young people, or people the same age as me, would feel that it's important to them as well. But I see that some fellow South Africans feel it's time to emigrate, and I think: 'No, you can stay and contribute what you can to a country that reared you when you were young.'

Both Themba in *Shameless* and Nonceba in *Do Not Go Gentle* were born in the United States and decide to come to South Africa in order to gain knowledge about their parents' and grandparents' country of origin. To what extent does your fiction engage with the search for one's roots and the (spiritual) return to Africa?
I think it plays a role. It is something that actually fascinated me. When I started university, we were getting all these people who would have a name like Themba or Sipho, but they couldn't speak a word of Zulu. Then you found out they actually grew up in exile because their parents had to leave the country. I always found that most of them felt they couldn't belong in this country. The local people were saying: 'Well, okay, we understand, but you had a nice life when we were dealing with apartheid. You don't know what really happened while you were away in the US.' And I can sense and feel their anguish of wanting to belong, but feeling discriminated against, not just by black people but by white people as well, who see them as just black people. They have the Zulu surnames like all of us. Okay, they speak sophisticated English, but they don't really belong with the white people either. So they have this search for home and I get the sense that they get very disappointed. They come out here feeling as if they will be welcomed like kings and queens, but they find that no one is really interested in knowing their story. It's painful that you can grow up, having this idea of a romantic Africa

that you're going to visit one day. You're going to meet your aunts and uncles and make new friends over there, and then you find out no one is actually interested in knowing you. Before studying, I did a one-year visit outside the country. For three months I spent time in Chicago. I met a lot of African-American people and went to their churches to see how they worshipped. It was interesting to see because in their worship they would use some of the Zulu words, snippets of things, just trying to hold on to something, a small something that they can find. I felt very sad. Here were these people trying to find a small piece of Africa, but some of the things were not making sense. It was Zulu words and I could hear that it was Zulu words, but they were not making any sense. But for them it was something sacred, something that they were getting into. And I . . . as much as I felt sad, I also felt lucky that I actually come from this country where I can trace myself further back than they could. They had a certain hunger, a spiritual hunger for a home that's neither here nor there for them.

In comparison to Johannesburg and Cape Town, Durban is far less often optioned as the setting for South African novels. How important is the representation of Durban as a place in your writing?
The first book was set mostly in Pietermaritzburg because that's where I grew up and then there was that movement to Joburg. In 1996, I spent a whole year in Durban and then I left. I came back to Durban from 2003 to 2007, and so *Do Not Go Gentle* is set in Durban because it's a place that I got to experience, so in that book it's central. It's one of the places that I portray. The problem is that with Johannesburg it has this history of where the revolution started, the uprising in Soweto in 1976, but the truth of the matter is that it wasn't just Johannesburg where things were happening. They were happening everywhere and Pietermaritzburg and Durban were hit the hardest, especially around 1994 when Mandela was coming into power. There was a division in KZN [KwaZulu-Natal] between what was then called the United Democratic Front and the Inkatha Freedom Party (IFP). There was a lot of violence that happened around that time and a lot of people died. So I do feel that there are many stories that need to be told about Durban because a lot of things happened in Durban then. There is a lot of richness that could be utilised with Durban as a location. And I was telling you about Mandla Langa's

The Texture of Shadows (2014). Some of it is based here in Durban, in the townships of Durban, where violence was occurring in the hot spots, so, ja, I think there's still a lot more stories that could be told about Durban.

As far as we know, *Do Not Go Gentle* is the only contemporary novel – apart from Zakes Mda's *Ways of Dying* (1995) – which focuses on people who live in an informal settlement. What were your reasons for choosing this particular setting?
As you've just said, besides Zakes Mda, I haven't read of any other stories that are told about living in the shacks, but there's richness! I mean, there is so much richness of life and things that happen in the shacks. I'll tell you one story: when I was a journalist, we went and did a story on flash floods. In these flash floods it rains really hard for two hours and then you get this body of water that just comes and wipes things out. So just up north from here, in Inanda, the flash flood did that. It wiped out houses, and a grandmother and a daughter were found two kilometres away and they were gone. It was terrible. There was mud everywhere, people trying to get their lives together. Life was still just going on and you think that no one outside of here knows the hardship these people face because now there are class issues besides racial issues, where you get rich black people who don't know poverty. They just grew up at the time when their parents were coming right in life. So they don't know about the shacks themselves. I feel it's a story that needs to be told. It's a story that needs to remind people where some of us started, and that there are people who are still stuck in this cycle. I know that people say: 'Oh, people are lazy and they make excuses, they can get out of it.' But, once you're actually in it, it's very difficult. You really have to have strength of mind to move out of that situation and make something of yourself. And people do. People manage to do it. But those who are left behind, it's like: 'Well, forget it, they're left behind, what can we do?' I don't think I can sleep well at night and enjoy my life knowing that there are people who are still dealing with these issues. So, ja, it's really important. I think it's not the last book I'll write about the shacks.

Considering Alan Paton[1] and Peter Abrahams's[2] prime examples of the Jim Comes to Joburg genre and its (post)apartheid rewritings – particularly Phaswane Mpe's *Welcome to Our Hillbrow* (2001) and Kgebetli Moele's *Room 207* (2006), among others – this trope can be described as a predominantly male narrative. In what ways is *Shameless* a female and/or feminist version of the genre?

When I was writing, I wasn't even thinking or comparing in terms of what was out there around this theme. It depends on the interpreters because really, I didn't have it in my mind that the theme is about Jim Comes to Joburg or Jane Comes to Joburg. It was simply about this woman moving to Joburg. But there was a time when I was a Jane moving to Johannesburg as well, when I started working at the newspaper. I had been living in Durban and then I went to the very small town of Grahamstown, to Rhodes University. It's a small town. It's safe and you feel like everything is fine. Then, when I was called to work for the *Sunday Times* in Johannesburg, what do I do? Not understanding what's happening in Joburg, I booked a place and I stayed in Yeoville. A few weeks into living in Yeoville I was walking to my editor's car because she lived just near the place where I was living, but on a fancier side, a suburb side. And two boys stopped me and they calmly asked for a cell phone. They just produced a knife and they said: 'We want a cell phone from your purse.' So I gave it to them, and I was all over the place. It was a typical Jim Comes to Joburg kind of shock. I was standing in the road crying and a man drove by and asked what had happened. I told him the story. We then got into his car and we followed them. They didn't see us. We followed them and they were walking past the police station. The police came out and they ran after them and they didn't know what had hit them. The next thing the police were on them and I

---

1. Alan Paton (1903–1988) was a Pietermaritzburg-born author. His most famous works include *Cry, the Beloved Country* (1948) and *Ah, but Your Land is Beautiful* (1981). *Cry, the Beloved Country*, which is centred around Reverend Khumalo who leaves his rural home in order to find his lost son in Johannesburg, is one of the prime examples of the Jim Comes to Joburg genre.
2. Peter Abrahams (1919–2017) was a novelist, poet, short-story writer and journalist. His novel *Mine Boy* (1946) is, alongside Paton's *Cry, the Beloved Country* (1948), one of the early examples of the Jim Comes to Joburg trope. The novel focuses on a young man who leaves his rural home for Johannesburg where he is confronted with the violent pre-apartheid social realities of South Africa.

got my phone back. That was my Jim Comes to Joburg story. Sometimes you bleed yourself into a story. So I think part of it just comes from my experiences of bumbling around in Joburg, but, no, I wouldn't say it has a feminist view of going to Joburg at all.

Zonke and Thandiwe in *Shameless* and Mvelo in *Do Not Go Gentle* are sexually molested during their childhood and teenage years. Your novels show the girls' struggles for survival after they have been violated. In what ways is your fiction dealing with the topics of mourning, resilience and empowerment?

You know, this issue of sexual violence against women in this country really breaks my heart. I feel I have to get involved. I don't know if you noticed that in both of the novels the people who violate women die. I feel like these children are so vulnerable and they have no way of defending themselves. They have no way of avenging what happens to them, but at least I get the satisfaction when I'm writing a book and I plot it and set it up in the way that: 'You've got to pay. You're going to pay for violating these children.' So part of it is to show that this is happening. You raise awareness, but you also show that, whoever reads it who has been through that experience, they're not victims forever, that they can get to the point of saying: 'I'm no longer a victim and I can try and find a way to move past this thing that happened to me.' I also get bothered when people want to become victims or say: 'Oh, but this happened to me, so now my life is over.' There is so much more to life than just getting to the point where you're saying: 'I give up. I was raped, so life is over for me.' I'm always trying to find imaginative ways of showing that you can actually go beyond what has happened.

In *Shameless*, Thandiwe, one of the protagonists, is a prostitute. To our knowledge, this is a rare fictional example in contemporary South African writing. Also, your fiction touches on virginity testing and female circumcision. In hindsight, where do you see yourself having broken taboos in your fiction?

When I grew up, I was living in a location, a village, that was controlled by a chief. In this place they wanted everyone to be part of the IFP. But my father didn't believe in being partisan or getting involved in politics. So he didn't get the IFP membership cards. When they started attacking people, we got attacked and I actually became a victim of that. I got injured quite badly. If they hadn't found me, I would have been gone in an hour. That's what the doctors were saying. So you get all these people saying: 'Oh, you must thank God, your life has a purpose.' So I became brainwashed into a raving, born-again Christian. As you grow up, you realise that this is not helping you either. It makes you feel very robotic. Your life is organised for you and decisions are made around you without you really applying your mind. So part of it was just rebelling against all of that, against that Christianity that was just too stifling for me. So when I wrote this book, it was a flag of freedom, writing about what I saw without caring a bit about who was going to judge me or what I was writing about. When I wrote the story of Thandiwe, it was symbolic of what was happening with the graduates who go into the workplace and it's like Thandiwe telling Kwena in *Shameless*: 'You're no different from me.' I felt like I was breaking a whole lot of rules and I was enjoying myself enormously [*laughs*] because it was such a freeing experience. I wasn't planning on doing it, saying: 'Oh, I haven't seen anyone breaking these rules.' I was doing it for my own freedom, for my own mental and emotional freedom, of just getting over all these things. And then there's the issue of female circumcision. It also talks about things that I don't think people outside the African continent understand. For some women it is circumcision, for us here in South Africa it's virginity testing, where someone has to watch you at all points to ensure that you're still 'pure'. So someone is controlling our sexuality.

Although South Africa is recognised as having one of the most liberal constitutions in the world, its society is still largely conservative. What taboos do you think have yet to find their way into contemporary South African literature? And, what other delicate issues do you still want to tackle in your own writing?

I think the biggest thing that I haven't seen happening, it may be out there, but I haven't come across it, is this issue called *ukuthwala*, where a man decides that he likes a certain girl, but he doesn't think he stands a chance. So what he does is he comes with his uncle. It happens in rural areas, not so much in urban areas. They would come and they would stalk you and watch you going to collect water in the river somewhere and then they would come and pounce, basically grab you and kidnap you into his house and then send people into your house to say: 'We've taken so-and-so, now you can come and negotiate that we arrange a marriage with this person.' Now, what bugs me is that it's normally an old, ugly person who can't find a girlfriend, who then decides he will just choose some young innocent girl and by the time the family comes, he would have sexually molested her already. It's like with a child: when you like a chocolate and you want to grab it and put it in your mouth, and then you take it out and no one else would want it again because you've had a taste of it. It happens a lot in the Eastern Cape, in the rural areas of the Eastern Cape. It used to happen a long time ago here in KZN. I was speaking to my mother about it and she was telling me about some fat guy who was after her. She spotted them and she ran like hell to get away from them, to get home. So she escaped the kidnapping.

Another thing I'm looking at is the role of black women in the South African War. It's scary to me how you can kill off a whole lot of a population by just not saying anything about them. It's as if they were not there, as if they didn't exist. Meanwhile, they were there, and they existed, and they contributed to what was happening. It's stories like this that I think need to be told.

In your opinion, what might be some of the new voices or perspectives that we can see developing in South African literature?
You know, I think I would be interested to hear from young people born in the mid-nineties. I won't call them born-frees because they were not free, but I would say children who were born when we got our democracy. I would love to hear what they have to say and know more about their perspectives and their views of what's happening. I think there could be some really interesting stories that we would not understand, but they would have a clear understanding of what was happening. So I'm looking forward to that. There is Malaika Wa Azania's *Memoirs of a Born Free: Reflections on the Rainbow Nation* (2014).[3] Their perspectives are interesting. I think they can teach us something about what's happening in our country.

---

3. The book contests notions of freedom for young people who were born into a democratic South Africa. It also challenges the image of the 'rainbow nation' and highlights the struggles of young black people who face discrimination in terms of race, gender and class.

Which different genres do you see becoming more prominent as an attempt to break away from realist conventions?

There's Lauren Beukes, who is venturing into science fiction. It's also a commentary on what's happening in society, but it's just different, fresh, interesting and new. I think that's coming up. I guess we can say it's like a South African *Men in Black* kind of thing. Also, there's potential for a whole lot of different things, maybe later on we will get the Harry Potter character of South Africa. If people imagine those things it could be interesting to see how and what they come up with. It's not something I identify with, but I think it can be very exciting for kids.

There actually is a South African version of Harry Potter in Charlie Human's *Apocalypse Now Now* (2013) and *Kill Baxter* (2014).

There you go! So it's already starting. It's exciting though. We live in an exciting country and there are so many opportunities for things to happen.

What are some of your current/future projects?

I think I've mentioned it already: I'm looking into the role of black women in the South African War. I still have it in my head as the Anglo-Boer War and I'm learning that it's actually the South African War for it to be inclusive of all who took part. It's going to be fiction. I'm not interested in just staying with the dry historical facts, but I'm looking into it. I've been doing a lot of research on it. During that time, there were a group of women who were called *bittereinders*, which, if you translate it into English, means 'to the bitter end'. They didn't want to move from their farms. They fought the British soldiers as much as they could and I want to write a story around their relationships in that camp where they were. I also want to look at the black women who were involved, who were in there, because actually there were very good relationships between black women and Afrikaans women in the concentration camps. I'm looking at that, just to find out what happened. I'm sure it's going to piss off a lot of people but I don't care.

⧠

References

Abrahams, Peter. 1946. *Mine Boy*. London: Dorothy Crisp and Co.

Langa, Mandla. 2014. *The Texture of Shadows*. Johannesburg: Picador Africa.

Mda, Zakes. 1995. *Ways of Dying*. New York: Picador.

Moele, Kgebetli. 2006. *Room 207*. Cape Town: Kwela Books.

Mpe, Phaswane. 2001. *Welcome to Our Hillbrow*. Pietermaritzburg: University of Natal Press.

Paton, Alan. 1948. *Cry, the Beloved Country: A Story of Comfort in Desolation*. London: Jonathan Cape.

———. 1981. *Ah, but Your Land is Beautiful*. London: Penguin.

Wa Azania, Malaika. 2014. *Memoirs of a Born Free: Reflections on the Rainbow Nation*. Johannesburg: Jacana Media.

'I think everybody's writing politics. Everything you write about can be political.'

Niq Mhlongo (photo: Olivier Moreillon)

Danyela Demir and Olivier Moreillon

In Conversation with Niq Mhlongo
(b. 1973)

We met Niq Mhlongo on an early Sunday morning for a coffee at Poppy's on Seventh Street in Melville. So far, Niq has published four novels, *Dog Eat Dog* (2003), *After Tears* (2007), *Way Back Home* (2013) and *Paradise in Gaza* (2020); two short story collections, *Affluenza* (2016) and *Soweto, Under the Apricot Tree* (2018) and he has edited a volume of essays, *Black Tax: Burden or Ubuntu?* (2019) as well as a collection of short stories and essays, titled *Joburg Noir* (2020). *Dog Eat Dog*, which was translated into Italian and Spanish, won the 2006 Mar de Letras International Prize. *After Tears*, in turn, was shortlisted for the Sunday Times Literary Award in 2008, translated into French and published by Ohio University Press in 2011. In 2012, Ohio University Press also published his first novel, *Dog Eat Dog*. Niq's third novel, *Way Back Home*, was translated into German by Verlag das Wunderhorn. His second short story collection, *Soweto, Under the Apricot Tree*, won the 2019 Herman Charles Bosman Prize for English Fiction.

Niq was born in Soweto in 1973. In 1996, he graduated in Political Studies and African Literature from Wits University. The following year, he started a postgraduate degree in law at the same university. He transferred to the University of Cape Town in 1998, but dropped out in his final year, deciding instead to become a writer. Until 2017, he worked for the Film and Publication Board, where he classified films. In addition, he has been writing journalistically for magazines such as *Fairlady*, *True Love*, *Getaway* and *The Johannesburg Review of Books*, among others.

Asked about his likes and dislikes in the writing process, Niq says: 'When I have a story in my head, I really want to get it out. It clouds everything else that I have in my mind. Ultimately, I cannot think of other things except that story, so it's like a disease, you know? You get that story, it's in your mind, and you feel like you're sick. But once you are in the process of writing it, you feel like you are relieved of that disease.' He consciously bases his writing on South Africa's current affairs, with a particular interest in quotidian stories from Soweto. 'In order to get such stories,' according to Niq, 'you have to live around people . . . You walk around, you talk to people, you open the newspaper and there's a particular story which you feel you can develop.' Niq's finger-on-the-pulse reports of post-apartheid South Africa's social complexities and challenges have rightly established him as part of the post-apartheid generation of South African writers.

Most recently, Niq has read *Hadji Murád* ([1912] 2003) by Leo Tolstoy, which tells the story of the Russo-Chechen war in the mid-nineteenth century. Niq liked how the book 'gives you a perspective of what was happening at that particular time', and he was surprised by the novel's setting, which he 'didn't expect'. In terms of music, he listens to all kinds, ranging from Hip Hop, to Reggae and Dance Hall. 'It actually depends on my mood,' Niq says.

Among his favourite places in Johannesburg is Braamfontein because of its vibrancy and youthfulness. In Soweto, he likes hanging out in the parks, which is where he keeps up to date with the latest trends and gossip. Niq explains: 'I won't go to a place for nothing. I go to a place because I want to research a story.'

❧

Works

————. 2004. *Dog Eat Dog* (Kwela Books)
————. 2012. *Dog Eat Dog* (second edition, Ohio University Press)
Set during the time of South Africa's first democratic elections, *Dog Eat Dog* tells the story of Dingz, whose student life is turned upside down when he faces expulsion from his campus residence and is then faced with an impending return to Soweto and his family's disappointment. Covering themes such as racial subjectivities, financial precariousness and the HIV/AIDS pandemic, the novel depicts the hopes and fears of South Africa's youth of the 1990s.

————. 2007. *After Tears* (Kwela Books)
————. 2011. *After Tears* (second edition, Ohio University Press)
After Tears revolves around university dropout Bafana who stumbles into an entanglement of lies and hustles as he sets up office as a lawyer in

order to keep up the pretence of having graduated from his family and friends from Soweto. Covering the events around the beginning of the Mbeki presidency, the novel can be seen as a continuation of *Dog Eat Dog*, particularly in terms of its themes.

————. 2013. *Way Back Home* (Kwela Books)
Way Back Home tells the story of Kimathi, a former uMkhonto we Sizwe (MK) soldier, who returns to South Africa from exile to become a successful businessperson, profiting from the government's Black Economic Empowerment scheme. His MK past, however, soon catches up with him and Kimathi sees his world come undone.

————. 2016. *Affluenza* (Kwela Books)
This collection consists of eleven short stories, some of which have previously been published to international critical acclaim. Covering themes such land restitution, xenophobia, betrayal and dysfunctional relationships, to name but a few, *Affluenza* adds to the wide range of relevant socio-political themes covered in Niq's work.

————. 2018. *Soweto, Under the Apricot Tree* (Kwela Books)
Niq's second collection of short stories includes eleven stories and, like his previous work, aims at capturing life in Soweto in its multifaceted dimensions. Among other things, the collection tackles illegal mining, socially marginalised subjectivities and complicated familial ties.

———— (ed.). 2019. *Black Tax: Burden or Ubuntu?* (Jonathan Ball)
Black Tax is a collection of essays that discusses and questions 'black tax' and its implications for black South Africans. Through personal accounts, the contributors negotiate the phenomenon and debate whether 'black tax' is a familial duty or a financial strain.

————. 2020. *Paradise in Gaza* (Kwela Books)
Paradise in Gaza tells Mpisi Mpisani's story during the height of apartheid. Mpisi has to straddle both his life in Johannesburg and his home village in Gaza. In both places, Mpisi has a wife and children. The conflict between the two very different lives intensifies when his son Giyani, whom he brought with him to Gaza for his mother's funeral, disappears.

_____ (ed.). 2020. *Joburg Noir* (Jacana Media)
Joburg Noir is a collection of 22 short stories and essays by different South African writers, which shows life in Johannesburg in different places and from various perspectives both past and present. The collection is a South African instalment of the well-known Noir Series.

ॐ

You have published both novels and short stories and you have had experience in non-fiction writing, in terms of journalistic writing. What aspects of writerly freedoms and limitations respectively do these different genres either grant you or impose on you as a writer?
Let me just speak about the work that I do. I've been trained as a journalist. In 2004, I was an intern at *Fairlady* magazine, one of the women's magazines in South Africa [*laughs*]. It's too white in terms of the things that they cover. It covers women's fashion, women's successes, but is normally focused on white people. So that's where I come from. I also write for a magazine called *Getaway*, for which I covered Soweto, Dar es Salaam and other places. These pieces are very difficult to write because you have to think about a brief that you are given. You also have to think about the target audience. *Getaway* magazine targets South Africa's middle class, both black and white. You don't have the luxury of picking particular words, particular dialogues. You don't have the luxury of making characters offensive. That's the limitations of it. Coming to fiction, I don't have a specific audience. Sometimes, I don't write with an audience in mind. I write with a story in mind, a theme normally, but you also have to make the characters as lively as possible. When I write fiction, I write my stories without being concerned about what other people might say, my editor or my publisher, for instance, because it's easier. I'll simply take my story to someone else if ever they say they don't like it.

What do you prefer to write, novels or short stories or do you feel at home in both genres now?
I think it's very, very difficult to write a short story because you don't have the luxury of developing your characters or themes. Sometimes your story will be misinterpreted. So you have to be very careful about that, and you have to be concise. You'll see that some of my stories are longer than the others, simply because I didn't know where to stop.

Take 'Passport and Dreadlocks',[1] for example; I didn't know where to stop. I wanted to stop but I found that the story that I intended to talk about was still missing. Sometimes, you'll find that you've written 7 000 words, still not having completed the story. That's why I find it difficult to write short stories. I'm fine with novels because you don't care how many pages you have in the end, but with short stories you have to stick to your theme. You can't flesh out your characters. That's why I choose a particular theme for my short stories and then stick to it. My short stories are more theme-driven than character-driven, unlike my novels.

Your first two novels were predominantly set in the township whereas many contemporary South African authors have favoured Hillbrow instead. What is your response to the fact that some critics label you as a township writer of the Kwaito generation?
The problem with labelling is that if somebody writes about the Holocaust, for instance, it doesn't mean they're a Holocaust writer. You just choose a particular subject. I think people should be free to choose whichever thing they want to talk about. I write from within. That's a strength. When I talk about a township, I write from within. But if you look at it, the stories that I write about are not only stories about the township. If I talk about HIV/AIDS, for instance, it's not a black or white issue. Anybody can get it. Then it's just a setting. You have to find a particular place to set your stories. I like settings that I am familiar with. I wrote my first two novels because of the settings that I am familiar with and also the stories that people normally overlook. Maybe it's just that it shocked people that the stories I write are supposed to be everyday stories from the township – the critics, for instance. Critics can talk about anything, but the stories that I write are not different from stories that any so-called 'important' writer has written about. I also write about love. If you look at *After Tears*, for instance, it is also a story about love and so is *Dog Eat Dog*, but the particular genre that I chose is a genre that people overlooked. Authors will be labelled over time, you know. That's why I'm so surprised that now that I've written *Way Back Home*, which is not set in the township, critics have stopped

---

1. 'Passport and Dreadlocks' features in *Affluenza*. It is the collection's longest story at 47 pages.

labelling me a township writer. Critics no longer seem to know how to label me because *Way Back Home* is not set in the township.

What are your thoughts on the term the 'Kwaito generation'? That really seems to be the term to describe writers like yourself, Kgebetli Moele or Sifiso Mzobe.
Well, maybe I have a different understanding of what they mean by the Kwaito generation. I thought when they talked about the Kwaito generation, they meant that my books were talking about that particular generation that came after democracy. So it's because of the music that was popular around that time and also the fact that I feature this kind of music in my books that makes it to be kind of musical as well. But, it takes the particular historical context of South Africa: what was popular back then was Kwaito, but it would be wrong to say Sifiso Mzobe writes about the Kwaito generation because during his time it was House music!

Maybe it's because I'm older than Sifiso. He was born in the eighties. I was born in the seventies. Around my time, Kwaito was a dominant thing. What happened with Kwaito is that it came around the time when it was 'free' music with lyrics that were against censorship. Just think of Arthur saying, 'Don't call me kaffir',[2] for example. So the way Kwaito looked at apartheid was unlike House music. House is just contemporary for me. It has got its own beat. We just accept the label for the sake of accepting it, but I think whoever coined the word Kwaito generation should come back and expand it further, so that we really do understand what it all means because it gives people the wrong impression.[3] Now, for instance, when I go out and present, people think I'm a musician because of that term. I would always be asked to recommend Kwaito songs and people are not aware that Kwaito has since died. In the end, I may be labelled a writer of the Kwaito generation, but what happens

---

2. 'Kaffir' is a song by Kwaito artist Arthur Mafokate, first released in 1995. The song, which sold over 150 000 copies upon its initial release, is commonly regarded as the first Kwaito hit. See https://1001sasongs.wordpress.com/2011/05/30/kaffir-arthur/ (accessed 8 April 2018).
3. See http://www.oulitnet.co.za/youngwriters/niq_mhlongo.asp (accessed 11 March 2015) where Niq Mhlongo talks about the Kwaito generation: 'This is the new national, hybrid generation that is united in a new kind of struggle: against Aids, poverty, xenophobia, unemployment, crime etc.'.

now that Kwaito is no longer around? Am I still a representative of the Kwaito generation? Or does it mean that I'm dead as well [*laughter*]?

To what extent would you agree or disagree with the statement that music can work as a signifier of a specific space and time in connection to your writing?
I would agree. Music makes it easier for us to categorise things. If you want to understand South Africa in the time of apartheid, of course you look at the dominant music genre. If you want to set your book during apartheid and want to get the mood of what was happening around that time, music will help you to achieve this. Sometimes, certain beats will trigger certain memories.

And how do you think your treatment of music in your writing has changed over time?
It hasn't changed. I choose specific music to create a specific mood. In *Way Back Home*, for example, the protagonist, Kimathi, listens to jazz. It's all about class. Kimathi listens to jazz not because he likes it, but because he relates jazz to belonging to South Africa's upper class. Or *Dog Eat Dog*, for instance, is set around the Kwaito time. It gives you that feeling of freedom that Dingz, the protagonist, is looking for. I chose Kwaito because it symbolised a new kind of freedom back then.

Perhaps we could go back to Soweto. To what extent do you think that Soweto has become integrated into the greater Johannesburg metropolis?
If you look at the road to democracy in South Africa, they say it starts in Soweto. Look at the kind of leaders that we have: they are mostly from Soweto. Whenever anything is happening in Soweto, it's taken seriously. Like the xenophobic attacks, for example, are taken seriously because they know it can explode into something bigger, which might lead the country to be ungovernable.[4] If they happened somewhere else, I don't

---

4. In January 2015, a wave of xenophobic attacks hit Soweto and then spread to Alexandra, a township north of Johannesburg. While the unrest calmed down in Gauteng Province, the violence spread to other areas, such as Limpopo and KwaZulu-Natal provinces, between February and April 2015. See http://www. sahistory.org.za /article/xenophobic-violence-democratic-south-africa (accessed 8 April 2018).

think there would be too much of a noise to quell. The ANC [African National Congress] knows that if it doesn't take care of Soweto, they might lose quite a lot. If you lose Soweto's votes, you lose the elections. So, that is why Soweto is taken care of. That's why Soweto plays a very big role, not only in greater Johannesburg but in South Africa as a whole and even in world politics because people around the world know exactly what happened in 1976. What happened in 1976 is what has led towards our democracy, which started in Soweto.

How important is the representation of space and place in your writing?
As you know, I also work in the film industry. Perhaps that's why my writing normally is visual. So when I write, I'll sometimes unwittingly put space in it because I used to write scripts for TV and I also wrote for film. Space is very much a part of my writing, so that people have a feel and a taste of what's happening. That's my kind of writing. I'm not the kind of person that likes to imagine things; I'll have to be shown things. That's why the visual has also got into my writing. I like that because of my background in film. But even before I went into the film industry, I was a person who was always more visual.

How important are aspects of home and belonging to a place for your writing?
I think my writing draws a lot on African culture. We're communal people. For instance, there is a saying that a child doesn't belong to one person. I can sit somewhere and call a child, anybody's child, and send the child to go and buy me something without asking permission from the parents. And whenever I see a child hungry, I give that child something to eat. That's how communal we are. At Christmas, for instance, you'll find that black people walk around in the township, asking for Christmas gifts and people will give you a small Christmas gift. It is difficult for you to do that if you can't relate to that particular sense of community. We are not insular. We just belong to a specific community. So my writing is embedded within that tradition.

One of the main differences, I find, between black communities and white communities is that within the white communities you'll find that a person can live in Switzerland, for instance, and come and settle in South Africa without going back home anymore. You'll have your family here and you'll get married. You no longer go home. For black people it's very, very different because home is where your ancestors are, where your grandparents are from. So, you'll find that I was born in Soweto, but since my mother is from Limpopo, my home is there. I might not know anybody that side. Home is not where you live with your wife. Home is where the communal people live. That's why on Christmas and New Year's, people flock to different rural parts of South Africa because that's where home is.

According to Chekhov, a writer has a responsibility to 'describe a situation so truthfully that the reader can no longer evade it'.[5] To what extent do you agree or disagree with this statement and how political a writer do you consider yourself to be?

A political writer [*laughter*]? Let me start with that: I think politics has to be redefined. What is politics anyway? I think everybody's writing politics. Everything you write about can be political. Politics has to do with things that we live every day. If you write about identity, space, hunger, unemployment or drug addiction, you are always writing about politics too. In that sense I think Chekhov is right. You can't look at post-apartheid South Africa without looking into townships, for instance. The township has again become a space of political and economic debate.

So would you then say that writers have a responsibility to write about those places that were silenced or ignored?

Definitely! If you want to understand a country better, you have to write about previously silenced or ignored places, such as South Africa's rural areas. Even though it is changing now, South African authors should write more about rural areas. When people talk about South Africa or think about South Africa, they often mean Joburg or Soweto. If somebody had written a powerful story about what's happened in a very, very deep rural area, we'd be able to further our understanding of South Africa's politics and the economy more generally. People, at the moment, consider townships as poor areas and the suburbs as richer areas, but they are forgetting there are villages that are really poor. How often do we think about villages? That's why, as writers, we should not

---

5. See Berlin (1978: 303).

be limited to only a few spaces. Authors also write to educate the world about what we think the South African society is all about and that includes the country's rural areas.

How gender-aware are you when constructing characters?
It's very much an unconscious thing, actually. In my writing, I love to portray things the way they are, the way I believe things are. So, I won't try to write about women being emancipated in South Africa if I know, experience and observe them not to be. My female characters are mostly driven by the story. It will come from within the communities that I'm living in. I will single out that particular individual, a woman, but she will still be living under the conditions that are determined by the males around her.

Some of the short stories in *Affluenza* have been published previously and the collection seems to have taken shape over an extended period of time. How did the golden thread that inspired the book's title come into being?
Affluenza is in a sentence that I used in *Dog Eat Dog*, describing a particular white student at Wits University, who suffers from 'affluenza'.[6] I find that when trying to get extensions to submit essays, for instance, a white student will use, what I call, a frivolous kind of excuse, saying: 'My cat has died!', whereas a black student will say: 'My mother has died.' It's not necessarily the biological mother because whoever is the same age as my mother is also my mother. So, that's where affluenza comes in. If a white person's pet dies, it's something huge, but for a black person it's just a pet.

Looking further at your short story collection *Affluenza*, affluenza also becomes 'a condition of the black middle class'. What has changed from the time that you first dealt with this condition in *Dog Eat Dog* to *Affluenza*, twelve years later, where affluenza seems to be ubiquitous, where it has infected everyone?
I think there have been quite a lot of changes. You'll find that, at the moment, there's a particular subculture within South African society.

---

6. See Mhlongo ([2004] 2012).

I'm not sure if you've heard about this notion of 'blesser' and 'blessee'? This is where a young person wants to have an affluent person, no matter how old they are, take care of them financially. So there's this notion that has developed in South Africa, people do whatever it takes to meet the standards that they've set for themselves. We can see the emergence of wealthy black people and those have become role models for our youth. If you don't have a car, you're considered just a loser. Young people want to pass as being rich. In the short story 'Affluenza', for example, the three ladies become criminals because they want to reach a particular standard of living. It's all about money, not their money, but some other person's money.

Although South Africa is recognised as having one of the most liberal constitutions in the world, its society is still largely conservative. What taboos do you think have yet to find their way into contemporary South African literature? What has not been written about yet?
I think in South Africa we are very apologetic in tackling issues that we feel will offend another race or other people. Say, for instance, I wanted to talk about landlessness and I said: 'Ah, but land grabbing is the best option.' I might not want to say it in front of white people because they might say: 'Ah, that one must be Malema.' There's no integration yet between white and black people. People are still afraid of writing about what causes that disintegration. We feel like we might offend white people. They still own the means of production, so they might not interview me. When I write a book about these issues, they might not publish it. So I must not take on these kind of issues. I mustn't talk about this racist bastard, who is white. I mustn't write about him because it will offend my friend. We are still not easy with ourselves, in terms of such issues. People just like you to talk about corruption, but popular beliefs are that if you want to write about corruption, as a black person, and say that the ANC is corrupt, they might not give me a tender next year, or they might hammer me. I mustn't talk about that. So, you have to find a middle ground.

Are there any taboos or any topics that you feel that you still want to address? You've obviously mentioned the landlessness in your upcoming work, but anything more than that? What is on your agenda that's pressing you?

Contemporary issues – the issues of homophobia and gays and lesbians. Those are the kind of issues that I want to write about. Some of these things are happening because the society is failing to understand that we are not static. It might help to talk about these issues. The most important ones are definitely homophobia and xenophobia. People are dying because other people are afraid of their spaces being encroached upon. I travelled to Europe several times where these issues are treated more openly. I'm not glorifying Europe in terms of progressiveness, but I think sometimes when I write, I want to make it a point that some of our traditions, which we think belong to our customs, in fact don't.

In your opinion, what might be some of the new voices and perspectives that we can see developing in South African literature?
There are quite a number of them. I think the one that I really like is Tshifhiwa Given Mukwevho and his books *A Traumatic Revenge* (2011) and *The Violent Gestures of Life* (2014) – great books about juvenile delinquencies. He, himself, was sentenced to ten years in prison. He comes fresh with a new perspective about how we should look into South Africa. He talks about, among other things, the causes of xenophobia. It's about drug addiction, for instance, which is quite a serious problem at the moment. In KwaZulu-Natal, people mix whoonga [a form of black tar heroin] with antiretrovirals (ARVs) and Rattex and whatever else. People are being robbed of their ARVs in order for these drugs to be made. Addiction has to be tackled, and unemployment among the youth, for instance, has to be tackled as well. Those are the things that one has to look into. You mentioned the new generation of writers. Thando Mgqolozana belongs to the new generation of writers that you have to know about. There are other writers that are self-published. I've read a number of their works. Mofenyi Malepe, for instance, has come out with a book called *283: The Bad Sex Bet* (2014). He writes about why young men are competing to sleep with as many women as possible in order to win the bet. That's what the book is all about.

You have mentioned several male writers. What about women?
I think Angela Makholwa, for instance, has written great books. *Black Widow Society* (2013), which is about spouses killing their men for insurance purposes, is very interesting. Or Futhi Ntshingila's *Shameless* (2008), which is set in rural KwaZulu-Natal.

Which different genres do you see becoming more prominent as an attempt to break away from realist conventions?
Are you thinking of Lauren Beukes [*laughter*]? I think nobody has ever attempted what she's done. I think she is doing quite well for herself. It's working for her. What kind of genre is that by the way?

Speculative fiction.
Ja, speculative fiction. And also crime writing is very popular. But if you ask me about black South African writers, we haven't attempted these kinds of genres yet. I just feel that writing crime fiction amounts to following the trend of writing within a bestselling genre. I would love to venture into what Lauren has done. I think she has done a great job, but at the moment I still have lots of things that I want to write about that mean a lot to me, such as homophobia and xenophobia. But I think speculative fiction works.

What are you currently working on in terms of fiction? What can we expect next from Niq Mhlongo?
I'm writing a book which is about 70 or 80 per cent done. I don't have a title yet, but the book resonates more or less with my life: being born in an urban area but having had to live in the rural area because of apartheid. Nobody owned property in Soweto. All houses were leased housing so that the government could easily say that every black person had to have a homeland. The book is about a person who goes in and out of those spaces. I'm trying to show some aspects of rural life because I used to live in rural South Africa. I am writing about when there were strikes in Joburg during the 1985 state of emergency, the uprisings, and how these events affected people's schooling, for instance, because at some points schools were closed. I'm also showing that the protagonist's father has two wives. There's a rural wife and an urban wife. The protagonist is the urban wife's second-born, who resembles her late first-born child to such an extent that she cannot bear it, disowns her second-born, and sends him away to the countryside to be brought up by the rural wife. It turns out that the rural wife also has a six-month-old baby. So, the two are brought up as siblings.

ॐ

References

Berlin, Isaiah. 1978. *Russian Thinkers*. London: Penguin.

Makholwa, Angela. 2013. *Black Widow Society*. Johannesburg: Pan Macmillan.

Malepe, Mofenyi. 2014. *282: The Bad Sex Bet – Temptation Gets an Upgrade*. Johannesburg: Koma Publishing.

Mukwevho, Tshifhiwa Given. 2011. *A Traumatic Revenge*. Polokwane: Timbila Publishing.

———. 2014. *The Violent Gestures of Life*. Pietermaritzburg: University of KwaZulu-Natal Press.

Ntshingila, Futhi. 2008. *Shameless*. Pietermaritzburg: University of KwaZulu-Natal Press.

Tolstoy, Leo. [1912] 2003. *Hadji Murád*. New York: The Modern Library.

'If women are the biggest book buyers, what the hell is chick-lit, particularly when we don't have dick-lit?'

Zukiswa Wanner (photo: courtesy Zukiswa Wanner, taken by Fungai Machirori)

Danyela Demir and Olivier Moreillon

In Conversation with Zukiswa Wanner
(b. 1976)

The following conversation with Zukiswa Wanner took place at Belaire Hotel, Durban, during the Time of the Writer Festival 2016. The full-time writer, who is half South African and half Zimbabwean, is based in Nairobi, Kenya, where she lives with her partner and son. Zukiswa is the author of four novels: *The Madams* (2006), *Behind Every Successful Man* (2008), *Men of the South* (2010) and *London, Cape Town, Joburg* (2014); three children's books, *Jama Loves Bananas* (2013), *Refilwe* (2014) and *The Black Pimpernel* (2021); as well as three books of non-fiction, *8115: A Prisoner's Home* (2010, co-authored with Alf Kumalo), *Maid in SA: 30 Ways to Leave Your Madam* (2010) and *Hardly Working: A Travel Memoir of Sorts* (2018). Her debut novel, *The Madams*, was shortlisted for the K. Sello Duiker Memorial Literary Award. *Men of the South*, her third novel, was shortlisted for both the 2011 Commonwealth Writer's Prize and the Herman Charles Bosman Award. For her fourth novel, *London, Cape Town, Joburg*, Zukiswa won the 2015 K. Sello Duiker Memorial Literary Award. In 2020, she received the Goethe Medal for her exceptional work for arts and culture as well as her commitment to fighting restrictions both on a political and a societal level.

Zukiswa studied journalism at Hawaii Pacific University in Honolulu. Her journalistic work includes articles for *Oprah*, *Elle* and *Juice* magazines; literary reviews and essays for the *Afropolitan*, the *Mail & Guardian*, the *Sunday Independent* and the online journal *African Writing*. In 2018, Zukiswa co-founded the publishing company Paivapo, which focuses on promoting African literature across various languages. In response to the restrictions imposed on social life by the

COVID-19 pandemic, Zukiswa founded and curated several instalments of the Afrolit Sans Frontiers Festival, a virtual literary festival.[1]

Commenting on her writing process, Zukiswa says: 'I actually don't have any dislikes about the writing process because I'm not the type of writer who does 1 000 words a day and forces myself to write. I only ever write when I think I have something to say . . . I don't struggle with the blank page because I have erased all my blank page days by not writing on those days [*laughs*]!'

When she is not busy writing, Zukiswa reads whatever she can get her hands on. The most recent book she had read before the interview was Sorayya Khan's *Five Queen's Road* (2009), which she found to be 'a lovely book' and 'very enlightening about post-partition India and Pakistan'. She says about herself that she is an 'adrenaline junkie, so I do silly things like bungee jumping and hope that the rope doesn't snap, and because I live in Nairobi, I also do crazy stuff, like getting on a *boda boda*, which is a motorbike, because I enjoy that it eases me through Nairobi's hectic traffic'.

Among her favourite spots in Johannesburg are Melville and Soweto, the former because Zukiswa likes book stores and is a big fan of artistic spaces and the latter because of its rich history. She particularly likes to return to her late grandmother's house in Orlando West 'to chill with family, and just bond and have a lovely time'. She also enjoys hanging out at Busy Corner, which she loves because of its 'good music . . . and the all-South African tradition, the braai'. Her favourite spot in Durban is North Beach. When she is in Nairobi, she tends to be 'a homebody'. She explains that 'with all the travelling, when I'm home, I generally invite people home, and I cook, and then we laugh and talk books and we have some beers or some wine'.

☙

Works

———. 2006. *The Madams* (Oshun Books)

The Madams deals with the intricate relationship between middle-class women and their domestic workers as well as the different responsibilities

---

1. See https://afrolitsansfrontieres.com (accessed 18 December 2020).

of successful black women in post-apartheid South Africa and the hurdles they face.

————. 2008. *Behind Every Successful Man* (Kwela Books)
Behind Every Successful Man continues with some of the issues raised in *The Madams*, shifting the focus, however, to the hopes and expectations of Black Economic Empowerment wives and their striving for self-fulfilment that leads to tensions between themselves and their patriarchal tycoon husbands.

————. 2010. *8115: A Prisoner's Home* (with Alf Kumalo) (Penguin)
This biography of Nelson Mandela, the title of which makes reference to 8115 Vilakazi Street, Soweto, the home of the Mandela family, collects some of the most precious photographs of the Mandela family's life by renowned photographer and close family friend Alf Kumalo. Zukiswa provides commentary and contextualisation for the book.

————. 2010. *Maid in SA: 30 Ways to Leave Your Madam* (Jacana Media)
Maid in SA continues to engage with the relationship between domestic workers and their madams, satirically shedding light on mutual stereotypes and biases of this complicated type of relationship.

————. 2010. *Men of the South* (Kwela Books)
Men of the South tells the stories of three men from different social backgrounds. The three interlinked storylines, which can be read as a novel or individual stories in their own right, tackle concerns such as breaking with gender stereotypes, the problems of coming out within the patriarchal hierarchies of South Africa's black society and issues of migration.

————. 2011. *Jama Loves Bananas* (Jacana Media)
Jama Loves Bananas is a children's book.

————. 2014. *London, Cape Town, Joburg* (Kwela Books)
London, Cape Town, Joburg tells the love story of Martin O'Malley and Germaine Spencer. During their marriage they move to South Africa, the 'homeland' of Martin's mother. The ups and downs of Martin and

Germaine's lives reflect the turbulences within democratic South Africa. The couple's life is further complicated by the various secrets around Martin's South African family.

————. 2014. *Refilwe* (Jacana Media)
Refilwe is an African retelling of the Rapunzel tale.

————. 2018. *Hardly Working: A Travel Memoir of Sorts* (Black Letter Media Publishing)
Hardly Working is the result of six months of extensive travelling with her partner and son on the African continent as well as her own trips within Africa and Europe.

————. 2021. *The Black Pimpernel: Nelson Mandela on the Run.* (Pushkin Children's Books)
The Black Pimpernel is a children's book that traces Nelson Mandela's path towards becoming a resistance fighter in the anti-apartheid movement in the early 1960s.

ॐ

Besides your adult fiction, and your non-fiction book *Maid in SA*, you have written three books for children. What prompted you to go into writing children's fiction?
I was asked. And because I hadn't done it, I did. I'm always up for a challenge. So when somebody says to me, can you write a piece for *Science Today*, or whatever, I am likely to be that person who says: 'Give me enough time and I'll do research on this issue and I'll write on it.' I'm always hungry to learn new things and to experiment and to find out stuff. The Little Hands Trust had asked me to do a baby book, and my son is a big fan of bananas, so I did the baby book *Jama Loves Bananas* because he is called Jama Hintsa. It was obviously a hit with him because he always calls it 'my book'. And then with *Refilwe*, there was a project that was happening where established writers took stories, traditional fairy tales, and did something with them. You know, my great-grandfather is German and perhaps that's where it comes from. The Rapunzel tale has always fascinated me because I always wondered whether the roots of her hair hurt, that type of thing. I really wanted

to retell Rapunzel, but I wanted it to have an African feel. It's actually not set in South Africa and that's why I wanted to do it. I wanted to set it in the mountain kingdom of Lesotho and part of it was because of the geography of the place, but I also hoped that when children read it, they'd become curious about their neighbouring countries. I often say about us South Africans that we are the Americans of Africa. We're so insular and we think we're self-sufficient and that we don't need to know the rest of Africa. We don't care to engage with the rest of the continent. And so this was my little contribution. I really wanted to make it work, so instead of a princess on top of a tower, I had an ordinary girl with dreadlocks in a cave on top of a mountain.

One of the recurring patterns within your novels is that they are structured around love and relationships. What is your response to the fact that some critics label your writing as chick-lit, while your male counterparts in South African fiction, such as Niq Mhlongo or Kgebetli Moele, have been grouped under the term Kwaito writers, and Thando Mgqolozana or Nthikeng Mohlele, for instance, are writers of literary fiction?

You know, when asked about this I have often said that the biggest book buyers, as you well know, all over the world, are women. If women are the biggest book buyers, what the hell is chick-lit, particularly when we don't have dick-lit? That said, I don't really care very much what people label my work, and I'll tell you why. When I finish a manuscript and it becomes a book, if you are reading it or you buy it or whatever, it is no longer my work. It's your book, and you interpret it the way you want to. I'm not responsible for the way someone interprets a piece of art. Different people will respond differently to stuff. It used to rile me when I first started writing. But, to be honest, after *The Madams* and *Behind Every Successful Man*, now it's not a big issue with me anymore. I just say, if this is how you feel about something, then it's okay. I don't expect everybody to like my work. I don't write for everybody. But then the reality of that, and we can't ignore it, is that there's a hierarchy in literature, isn't there? There is literature that is white and male, and then there is women's literature. There is African literature that is black and male, and so forth.

In South African literature, this hierarchy seems to be particularly entrenched in contrast to other places on the continent. NoViolet Bulawayo, Chimamanda Ngozi Adichie and Taiye Selassie, for example, are internationally renowned. They are probably even better known than some of their male counterparts.

Absolutely! I don't say it often enough, but I have said it every now and again, that word for word, women on this continent for the last five or ten years, have been out-writing the guys in terms of output. That's up for contention [*laughter*]. That said, you know, it's what happens, and sometimes when they say to you that you have to work twice as hard to get half the recognition, it happens a lot of times.

How important is the representation of space and place in your writing?

I think space and place are important, but they are important only in that they move the narrative forward. I like the idea about writing the familiar, so I will set something in my favourite city in the world, which is Joburg. I always picture my characters in the places that I love.

What different aspects of home, belonging and community do you engage with in your fiction?

I think a lot, you know, as I mentioned before. I think identity is the one thread that goes through my writing. Home itself – I had a weekly column in the literary pages of Kenya's weekly *Saturday Nation* that was called 'Outsider Looking In'. It was my commentary about where I am. Even if I'm in South Africa, I write 'Outsider Looking In' because I think my whole identity itself – my father being South African, my mom being Zimbabwean, and me having been born in Zambia – has always allowed me the external gaze. I am also allowed the intimacy because I have a relationship with each of these countries. So, for instance, South Africa has been incredibly generous to me, as has Zimbabwe, as has Zambia, even Nigeria now and Kenya. They permit me to – sometimes satirically, sometimes seriously – critique them without showing the deference you would usually show someone if they're not from that community. They've opened up to me that way and they've allowed me that space, so I'm very lucky and privileged. I am this nomad who is loved enough by the people that I've encountered that they allow me to critique them, laugh about them, laugh at them and with them, without necessarily feeling like I am doing it out of malice. I think they realise that I am generally doing it out of the love that I feel for the place, and just essentially because I'm an African, and I enjoy that. I enjoy my places. I enjoy making fun of them. I also sometimes look at them and hope that my criticism will help us become better people.

Particularly in *Men of the South*, traditional or patriarchal understandings of masculinity are undermined. How vital is it, for you as a writer, to deconstruct hegemonic notions of masculinity as well as of femininity?
It's always been very important for me to question, so I always think of *Men of the South*, for instance, as a counterpart to *The Madams* because *Men of the South* questions the patriarchal notions of manhood, which, in a country like South Africa, can be very debilitating, but also absolutely horrible if you consider that there are a lot of female-headed households. It was also very important for me to get the reader to perhaps be lured in, but also to question. There are misconceptions and there are biases, and what is manhood? What is nationality? That was an important part of what I was writing and I do hope that it came out that way. Sometimes, I think it did because there's a friend of mine whose husband read it, and then he called me and I answered and he wanted to know whether I was Zukiswa. What had happened was that he thought his wife was having an affair and that I was a man. He had read *Men of the South* and thought there is no way that a woman could have written it [*laughter*]. He ended up apologising, but that was just one of those weird moments.

I guess, as a writer, you're exposed to these strange things. People mixing fiction with reality. How important are issues of race, racism and white privilege for the plot of *London, Cape Town, Joburg* and *The Madams*, in particular?
I think it's difficult to engage with South Africa without engaging with race because it's such an important component of our history and our present as well. So they were important for me, but I also wanted to show that it's possible to have interracial relationships and friendships if you are actually willing to engage. Too often people close themselves up in their little cocoons and they don't take the time to engage and they are stuck with their stereotypes of what they believe the other is like. So, for instance, Lauren in *The Madams* is very quick to question the employment of Marita, but she doesn't question her relationship with

a black domestic worker. Sometimes, jokes help to question how we perceive things. Even when we think we are liberal, there are undertones of prejudice. Homophobia, for instance, in both Martin and Germaine when they engage with the idea of Anil, you know?[2] With regards to homophobia and race, according to our constitution, we are all supposed to be holding hands and singing 'Kumbaya', but it's not the reality on the ground. The University of the Free State and a lot of the things that were happening during #RhodesMustFall and #FeesMustFall enlighten us and show us that maybe it's not as we think it is.

In terms of white privilege, I just think of the scene where Germaine goes into the township and tries to open the studio with the other ladies, and in the beginning she makes all these stupid mistakes and she doesn't want to be called madam, but she also has the luxury of having a domestic worker. To me, it seems that there is this development in your fiction, say from *The Madams* to *London, Cape Town, Joburg*, where the topic of white privilege is pivotal.

Absolutely, because here's the thing. Noma has been in this community for a while. Noma is an intelligent woman who has all these things going for her. She has a degree, but she is unfortunately this black woman who is not allowed to be able to be and do what she wants. She's busy being a bookkeeper for some shops in the townships because nobody will allow her the space to do what she's qualified to do. But on the other hand, Germaine can come through from England and just be able to go in the townships and everybody supports her. It's not something that we interrogate often, but I think it's something that we need to interrogate more. There's a default setting in society, and I'm talking black and white, that expects that a white person needs to totally and absolutely fuck up before they can be considered wrong. On the other hand, a black person needs to fuck up just once and they're written off, you know? And that happens, and even when Germaine comes to Joburg, it's not as hectic a transition for her as it would be for a lot of people. There are a lot of black people transitioning from one city to another and they have to create a niche for themselves. Speaking for myself,

---

2. Anil marries Germaine's best friend Priah in order to keep up appearances with his family and quell the suspicions with regard to his homosexuality, while both Priah and Germaine are well aware of Anil's relationships with men.

it took me at least two years of living in Nairobi before I was invited to literary events. On the other hand, I think that a white writer who doesn't have the same body of work that I have would be more likely to be welcomed into that space.

To our knowledge, you are one of the very few writers in contemporary South African fiction who focuses strongly on the relationship between domestic workers and their employers in various shapes and forms and the things that come with it. What were some of the reasons for choosing to write about such a 'loaded' theme?

I think too often we talk about how terrible things are. I'm a feminist, but we often cry about how women are at the bottom of the table, and in a lot of situations, they are. What then happens when a woman is the one who is stepping down on another woman, like in a domestic situation? A husband will go to his wife to complain about the fact that the domestic worker has burnt his shirt. So it's then the woman who goes and complains and as far as the domestic worker is concerned, it's her female employer who is bad and not the husband. So there is that quandary. But also, if you have a bottle of whisky that costs R4 500 in your home on a weekend, and your domestic worker is being paid R2 500 per month, there is something wrong with that situation. There is something wrong with the fact that the person you trust to look after your most precious possessions – never mind your children – is the person that you decide doesn't deserve to be paid enough. That's problematic.

Although South Africa is recognised as having one of the most liberal constitutions in the world, its society is still largely conservative. What taboos do you think have yet to find their way into contemporary South African literature? And are there any topics you feel you cannot write about yet?

I don't think there's anything I can't write about. It's been done in African literature before, from within an even more conservative society than South Africa – Zimbabwe, but I would like to explore the idea of an intersex or transgender person, you know? It's an issue that's important to me and one that I think should be important to people because it's a human right, and it's something that I'm very keen to explore in literature.

In your opinion, what might be some of the new voices or perspectives that we can see developing in South African literature?
There are too many: Nakhane Touré's *Piggy Boy's Blues* (2015), Songeziwe Mahlangu's *Penumbra* (2014). Then there is this one book set in Durban that I love, *By Any Means* (2014) by Kurt Ellis. Rehana Rossouw's *What Will People Say?* (2015) is a beautiful book. Who else? Panashe Chigumadzi's *Sweet Medicine* (2015). Penny Busetto is on the shortlist of the Etisalat Prize with *The Story of Anna P, as Told by Herself* (2014). Paula Marais: you need to read her *Shadow Self* (2014). It's a lovely book. There's Masande Ntshanga's *The Reactive* (2014). There's just so many people right now. It's exciting! Yewande Omotoso's second book, *The Woman Next Door*, is coming out [published in 2016]. I have been privileged to have read the manuscript and she just takes it to another level.

Which different genres do you see becoming more prominent as an attempt to break away from realist conventions?
Well, crime fiction has been very popular in South Africa. We just have really great material, don't we? I've been seeing a lot of science fiction as well, and I actually fantasise about doing crime fiction. I've done a crime fiction short story, 'To Kill a Politician', in *Home Away: 24 Hours, 24 Cities, 24 Writers* (Greenberg 2010), and I fantasise about writing a crime fiction novel. My fantasy would be a whodunnit, and a publisher is killed, or a bookseller or something [*laughs*].

Last question, what can we expect from you? Future projects?
I want to avoid jinxing stuff so less about future writing but hopefully publishing in the not-too-distant future.

Is there anything else?
That novel, and then because right now I have access to the rest of the continent, I'm just really keen to write maybe two or three manuscripts a year? Maybe set up a publishing firm at some point in the future, maybe within the next two or three years, and I'll tell you why. I am actually so *gatvol* with the way publishers, in South Africa particularly but even on the continent, have failed to use up the space they have.

Many editors miss nuances. Sometimes, though, it's not even missing it. Sometimes you are assigned an editor who is just happy to get their little money, and also, depending on the name of the writer, they are just in awe and are happy to do it. One of the reasons that I love *London, Cape Town, Joburg* so much was because when James Woodhouse was at Kwela, he was amazing because he allowed me to choose my own editor, and I went with Jacqui L'Ange. She is the person who edited *The Madams* for me.

That was a different publisher though, right?
It was a different publisher, but I decided I didn't want anybody else to edit this book except her, and part of the reason was I knew she wouldn't bullshit me. I knew she wouldn't be in awe of me, and, as far as I'm concerned, the relationship between an editor and a writer should be a hate/hate relationship during the editorial process, and then a love/love relationship when the book has come out.

References

Busetto, Penny. 2014. *The Story of Anna P, as Told by Herself*. Johannesburg: Jacana Media.

Chigumadzi, Panashe. 2015. *Sweet Medicine*. Johannesburg: Blackbird Books.

Ellis, Kurt. 2014. *By Any Means*. Cape Town: Human & Rousseau.

Greenberg, Louis (ed.). 2010. *Home Away: 24 Hours, 24 Cities, 24 Writers*. Cape Town: Zebra Press.

Khan, Sorayya. 2009. *Five Queen's Road*. New Delhi: Penguin Books.

Mahlangu, Songeziwe. 2014. *Penumbra*. Cape Town: Kwela Books.

Marais, Paula. 2014. *Shadow Self*. Cape Town: Human & Rousseau.

Ntshanga, Masande. 2014. *The Reactive*. Cape Town: Umuzi.

Omotoso, Yewande. 2016. *The Woman Next Door*. Johannesburg: Penguin Random House.

Rossouw, Rehana. 2015. *What Will People Say?* Johannesburg: Jacana Media.

Touré, Nakhane. 2015. *Piggy Boy's Blues*. Johannesburg: Jacana Media.

'I think that there is an unfortunate perception that African writers are confined to issues that happen on the African continent and their immediate surroundings.'

Nthikeng Mohlele (photo: courtesy Nthikeng Mohlele, taken by Oupa Nkosi)

Danyela Demir and Olivier Moreillon

In Conversation with Nthikeng Mohlele
(b. 1977)

We met Nthikeng Mohlele the day after the Johannesburg launch of his novel *Michael K*. It was a balmy April evening in Rosebank, where we chatted about his work over a glass of red wine.

Nthikeng is the author of six novels: *The Scent of Bliss* (2008), *Small Things* (2013), *Rusty Bell* (2014), *Pleasure* (2016), *Michael K* (2018) and *Illumination* (2019). *Small Things* was translated into Swedish as *Joburg Blues* in 2014. *Pleasure* won both the 2017 University of Johannesburg Main Prize for South African Writing in English and the K. Sello Duiker Memorial Literary Award and was longlisted for the 2018 International Dublin Literary Award.

He grew up in Limpopo and Tembisa and later studied Dramatic Arts, Publishing Studies and African Literature at Wits University. He currently lives in Johannesburg.

Maybe somewhat uncharacteristically, Nthikeng likes everything about the writing process, including aspects that other authors might consider taxing. In his opinion, 'it can be very slippery to pin down specific things that you want to write about. It can be very lonely. It's very demanding on time and social aspects of one's life because it is such a solitary art.' At the same time, it is the writing's 'posterity, self-expression, reflection, depth and contribution to culture' that make it fascinating and worthwhile for Nthikeng.

Asked about what he does when not writing, he says: 'I think. I read. I take a lot of photographs.' His most recent read at the time of our meeting had been *Seize the Day* (1956) by Saul Bellow, which he found 'brilliant'.

He does not have a specific favourite place in Johannesburg, but he likes the motorways because he enjoys 'driving in open spaces late at night when it's just the city lights'. He adds, however, that he does like the Telkom Towers in Pretoria for their 'very nice view of the city'.

੭

Works
———. 2008. *The Scent of Bliss* (Kwela Books)
———. 2019. *The Scent of Bliss* (second edition, Kwela Books)
The Scent of Bliss tells the story of Q, a literature lecturer who lives in the fictitious Lumumbaville. He was orphaned as a teenager and suffers from General Anxiety Disorder. Struggling to find his place in the world, he enters a relationship with Bernice, an older woman, finds his life uprooted and stumbles into chaos, trying to find his feet.

———. 2013. *Small Things* (University of KwaZulu-Natal Press)
———. 2018. *Small Things* (second edition, Jacana Media)
Small Things centres on an unnamed narrator who spent eighteen years in jail during apartheid for an unspecified crime. In post-apartheid South Africa, the narrator roams the streets of Johannesburg, playing the trumpet, in the company of his scruffy dog. Torn between two women, Desiree and Mercedes, he ultimately cannot give up his obsession for the former and plunges into an existential crisis.

———. 2014. *Rusty Bell* (University of KwaZulu-Natal Press)
———. 2018. *Rusty Bell* (second edition, Jacana Media)
Rusty Bell tells the story of corporate lawyer Michael, aka Sir Marvin, whose relationship with his wife and son is deteriorating and rather on the frosty side. With Michael on the couch of his long-time psychologist, readers find out about his sex addiction, behind which lies a tragic and seemingly long-lost memory linked to his childhood in Alexandra.

———. 2016. *Pleasure* (Pan Macmillan)
Pleasure circles around Milton Mohlele who is a writer living in self-isolation. He spends much of his time contemplating his relationships and various forms of pleasure and unease that he has experienced with different women. Throughout the novel, Milton sees present-day Cape Town in a different light as he dreams of Nazi Germany, consequently drawing parallels between South Africa and Germany's troubled histories.

————. 2018. *Michael K* (Pan Macmillan)

Michael K could be described as a continuation of J.M. Coetzee's *Life and Times of Michael K* (1983). The novel's narrator, Miles, spends two-and-a-half years on Dust Island, where he meets Michael K. In an attempt to fuel his creativity, he observes Michael K's daily life and profound connection to nature on the island. In his perpetual quest for inspiration, Miles' initial curiosity soon turns into an obsession that persists once he moves to Johannesburg.

————. 2019. *Illumination* (Pan Macmillan)

Illumination tells the story of the renowned jazz trumpeter Bantubonke, whose professional success takes a substantial toll on his private life. His excessive focus on his artistic career not only encumbers his marital life but also has far-reaching effects on his mental health.

৵

The intersection of music and writing is particularly important in *Small Things* but resurfaces in your other work. Where do you see crossovers between music and writing in general and in your writing in particular?

I think it's at a very automatic level because I don't think that art is mutually exclusive. So I look at music, literature, visual arts, motion pictures and the theatre as a continuum of artistic expression. I read music in the same way as I would read poetry. Music is timing and literature is words and there is space between words and notes. That's the position I have.

How important is musicality for (your) language?

Well, musicality is everything to the language that I use because it helps me to write in such a way that the stuff is not dry. It gives the language, I believe, a certain flair, a certain originality and unpredictability. It gives it a certain ambience and that is why I really associate music very much with words and not only words, but the emotive too.

Many of your female characters seem to be unreachable or undecipherable for most of your male characters. What importance would you attribute to this general disconnectedness between women and men in your *oeuvre*?

I think that women are very complicated people – complicated in inverted commas – in that they've been rendered by civilisations, by time, by cultures, by scholars, by sociological determinants, as one-dimensional. But I think that which we don't understand is not necessarily one-dimensional and I didn't want women that were ogres in my narrative. I wanted women that were strong without being brutal.

The protagonist in *Small Things* claims at one point: 'Martyrdom is not only when you are dead and buried; there are many walking dead, bruised by the revolution. A revolution which, by the look of things, has lost its way – in the *Animal Farm* (1945) and Kafka-esque sense' (2013: 74). We could claim that your work, in comparison to other contemporary South African writers, is maybe less obviously political. However, to what extent are the themes of love, sex and desire in your writing entangled with political issues of South Africa's past and present?
I think that my fiction tries to delve into the complexities of existence itself. In trying to unpack that relationship between society, private citizens and the powerful institutions that govern or affect their lives, which impact on their lives, you get very interesting tensions and linkages from there. The nature of how a country and a time period function actually has a direct bearing on the kind of relationships that people have. Whether they be private relationships – the sexual as you have alluded to – or whether they be about ideas, which are ideological stances, as you say, with regards to politics and history, all those accents are interdependencies for me and many sides of the same coin.

There is a passage in Eusebius McKaiser's *Run Racist Run* that says: 'If you're black, you can't write what you like' (2015: 24). And yet, with you it is very different. It is speaking to ideas more than to plot in a way. And this stance of writing about ideas, perhaps in a more abstract way, to what extent would you say this is a very different form of actually decolonising literature than what many other people would understand?
I don't think that it's necessarily a decolonising project per se. I think it is stylistic adventurism, if I were to put it that way, and putting a personal imprint on contributions to a literary stream. Remember, literature is not a one-dimensional thing and it doesn't come from one writer. So, we're all contributing to the multi-stream of literature based on a heritage

of our own specific contexts within South Africa and on the African continent. But it is informed by, and reflecting on, global literature as it were. So, I don't think it's intrinsically decolonising – it might have those accents, but my emphasis is to try to write away from established and well-known formulas of what constitutes an African novel.

The Holocaust has repeatedly been mentioned as a historical precursor to apartheid. One thinks of works such as Richard Rive's *'Buckingham Palace', District Six* (1986), Lesego Rampolokeng's *Bantu Ghost* (2010) but also the comparison of the Truth and Reconciliation Commission (TRC) with the Nuremberg Trials.[1] Why do you think that writers keep making this comparison and what made it fruitful for your own work?
I think that there is an unfortunate perception that African writers are writers that are confined to issues that happen on the African continent and their immediate surroundings. Whereas ideas and humanity and existence are quite transcendent things. I found the Holocaust very important because it's a profound moment in history, in the sense that something so terrible could happen. But I also used it to illuminate the holocausts that happened on the African continent itself that are less written about, less articulated, less recorded in terms of proper archives of human tragedy. I needed to actually focus on themes of war and how they devastate societies and the private lives of individuals, and I needed to contrast that with pleasure, which is expected to have some luminescence, some beauty, some sensuality contrasted with this brutality that happens. Whether in times of war or under dictatorships, such as Uganda or Germany, for instance, or the trans-Atlantic slave trade, there are these various moments in history that interest me. History features very strongly in my fiction, I believe.

How important is the representation of space and place in your writing?
It's very, very important because I try to defamiliarise spaces that I work with or I choose obscure angles of that space because I think that gives the created work its natural speech.

---

1. For a discussion of the recurrence of this comparison, see Robins (1998).

There's a certain defamiliarisation in *Rusty Bell* and *Small Things*, but then *Michael K* has concrete spatial markers that are very, very palpable, such as the Sunninghill area, and even when the characters walk into a café, the readers can almost smell the coffee. So, on the one hand, space and place is in the background, but on the other hand, it's so much in the foreground. As Eusebius McKaiser said during the launch of *Michael K*, Johannesburg becomes a character in some of your novels. And Cape Town is this elusive person in *Pleasure* because we don't really see Cape Town all that much, we hear it more than we see it, right?

Yes. And that was a very deliberate choice in terms of Cape Town because Johannesburg, for me, has a certain class and a certain energy. Cities are very much like people. You're right in saying that they're all like characters in that each has got its own character traits. It was very important for me to bring out the sensual aspects of things that Michael K would not necessarily care about. I don't think he cared about coffee or culture, for instance. There's a line that I alluded to which asks whether he would make a difference between 'Amazing Grace' and 'I Shot the Sheriff'. I didn't think he would care about that because he is that sort of material; detached, introverted, but very metaphorically complex.

Considering that *Michael K* is a patchwork quilt of so many references, in what ways are you writing back to J.M. Coetzee and perhaps to a broader discussion about *Michael K*?

I don't think that it's writing back per se. It is more a continuation of that artistic project. It's an act of reinvention through a borrowing of the dominant tropes in the original text. But I don't think it's writing back. In terms of a 'patchwork of references' I tend to agree with that. I wouldn't see it necessarily as patchwork, but I'd see it as giving that guy the persona of John Coetzee himself. Because remember, as much as he appears as a character in *Michael K*, he is a real-life person. So you're not going to make J.M. Coetzee into James Bond all of a sudden, you know what I mean? So you are confined to the biographical information that is there and to present it in such a way that it ties up with him being a character, him being a reference point as well as the body of work that surrounds him being inserted into the book – which is quite a delicate balance to work through.

I didn't so much mean J.M. Coetzee as patchwork. I meant the many other impressive references that a lot of reviewers are not really seeing. Maybe it's got something to do with the marketing strategy? But for me Dambudzo Marechera is important, Keorapetse Kgositsile is important and James Baldwin – the patchwork quilt of other texts dancing around *Life and Times of Michael K*. Is it a different continuation of taking *Michael K* into a very different direction?

I think so. But the references, remember, are not isolated. There are strong thematic connections in the references that I have chosen. And you're right, maybe the reviewers might miss that. But remember, reviewers have certain interests as much as writers do. So they will take an angle of what they connect with in the book and reflect on that, which is not necessarily exhaustive or conclusive.

What different aspects of home, belonging and community do you engage with in your fiction?

I focus on the self, primarily, and the self is what drives me to think through how it reacts to the social, cultural, economic and historical contexts in which that character exists. From that point of view I'm able to draw parallels with other geographical localities around the world because we live in a globalised world. It's not possible anymore to just confine stories to their context of origin. There are always linkages or influences that we encounter, and subcultures that emerge from those fusions that happened in the natural progression of societies in an interconnected world.

Many of your characters seem to display some sort of mental dis-ease. What function do these different forms of mental instability have?

I think they do have mental dis-eases. Narrative thrives on conflict. Anything that is hunky-dory would make a terrible read. There needs to be objective and subjective art for relevance and progression, as it happens in life. And that can be in the family unit, it can be in the personal space. And how that interfaces with the moral context of what happens when characters interrelate. Inevitably, there will be pressure-filled situations and some people become schizophrenic, and they lose their focus.

In what ways are these psychological issues an expression of the characters' existentialist lifestyles or ways of living?
I think it's a mirror of the societies that those characters live in. Maybe it's just that the characters I deal with are more sensitive, more brittle, and do not necessarily absorb those pressures and tremors as well as others do. Hence they become focal points of narratives that I deal with. But I believe they're well-balanced with very sane and normal characters, and sober ones.

Although South Africa is recognised as having one of the most liberal constitutions in the world, its society is still largely conservative. What taboos do you think have yet to find their way into contemporary South African literature? Are there topics you feel you cannot write about yet?
No. If I didn't write about something it's just purely because I don't want to write about it. I don't feel restrained as an artist at all. I don't think that I should produce offensive literature. I think I should produce competent literature and that is sufficient for me.

But do you think that some of your peers are breaking with taboos, or struggling with taboos, or do you see that there's a gap, that there are topics missing that we are tiptoeing around?
Homophobia is one of those topics. The complexities of present-day racism is one of those things. Economic imbalances is one of those other things that are not really written in the literature of now.

In your opinion, what might be some of the new voices or perspectives that we can see developing in South African literature?
I'm an old hat now, I know. I think that if I look at the literary landscape the leaning is more towards music than it is towards literature and I'm not saying that lightly. I'm thinking that as much as we've got Thandiswa Mazwai and Simphiwe Dana and what have you, their approach to music is one of reflecting on the old, but it's a reinvention, taking the music forward. And that – because I've got a musical approach to literature – is much more powerful than the individual texts of the new younger artists.

Which different genres do you see becoming more prominent as an attempt to break away from realist conventions?

I think that there is a need for sanitised historical fiction. Historical fiction does not necessarily need to delve into heavy subjects and morbid historical occurrences. I think something can be historical where you have history that happened as the faraway background, but bring to the fore a great love story, for instance, that is not bolted down by racism and apartheid and what have you. I think there are also no great novels, as far as I'm concerned, that actually competently handle the female character and the female form in South Africa. Women are not very strong leads in our literature and they play supporting roles of sorts, including my own, and I think that needs to be looked at in the literatures of the future where you've got women actually setting the agenda. I've been thinking a lot about that – where women shouldn't exist, because there are male counterparts around them, but women being pioneers and being innovative in terms of our societal formations and transformations. I think that is very much lacking. And the other thing is that there is a very concerning lack of biographical fiction in South Africa – if I can use that term – fiction that focuses on people that are prominent in the national discourse of South Africa and on the continent for that matter.

What are your current and future projects? Is there anything developing?
I've been taking mental notes [*laughs*]. So no, not at this point.

References

Bellow, Saul. 1956. *Seize the Day*. New York: Viking Press.

Coetzee, J.M. 1983. *Life and Times of Michael K*. Johannesburg: Ravan Press.

McKaiser, Eusebius. 2015. *Run Racist Run: Journeys into the Heart of Racism*. Johannesburg: Bookstorm.

Orwell, George. 1945. *Animal Farm: A Fairy Story*. London: Secker and Warburg.

Rampolokeng, Lesego. 2010. *Bantu Ghost: A Stream of (Black) Unconsciousness*. Johannesburg: Mehlo-Maya.

Rive, Richard. 1986. *'Buckingham Palace', District Six*. Cape Town: David Philip.

Robins, Steven. 1998. 'Silence in My Father's House: Memory, Nationalism, and Narratives of the Body', in *Negotiating the Past: The Making of Memory in South Africa*, edited by Carli Coetzee and Sarah Nuttall, 120–43. Cape Town: Oxford University Press.

'I just think that African spirituality hasn't been colonised, which is why it's not popular.'

Mohale Mashigo (photo: courtesy Mohale Mashigo, taken by Sydelle Willow Smith)

Danyela Demir and Olivier Moreillon

In Conversation with Mohale Mashigo
(b. 1983)

We met Mohale Mashigo at Café Jiran at Durban's North Beach just as the Time of the Writer Festival 2018 was coming to a close.[1] She is the author of *The Yearning* (2016), which won the 2017 University of Johannesburg Prize in the debut category. The novel was also shortlisted for the 2017 K. Sello Duiker Memorial Literary Award and was longlisted for the 2017 Barry Ronge Fiction Prize,[2] as well as the 2018 International Dublin Literary Award. Her second book, *Beyond the River* (2017), is a young adult novel, an adaptation of the eponymous South African film directed by Craig Freimond (2017). *Intruders* (2018), a collection of short stories, is her third book to date.

Besides being a writer of fiction, Mohale, who holds a BA in Journalism and Linguistics from Rhodes University, is also an award-winning singer-songwriter, performing under the name Black Porcelain. The born and bred Sowetan furthermore writes for the comic book series *Kwezi*, featuring South Africa's first superhero.

While Mohale likes creating characters who have to make complicated life choices because she is fascinated by the human experience, she does not like writing herself 'into a corner' and finds editing 'tough'. She explains: 'Editing is difficult because writing is solitary. I always say it's like you have a baby and somebody cuts your baby open and they say, "Oh your baby's liver is too big. Your baby doesn't really need that much liver."'

---

1. Mohale's given name is Kgomotso Carol Mashigo. Her pen name is her mother's maiden name.
2. Formerly the Sunday Times Fiction Prize.

The most recent book Mohale had read before our meeting was Jacques Pauw's *In the Heart of the Whore* (1991), which unearths the operations of apartheid's death squads and their murders of anti-apartheid activists. About Pauw's book she says: 'It's really ugly, but I think it's also necessary because there's a lot of revisionism happening right now in terms of what really happened.' To counterbalance the heavy read, she was simultaneously rereading Toni Morrison's *The Bluest Eye* (1970), which calmed her even though it was 'not really easy either'.

Mohale can be found wherever there is good food. She says she is a fussy eater and, adds jokingly, that whenever she goes through something she is always on the lookout for 'a place with ribs'. This is why The Smokehouse and Grill in Braamfontein or the Chef's Warehouse in Cape Town feature among her favourite places in the respective cities.

❧

Works

———. 2016. *The Yearning* (Pan Macmillan)
The Yearning is the story of Marubini, who lives in Cape Town and seems to have a picture-perfect life. When her childhood trauma and further family secrets start disrupting her present, both Western medicine and African spirituality help Marubini come to terms with her family history and her life.

———. 2017. *Beyond the River* (Pan Macmillan)
Beyond the River tells the story of Duma, a young Sowetan, who decides to leave his life of thievery to return to canoeing, his one-time passion. Struggling to regain his former skill at the sport, Duma strikes up an unconventional friendship across race and age with Steve, an experienced white canoeist who is struggling to live up to his earlier success.

———. 2018. *Intruders* (Pan Macmillan)
Intruders is a short story collection that retells various South African urban legends, such as Vera the Ghost, die Water Meisie and Pinky Pinky. It taps into speculative fiction and sends the reader on a journey with black girls finding themselves in a space ship, realising that they

are mermaids while on holiday in Durban or taking revenge on behalf of abused women. Besides the short stories, the book features the essay 'Afrofuturism is Not for Africans Living in Africa', in which Mohale takes issue with the term 'Afrofuturism'.[3]

⤫

What different aspects of home, belonging and community do you engage with in your fiction?
In *Intruders,* I am definitely exploring the legacies that define how we think of community and what happens thereafter, the kind of communities that we build for ourselves. I'm really interested in the legacies we can't control and how we build our communities, and what home means. For a long time I felt like I grew up around *black* people in *black* spaces, rural or urban. So, I'm interested in how the legacies affect what we call home, and how, when there is a change, we have to change our idea of home and our communities and how we relate to each other. What if there were no rules about what a person's body could do or what we could do with science? I don't necessarily think that would be a utopia. I think that black women in South Africa have been doing pretty futuristic things. You have people that were raised by women only in what is a women-only community because men are gone. The men are absent, either emotionally or physically. So, we have been futuristic actually!

How important is the representation of space and place in your writing?
That's a very interesting question. When I was looking for an agent for *The Yearning,* one of the things one of the agents said was that *The Yearning* doesn't have place, which I didn't understand because the novel is a very South African story that takes place in present-day Cape Town. The city has its own problems and Marubini is obviously trying to find her place there, which she eventually does. And then I realised that agents want to sell something that says 'Africa!'. Or they want an

---

3. See https://johannesburgreviewofbooks.com/2018/10/01/the-johannesburg-review-of-books-vol-2-issue-10-october-2018/ (accessed 5 April 2020).

immigrant story. But *The Yearning* is a very South African story. There's no 'I went to London and then I struggled with blackness in London'. Oh God! Now it sounds like I'm talking about *Americanah* (2013), Chimamanda Ngozi Adichie's third novel, transferred onto London [*laughs*]. I think right now international publishers and agents want a story that's *very* African, but one that doesn't take place in Africa. It also needs to be the Africa of their imagination. And I don't think that the Africa I am representing is the Africa that people imagine.

For me, Marubini is struggling with the move from her rural upbringing to living in a township, where culture and tradition are not necessarily important because people are just trying to survive. And then she moves to Cape Town, which is another kind of culture, a culture of erasing blackness and brownness and, on top of that, erasing women. So I like to explore the spaces that women occupy physically, but also in ways that we can't touch.

In *The Yearning*, the history and presence of South African social and political life seems to be reflected in the theme of sacrifice, especially by women. What sacrifices are made by which characters in the novel, and to what extent do these different sacrifices reflect gender relations?
When people read *The Yearning*, they often think Marubini's mom is not a nice person. But once you go look back and realise what she's had to give up and the dark place that she had to go to, you realise that she's the hero of the story. I'm very surprised when people say Marubini's dad is the hero of the story. I think he did some heroic things, but he didn't have to stay for what happened after the bad things. Marubini's mom has been through so much. She lost the love of her life. She lost all of her ideas of traditional healing. I think she's a little disengaged and she's also disenchanted with the traditions, understandably so, because this big ugly thing happened and they weren't able to use tradition to make it go away.

Marubini is the only person in the story whose life looks perfect in the beginning, but the sacrifice that she has to make is sacrificing all of these ideas that she's had about her family. That happens to a lot of us, for example, when our parents *lie* to us to try to make the world perfect, and we walk around thinking it is perfect until the wound festers. So, she starts to make sacrifices and she starts to see the sacrifices that the other women in her life have made. And I think that's one of the things

I love about *The Yearning*, you start to see that the women in this story are actually the heroes.

Marubini suffers from some sort of mental dis-ease. What function does this mental instability have in the novel?
It's so funny. I started writing *The Yearning* in 2006 and then I got my job in radio and things were hectic and I was kind of writing. Then in 2008 or 2009 I had a real mental breakdown. It was a terrible depression. I was not comfortable in my mind or my body. I wasn't eating. I wasn't sleeping. I was just wasting away. Then a friend of mine suggested that I write about it. And as I started writing about Marubini, I realised that I am so familiar with mental and physical pain caused by anxiety and depression and panic attacks. So, I pulled from my own pain and it worked really well because I think it was so personal. That really helped to build the character because sometimes if you write 'and she was sad', or 'and she was crying', it doesn't really work about a wound that you don't know, and which is festering. And you're uncomfortable, but you can't even touch the thing because you don't know where it is.

In order to relieve herself of her pain resulting from her mental dis-ease, Marubini is persuaded to first seek counselling with a psychologist instead of visiting a traditional healer. This becomes an option only later in the novel. Could you maybe comment on this position of Western medicine and traditional healing and their purpose in your novel?
My mom loves spirituality, whether it's church or cultural ways of communing with the ancestors, and I never felt those things were separate. It was my dad who didn't believe in anything. Now he believes in something, but he was a man who believed in nothing. I feel like certain illnesses need a specific kind of medicine and that there are different ways of healing. So yes, absolutely go to therapy. But if that doesn't work, it's okay to go for something else, and you don't necessarily have to go for what I'd call 'Western medicine'. I'm not saying if you've got cancer, you mustn't go to the oncologist. I just want people to start exploring their own lives and deciding for themselves how to deal with healing. I feel like: 'Yes, therapy.' And I'm famous for saying South Africa needs therapy, but for me therapy isn't just going to a psychologist or a psychiatrist. It's about seeking the things that work for you. I think that there are so many different ways to heal.

This is why I think *The Yearning* is so important because both trying to seek therapy and going the spiritual route have been stigmatised. People of colour, in general, see therapy as something for Western people who can afford this luxury while they need to soldier on.

I just think that African spirituality hasn't been colonised, which is why it's not popular. But I also feel like we need to seek help wherever and however we can. The only way to find out what doesn't work for you is to try it. I think that's what was so important because Marubini is in a lot of pain. She's even reluctant to go to the hospital, for God's sake. She's afraid to open up. She's just afraid of talking about her pain. And that's a very South African thing, where you can't say to people: 'Hey you know what, actually, being forced to assimilate into primary school, right at the beginning when they opened up schools, that hurt me. That harmed me because I was othered, because my little white friends at school had never had black friends and they said harmful things. And my teachers were not equipped to deal with a different child. And they did harmful things.' In this country we're so afraid to talk about the pain just in case it *offends* someone.

In what ways is *The Yearning* dealing with betrayal, guilt, complicity and responsibility?

When I first started, I knew that there had to be a secret because people stand around a secret, right? And when they're standing around a secret, they default, they abscond from their duties because keeping a secret is a full-time job. And also, keeping a secret means you have to lie to people. So a secret not only makes you abscond from the things you're supposed to be doing, especially with a child or maintaining relationships, but it also means you're constantly lying. You have to keep building this lie over years and years and years. The point of departure in *The Yearning* is a secret. You keep jumping between the past and the future and bits of the secret keep leaking out, and this is how you deal with the betrayal. Every time a little bit leaks out, you have a suspicion as to who might have done it, but when you actually get to the big secret, it's even uglier than you thought it would be.

Although South Africa is recognised as having one of the most liberal constitutions in the world, its society is still largely conservative. What taboos do you think have yet to find their way into contemporary South

African literature and are there topics that you feel that you cannot write about yet?

You know it's funny, I was talking to Unathi Slasha and he was saying that some of those early writers who were writing in *isiXhosa* were quite moralistic and it was because the original presses that were printing them were at churches, they were mission presses. So you couldn't talk about sex and nudity. Oh, the scandal! And I think South Africa is very conservative. I was very worried about *The Yearning*. It's not scandalous, but I also know that people are quite precious about their beliefs and about sex and about how people treat their parents. Marubini is particularly nasty to one of her parents. At one point she says: 'I wish you had died instead of my dad.' She's very harsh with her mother and I was also worried about other stuff that I was writing. In my short story collection there's one story that deals with abortion – forced and chosen, abortion and miscarriages. I feel like we don't deal with a lot of things. I don't know if there's anywhere I wouldn't go, to be honest with you. The place I wouldn't go is if it's not my story to tell.

Even though *The Yearning* does not tiptoe, it finds a very elegant way around breaking some sort of code of revelation.

I grew up in a family of healers, both religious and traditional. As a child I didn't realise I was growing up in a family of healers until I actually finished this book and somebody asked how I knew some of this stuff. When you're a child, you listen to parents discuss things and you think that's how the world works. I didn't realise that not everyone comes from a family of healers. I am also very respectful of the fact that there are things that I would never talk about because when you go *utwasa* [the process of becoming a traditional healer], it's things only meant for you and for those who have – now I was gonna say abilities, like they're superheroes [*laughs*] – those who have abilities, who have been chosen. I didn't want to talk about that stuff. So, I basically mixed up everything that I'd heard as a child that I thought I could say and I left out what I knew shouldn't be said.

In your opinion, what might be some of the new voices or perspectives that we can see developing in South African literature?

I think queer voices are doing things unapologetically and this is upsetting a lot of those 'straightees', as you know. Hey shame, it must be difficult to be so hetero and then you're not the focus of every narrative.

Can you give us examples?

You know, I'm not a poetry person, by the way. I struggled a lot with poetry. When I was a teenager, I thought I could be a poet, but I was a rubbish poet. But when I read Koleka Putuma's *Collective Amnesia* (2017), she's very – now I'm going to sound patronising if I say she's very unapologetic because why should she apologise for being a queer woman? – but she deals with having a religious family and being a queer woman who leaves home and goes to Cape Town and she's in a relationship with a Muslim woman. She really deals with her identity well. Unapologetically. I don't know if this would've been a popular book like maybe twenty years ago. I feel the same way about *The Yearning*. I don't feel like anyone would've read *The Yearning* twenty years ago, but there's just a time and an opening up of narrative. I think after Nakhane Touré's album *You Will Not Die* (2008), the film *Inxeba* (2017) and Nakhane's *Piggy Boy's Blues* (2015) as well, I just feel queer voices are coming up. And in Chwayita Ngamlana's *If I Stay Right Here* (2017), she experiments a lot with storytelling, but she deals with domestic violence between two women, and I just feel like queer voices, especially queer *black* voices – I'm not saying queer white people shouldn't write, by the way – that's the next opening up. Things will just keep opening up and I'm so excited. And also I feel like – I'm not saying *The Yearning* started this trend [*laughter*] – but I feel like people are starting to talk about traditional ways of healing, they are starting to trust their sangomas a little bit. In fact, I read Nechama Brodie's *Knucklebone* (2018) and there she deals with witches – I'm not sure if it's called Wicca – white witches and a sangoma and some evil witches from Eastern Europe. I love that we're going to places respectfully.

Which different genres do you see becoming more prominent in South African writing as an attempt to break away from realist conventions?

People will start experimenting. I'm seeing it currently happening. But also speculative fiction. I write for a comic called *Kwezi*, so superheroes are coming up and speculative fiction. Lauren [Beukes] has been doing it for a while, but people are really starting to write about monsters and stuff and I like that.

I have this opinion that Afrofuturism is not for Africans living in Africa. Afrofuturism makes people very angry. Afrofuturism is not our style as Africans living in Africa. Afrofuturism belongs to the diaspora. It's a vehicle for them. I can't imagine what it's like being a minority in a country and being divorced from your culture somewhat. I'm scared because South Africans are little cannibals. Now we don't call them tekkies, we call them sneakers or trainers. We're little culture vultures in that way because we're so easily influenced by what happens in the UK and the US. I'm afraid that people are going to start tinkering with Afrofuturism and I don't know what we should call our own thing. So what's coming up is superheroes, definitely.

What are your the current and future projects. When is the short story collection coming out now?
I'm working on a graphic novel that is based on two of the characters that I created for two short stories. One of them actually stems from the short story 'The High Heel Killer' that I wrote for the *Mail & Guardian* in 2016.[4] It's about a girl who's walking through Johannesburg. When you take public transport in Johannesburg, you have to wake up really early and you get home very late and the city is particularly violent to a certain kind of woman. Once you've gone through that violence, I think you snap. And this character snaps and the press starts calling her 'the high-heeled killer' because, after she fell into a dirty puddle and a man laughed at her, she kills him with her high-heeled shoe because she's frustrated. As she goes through her trial, she grows wings. It's about this woman and another character from a different short story in the city. So I am working on that graphic novel. It'll come out soon. I won't say this year, but at some point.

I'm also still building libraries for schools. It's a very tough project because I have no funding, so I'm really relying on people's kindness and their donations.

Ș

---

4. See https://mg.co.za/article/2016-08-25-short-fiction-by-the-yearning-author-mohale-mashigo-the-high-heel-killer/ (accessed 16 April 2018).

References

Brodie, Nechama. 2018. *Knucklebone*. Johannesburg: Pan Macmillan.

Morrison, Toni. 1970. *The Bluest Eye*. Austin: Holt McDougal.

Ngamlana, Chwayita. 2017. *If I Stay Right Here*. Johannesburg: Blackbird Books.

Ngozi Adichie, Chimamanda. 2013. *Americanah*. New York: Alfred A. Knopf.

Pauw, Jacques. 1991. *In the Heart of the Whore: The Story of Apartheid's Death Squads*. Cape Town: Jonathan Ball.

Putuma, Koleka. 2017. *Collective Amnesia*. Cape Town: uHlanga.

Touré, Nakhane. 2015. *Piggy Boy's Blues*. Johannesburg: Blackbird Books.

Music

Touré, Nakhane. 2008. *You Will Not Die* [CD]. Paris: BMG France.

Films

Beyond the River. 2017. Directed by Craig Freimond. Johannesburg: Heartlines.

Inxeba. 2017. Directed by John Trengove. Cape Town: Urucu Media.

'I feel that South African fiction is allowed more space to be whatever it wants to be now, and that's really cool.'

Lauren Beukes (photo: courtesy Tabitha Guy)

Danyela Demir and Olivier Moreillon

In Conversation with Lauren Beukes
(b. 1976)

We met with Lauren Beukes at Blue Café in Tamboerskloof in Cape Town. She had just returned to South Africa from a research trip to Haiti. Despite her busy schedule and still being jetlagged, Lauren took the time to sit down with us for a lively discussion on a sunny Monday morning.

She is the author of five novels: *Moxyland* (2008), *Zoo City* (2010), *The Shining Girls* (2013), *Broken Monsters* (2014) and *Afterland* (2020). *Zoo City* won the Kitschies Red Tentacle for best novel in 2010,[1] as well as the prestigious Arthur C. Clarke Award for Science Fiction in 2011, the Finnish Tähtivaeltaja Award in 2017 and it was shortlisted for several further international and South African literary prizes in 2010 and 2011.[2] *The Shining Girls* won the 2014 University of Johannesburg Prize and was shortlisted for the 2014 Sunday Times Literary Prize and the Tähtivaeltaja Award (Finland). *Broken Monsters* was shortlisted for the 2015 University of Johannesburg Prize and the 2015 ITW (International Thriller Writers) Thriller Awards and longlisted for the 2015 Barry Ronge Literary Prize.[3] Lauren is also the author of a collection of short stories and essays, *Slipping: Stories, Essays and Other Writing* (2016) and several graphic novels as well as a non-fiction volume, *Maverick: Extraordinary Women from South Africa's Past* (2005), which was nominated for the Sunday Times Alan Paton Award for non-fiction in 2006.

---

1. See http://www.thekitschies.com (accessed on 13 May 2016).
2. The novel was shortlisted for the 2010 British Science Fiction Association Award, the 2010 World Fantasy Award, the 2011 University of Johannesburg Literary Prize and the 2011 M-Net Literary Awards, and it was longlisted for the 2011 Sunday Times Literary Prize.
3. Previously called the Sunday Times Literary Prize.

Lauren is a trained journalist and holds an MA in Creative Writing from the University of Cape Town. She has extensive experience in the field of journalism and has contributed to Disney children's television programmes, such as *Mouk and Florrie's Dragons*, and she was the showrunner of the South African animated TV series *URBO: The Adventures of Pax Afrika*.[4] She likes writing 'when it flows and when the characters surprise you', but she dislikes starting. She says: 'I'll do anything to avoid starting. Once I'm actually writing for the day, it's okay. Things will happen. But I have to work up my nerves to face the blinking cursor. Even now. It's crazy.' Lauren, however, also posits: 'What pushes you to be a better artist is self-doubt and criticism. You just have to find a way that is not poisonous.'

As an avid reader, the Book Lounge in Cape Town and Love Books in Melville, Johannesburg, are among her favourite places in these two cities. In Cape Town, Lauren also likes going for a swim with friends at Beta Beach, a little, secret beach in Bakoven. According to Lauren: 'The water is freezing cold but it's so cleansing to go and have a swim in the sea there between the rocks.' She also likes Dias Tavern in Caledon Street, where they serve Mozambican beer and 'the best Trinchado' (spicy meat in a wine sauce), and Green Point Urban Park, which she believes to be 'the most beautiful place in Cape Town'. In Johannesburg, she enjoys Braamfontein, a neighbourhood she likes because of its 'urbanness' as well as 'its art galleries and little bars'.

Works

———. 2005. *Maverick: Extraordinary Women from South Africa's Past* (Oshun Books)

———. 2015. *Maverick: Extraordinary Women from South Africa's Past* (second edition, Umuzi)

This non-fiction book contains a series of short biographies on the lives of women, such as Krotoa-Eva, Sara Bartmann and Ruth First, all of whom left an indelible mark on South Africa's history.

---

4. For more information on Lauren Beukes's rich publishing activity, see her personal homepage at http://lauren beukes.com (accessed 24 May 2016).

————. 2008. *Moxyland* (Jacana Media)
Moxyland is set in a near-future Cape Town. The city is under the control of a number of corporate companies that police almost every aspect of people's lives. The novel follows the lives of four young Capetonians and their coming to grips with the city's corpo-governmental system.

————. 2010. *Zoo City* (Jacana Media)
Zoo City tells the story of Zinzi December, who is mysteriously bonded with a sloth after she gets her brother killed. With the help of the sloth, Zinzi finds lost objects for other people to support herself and repay her debts to her former drug dealer, for whom she also runs 419 email scams. When hired to find a missing pop star, Zinzi, unaware of the trouble she will find herself in, sees an opportunity to come up with the missing money and finally leave the crime-ridden Hillbrow, which, in the novel, is better known as 'Zoo City'.

————. 2013. *The Shining Girls* (Umuzi)
The Shining Girls follows the serial killer Harper Curtis. He travels through time by means of a boarded-up house that serves as a portal, and he kills girls he finds particularly gifted, captivating or compassionate. Harper seems to be untraceable until one of his victims survives and decides to track down the man who tried to kill her.

————. 2014. *Broken Monsters* (Umuzi)
Broken Monsters tells the story of the failed artist-turned-serial-killer Clayton Broom, who displays his victims as half-human, half-animal 'exhibition pieces'. For homicide detective Gabriella Versado, who is in charge of the investigations, the stakes are high, particularly once her teenage daughter gets caught up in the murder case.

————. 2016. *Slipping: Stories, Essays and Other Writing* (Tachyon Publications)
Slipping collects Lauren's short fiction and a number of non-fiction pieces. One of the stories featured in the collection that spans a wide range of topics and geographical locations is 'Ghost Girl', the precursor to Lauren's first novel, *Moxyland*.

————. 2020. *Afterland* (Umuzi)

Afterland tells the story of Cole and her twelve-year-old son, Miles. After a pandemic, 99 per cent of the world's male population has died and now the world is run by women. Within this new order, Miles, whose value as one of the few survivors of the male species has grown exponentially, is in grave danger. Disguised as mother-daughter-duo, Cole and Miles are on the run.

❧

What were your reasons for choosing speculative fiction as the genre to tell your stories?

The genre chose me. I just wrote the books that came out. I'm interested in social issues and in using these high concepts and weird ideas as a way of exploring that and commenting on the way the world is now, just putting a twist on it; enough that it makes it fresh and you can get over people's issue fatigue. Those are the kinds of stories I always like to read and to watch. I always bring up *District 9* (2009) as a classic example. If there had been a movie about actual xenophobia and refugees, it wouldn't have got the same attention it did. Using metaphor and allegory is very powerful. Jesus did it, Aesop's fables did it, we've always done this.

Besides being a writer of fiction you are also a filmmaker and have worked in various forms of media, including comics. How do these different fields of interest influence each other?

It's all storytelling, so you just have to learn a new medium. I was a freelance journalist for a long time. I'd be writing for a business magazine one week and a woman's magazine the next and then the World Health Organization the week after. They're all different styles and you have to be flexible and find the most interesting way into the story. Comics and animation have taught me to write shorter and sharper. I love dialogue, but in comics and in animation you're not allowed a lot of dialogue. If you go longer than two sentences, you're waffling. It taught me to think more formatically and more visually because in comics and animation you are writing for someone to draw. You have to explain exactly what's happening and what the characters are doing. You've got to come into the scene as late as possible and out as early as possible. Everything has to move the plot forward or say something about the character. It's an amazing discipline to learn, and that feeds into everything. Of course, my journalism feeds into my work because the research, the talking to people and using those details, is a big part of what makes my work mine. And I actually want to go to a place and walk around. I could totally do it on Google Maps and I can read some books, but I like to be able to go and feel the scene of the streets or nearly die in traffic in Haiti, on the back of my bike [*laughs*].

Your novels have a wide array of characters and multiple narrative perspectives seem to be one of the trademarks of your writing. How much research and planning goes into crafting both your plot and characters?
The characters kind of emerge themselves in the writing. Sometimes I'll have a very clear idea. Other times it is that subconscious, alchemical process where, as you're writing, things shift. That's the most exciting part; when the character shifts slightly and moves into a direction I hadn't been anticipating or says a line of dialogue, and I'm like: 'Oh, that's much better than what I was thinking you were going to say.'

I always know where I'm going. I always know what my endings are. But it just kind of develops, it evolves. I have an outline, I know where I'm going, but at the same time there's lots of flexibility, there's lots of space. In one of my books I was going to kill the main character at the end, but I grew to like her too much. It didn't feel right anymore to have the kind of ultimate Jesus sacrifice. E.L. Doctorow says: 'It's like taking a road trip at night. You know where you're leaving from. You know where you're going. And the rest of the time you can see 20 feet ahead of you in the headlights and you just have to stay on the road.'[5]

---

5. Edgar Lawrence Doctorow (1931–2015) was an American writer of historical fiction, editor and professor of English. Among his works is the award-winning novel *Ragtime* (1975). The original quote Lauren is paraphrasing here comes from an interview Doctorow gave in *The Paris Review*, where he said that writing was 'like driving at night: you never see further than your headlights, but you can make the whole trip that way'. See https:// www.theparisreview.org/ interviews/2718/the-art-of-fiction-no-94-e-l-doctorow (accessed 6 May 2016).

In your opinion, what do the numerous subjectivities contribute to your novels?

The world is complicated and your perspective on life is completely different to mine. We can't actually agree on anything. As human beings we can't agree on what love means, or on what happens in the afterlife. Everything is personal, which also means everything is political. And those different voices allow me different insights and different commentaries and it's also a nice play with the unreliable narrator, to have somebody see something from a different perspective and they're wrong. But you only see that when you see the same scene from somebody else's perspective. It's really about trying to find multiple ways into a story and trying to represent the world in some way.

Which characters did you find most rewarding or taxing to write about?

Harper in *The Shining Girls*, the serial killer, was the worst. I didn't want to make him a Hannibal Lecter because that's not real. Serial killers are not Hannibal Lecters. They are pathetic losers who only know about violence. They have major sex issues, but they're also impotent in the world. They feel powerless and that's part of why they do this. They're just not interesting. Of course, fiction is trying to make them more interesting because we want to believe that there's a reason for evil and we want to believe: 'Oh well, of course he turned into a psychopath. His family was killed by cannibals in the Russian snow fields.' But actually sometimes it's nothing. There is no good reason at all. To write someone who is that, who is just cynical and awful, to write about the violence and his perspective on the world, and about the compulsion, this twisted obsession that was eating him up, I hated it. But at least when I closed my computer, I could walk away from him. I knew he wasn't real. He was a figure in my head, but it was horrible trying to find that cynical germ inside myself and then bring that out. It felt like vomiting.

Which was the most rewarding character?

Most recently I really enjoyed Layla in *Broken Monsters*, but Zinzi is still one of my favourites. I really love Zinzi. I have a real soft spot for *Zoo City*. The book was the game changer, it changed my career, but it was also a really fun book to write.

While crime is a common denominator in all of your books, your work can by no means be classified as crime fiction. Additionally, your novels seem to evade any genre-specific classification. How conscious are you of genre blending when crafting your fictions and to what effect do you employ this blurring?

I just write the books I want to write and people tell me what they are afterwards. Sometimes it's a bit irritating because I didn't actually see it that way, but sometimes it's quite interesting. A lot of people read *The Shining Girls* as horror and I hadn't thought of it like that. I don't sit there and write a book thinking this is really going to be a top seller because I'm mixing genres. It would actually be much easier if I was just writing straight crime thrillers, if I stuck to a series, if I did a detective who kept coming back, but I get really bored of that.

Each of your novels is set in a different city. While *Moxyland* is set in Cape Town, *Zoo City* is set in Johannesburg. *The Shining Girls* and *Broken Monsters* shift to Chicago and Detroit respectively. Many of the locations in your South African-based novels, for example, can be pinpointed on a map, even though you have at times used some artistic licence and have added things and twisted real circumstances. How important is the representation of place in your writing?

It's very important, and in Detroit and Chicago you can also pinpoint places. A lot of the time, I'm writing about actual places that I've actually been to. My best example is when I went to Detroit. I'd done a lot of research before I went there. It was the second time I'd gone. I went before I wrote the book, then I wrote the first draft of the book, and then I went back again to find the stuff that I'd missed. I had read a lot about the Detroit Police Station on Beaubien Street and how it was falling apart and had weird stains coming through the ceiling and none of the computers worked. I went to visit the Beaubien Police Station with Detective Kenneth, the reverend gardener in his alligator skin shoes, and it was amazing. It was where Bonnie and Clyde were arrested. It had these amazing blue lights outside, these really ornate lamps, the interrogation room, and this manky, tiny little cell with like plywood board walls and people had written all over the walls, saying stuff like: 'Please God, help me, help get me out of here.' Or, 'I'm so sorry Jerry, I didn't mean for this to happen.' There were old filing cabinets and desks, and the wood and the glass was total rainbow charm. It was stunning.

But that's not the police station anymore. That is the old police station. There's like a skeleton crew there just maintaining the building.

They've moved to this shiny, new public safety headquarters, and the inside looks like a freaking *Dilbert* cartoon. It's cubicle city and everyone's got a working computer. There's a gym upstairs with TVs above the treadmills. I was like, 'No! No! I don't want to write about this!' I had already actually written all those chapters with the police station and I had to go back. I couldn't justify keeping the setting in the old, fucked-up police department because it wasn't truly Detroit. I've seen South Africa misrepresented so often and so badly and in such terrible clichés, and I didn't want to buy into that and misrepresent Detroit. So it was important to me that I get it right.

In both *Moxyland* and *Zoo City*, inclusion and exclusion are central themes. In what ways are these themes linked to aspects of home, belonging and community?
They're both apartheid allegories. *Moxyland* is a corporate apartheid and *Zoo City* is about South Africans' favourite dinner party conversation, crime. I was interested in finding the human stories within that, and I'm interested in poverty and segregation and class and the ridiculous things we find to divide ourselves. It is a theme in all my work.

And how do you see these novels as positioning South Africa in a more global and integrated context?
The rest of the world is not more integrated. The apartheid government went to Chicago to learn how to do segregation better.[6] In Detroit, a lot of people blame the fact that Detroit has gone so downhill on them having a black mayor and there's been a lot of 'white flight'. And Chicago had redlining that were crazy racist practices in the property business to try to stop black families from moving into neighbourhoods. So, I'm finding those commonalities. *The Shining Girls* and *Broken Monsters* are both riffs on the same theme. They're about exclusion and alienation. I think it's a big danger that we want fiction to be representative. It's the same as

---

6. See Nightingale (2012) and also https://www.chicagomag.com/city-life/January-2014/The-Parallel-Paths-of-South-African-Apartheid-and-Chicago-Segregation/ (accessed 6 May 2016).

having a black or a female character in a movie. As soon as there's only one, they become a stand in for everything that is female or everything that is black or everything that is gay. I don't want *Moxyland* or *Zoo City* to be representative of anything. Just because I've had international success with those books does not mean they're the final word on South African fiction. They are one take on that and that's what I think is so exciting about South African literature at the moment. It has been blasted wide open and we've seen all kinds of different stories and that feels much healthier and more sane.

I had someone interviewing me about Afrofuturism. I don't even know what Afrofuturism is. You can't just put a label on anything that is vaguely futuristic. I don't like labels generally and I don't like genres generally. I understand that we need to try to quantify the world and to try to understand it and pigeonhole it, but it's just irritating. It becomes representative.

Moving back to *Zoo City*. Your second novel draws on a broad spectrum of African myths and legends. How does this rich corpus contribute to your novel?
I wanted to write African magic in a way that felt real. I went to see a sangoma and I spoke to her. I know a sangoma, @noksangoma, who does consultations on Twitter. What I find most interesting about South Africa is the way we use technology and magic at the same time, that they're not counter-intuitive. It was the same when I was in Haiti. I went to see a *houngan*, a voodoo priest, and at one point he took out his phone, and I'm like, 'What? Is there an app for that?' [*laughs*]. But this is the modern world. We're not trapped in the past.

But I did want to use African magical beliefs and mythology. I grew up with this big book of African legends, Penny Miller's *Myths and Legends of Southern Africa* (1979), and it really played into my imaginative space, the same way all the other fairy tales and the Egyptian mythology and the Greek mythology and everything else I read did. It was up there in the pantheon of my mythology and I wanted to bring that back. I wanted people to get a sense of it. At the same time, I was also struggling with it a bit. Then I met Neil Gaiman very briefly in 2009, and I asked him how he did it with *American Gods* (2001) and *Anansi Boys* (2005). There's not a lot written on African mythologies. A lot of it was oral tradition. So I asked Neil: 'What do I do? Because I can't find enough written down on this.' He said: 'Just make it up.' That was really good advice. It was also really liberating because *Harry Potter* is not based on real stuff. That's what's interesting; the play between the real and the imagination. But the important thing is when you have the realities to ground it even more. Like if you're going to have crazy magic and magical animals or dreams infecting artists, then everything else needs to be as real and tangible as possible. You have to be credible before you can be incredible.

With your third and fourth novels, you move away from South Africa. They are set in the United States. What were your reasons behind this decision and to what extent did the new settings provide you with some form of artistic liberation?

I've made a lot of people quite cross. They feel I've abandoned South Africa or sold out. And I'm like, 'Whatever. Please!' David Mitchell is allowed to write about Japan and his only reason for writing about Japan is that he lived in Japan. We hold South African artists to these ridiculous standards. Somebody once described me in an interview, it was the *Mail & Guardian*, as an international bastard,[7] and that's how I feel. That's my accent, that's my experience of the world. I've travelled a lot and I've lived in other places. The world is global, it's not just here, and I want to be able to write about what interests me.

The reason I moved to the States with *The Shining Girls* was because I had this idea of a time-travelling serial killer and I knew immediately that it wasn't going to be 'Bill and Ted's Accidental Killing Spree through Time'.[8] I wasn't going to go from the dinosaur age to killing Hitler to 2030 with the space babes. I wanted to write about the twentieth century and how that shaped us and how women's roles, in particular, have changed. If I'd set that in South Africa, it would have immediately become an apartheid story because if you're looking at the

---

7. See https://mg.co.za/article/2013-03-01-00-lauren-beukes-at-the-forefront-of-the-global-invasion/ (accessed 6 May 2016).
8. Lauren is riffing here on the *Bill and Ted* franchise that consists of two films: *Bill and Ted's Excellent Adventure* (1989) and *Bill and Ted's Bogus Journey* (1991). Both films star Keanu Reeves, Alex Winter and George Carlin, and they are premised on the existence of a time machine disguised as a telephone booth. The telephone booth allows the two comedic slackers, Bill and Ted, to travel through time to change the course of history.

history of the twentieth century in South Africa, it is apartheid. That would have overwhelmed everything else I wanted to talk about. I also wanted to look at the invention of the skyscraper and I wanted to look at McCarthyism. Of course, McCarthyism is absolutely apartheid. It's my way of writing about apartheid and the war on terror. The same tactics they used then, they're using in the war on terror to frighten us, to get us to spy on our friends and to justify anything. I wanted to find these echoes of history and the States gave me a bigger canvas. Let's face it, the twentieth century was the American century.

Of course that made it immediately more commercial, which is not something I intended. I'd love to say I was that canny and strategic. My novel is set in America because America is where it's set. It's because I'd lived in Chicago. New York was too obvious and has been done to death. London didn't fit. So it turned out to be Chicago. Then my American publisher wanted me to write the next book set in the States. But the new book is set all over: it's partly in Haiti, partly in America, partly maybe in Dubai – I'm still deciding – and in South Africa as well. Doing these two American books has meant that I can now go wherever I want after this. A lot of my short stories since then have been set in South Africa and my comics have been set in South Africa. One of the characters in DC Vertigo's *Survivors' Club* series, a comic I wrote in collaboration with Dale Halvorsen, is South African.[9] I definitely haven't abandoned South Africa and really I'm writing about South Africa wherever I go.

To what extent are the social issues in America comparable to post-apartheid South Africa?
Oh totally! Everything is. We like to think we're a special snowflake and that we are the best at corruption and crime. In Haiti I met schoolteachers who haven't been paid in two years! That is how dysfunctional the government is. Detroit and Chicago have ex-mayors in jail because of the corruption. When I was in Chicago they had 40 shootings in one weekend! They have safety corridors to get kids to school through gang war zones because the kids have to walk to school and they try to protect them from getting shot. We think America is what we see in the

---

9. See http://www.vertigocomics.com/comics/survivors-club-2015/survivors-club-1 (accessed 23 June 2016).

movies, but it's not that at all. Look at what's happening in Ferguson at the moment, look at the #BlackLivesMatter protest. Racism is still a really big deal there. It's horrific. I've got a kid brother, Thabo, who grew up with us, who's obviously black, and he said to me a few years ago: 'I just want to go somewhere where my race doesn't matter.' And I was like: 'Thabo, I don't know where that is. I don't know where that is.' Of course urban environments and middle classes are much more integrated. I think it's become much more of a class thing, but the majority of poor in many places are still black because of historical circumstance and it takes centuries to recover from that. There's no easy fix. There's no magic wand. That is a universal theme. And those histories do have teeth and they do lurk underneath and come back to bite us.

In all your novels, many of your characters seem to be in varying states of motion. How important are different aspects of movement in your work?

I'm interested in complicated people who are dealing with trouble. Maybe it's trouble they got themselves into. Maybe it was trouble that fell on their heads. But that's where we're at our most interesting; when we're being tested. I got divorced recently and suddenly I had all these incredibly deep conversations with people: about tragedies in their lives, great sadnesses and things that they'd been through. It's true that happiness is banal. Of course I would like some banality, but it is the sadness and grief, times of trouble and hardships, the things that we go through and how we come out on the other side that make us who we are. That's where the stories are. It's that forge of life.

Moving away from your own fiction to the more general questions. The community of South African writers who work within the genre of speculative fiction seems to be particularly close and cooperative. Frequently, one finds recurring names in the acknowledgements, such as Sarah Lotz and yourself, among others. How does this community function and to what extent do the writers of this community work together to further the cause of the genre?

You pay it forward; you try to help out other young writers as they're coming up. I talk about South African fiction whenever I can. I used to have a guest space on my blog where African writers, whether they're speculative or not, can write about their new book and what inspired it. I do that sort of promotion more on Twitter now because it got very time-consuming. I get a lot of attention and it's a way of sharing the spotlight. But I do think it's an incredibly supportive and tight-knit community and it wasn't until *BooksLIVE* started.[10] Of course there were movements like *Die Sestigers* in the 1960s that were very political.[11] It's harder now because politics is muddier now. Back in the day, you were definitely fighting against apartheid and that was the 'big bad'. Everyone was throwing their weight behind that to fight this one thing. Now our social issues are so much more spread and more complex and more diffused that it's really hard to choose one enemy to fight. There's not one obvious bad guy. So we didn't have that unifying factor and suddenly South Africa and fiction were both kind of splintering through different genres and being blasted wide open and you had more interesting things and different kinds of writing coming through. And then *BooksLIVE* started. Ben Williams came here from the States and he started this writer portal. None of us knew what he was on about. He said: 'I want you to write a blog!' I was like, 'I don't even know what a blog is. Leave me alone.' He told me that I should get on Twitter. And I'm like, 'What? No! I don't want to tweet about my lunch!' And you know what? Twitter has been the best thing for me. *BooksLIVE*, before Facebook really took off, was where we sat and talked about books. We had arguments. People were supportive. People commented on blog posts. He really created that community and that really brought us together.

---

10. *BooksLIVE* is a forum on South African writing that provides book reviews on recently published books (both fiction and non-fiction), author interviews, as well as news on current literary events, such as local literary festivals, and it also contains blogs by different South African writers. See http://bookslive.co.za (accessed 6 May 2016).

11. *Die Sestigers* (The Sixtiers/Sixtyers) was an avant-garde literary movement of Afrikaans writers that opposed the National Party and its apartheid policy. They sought to subvert the status quo by directly addressing taboo topics, such as apartheid politics, (inter-)racial relations and sexuality, and by opening up Afrikaans literature to modern stylistic directions, such as surrealism and symbolism. Its founding members were Chris Barnard (1939–2015), André P. Brink (1935–2015), Breyten Breytenbach (b. 1939) and Ingrid Jonker (1933–1965). See https://diesestigers.wordpress.com (accessed on 13 May 2016).

Would you say that the sense of camaraderie is different within the speculative fiction group in comparison with other writing communities?
We're all geeks who are interested in weird mythology and horror movies, but we're also intimate friends. We all champion each other and South African fiction as a whole.

Although South Africa is recognised as having one of the most liberal constitutions in the world, you can, in many ways, say that in South Africa society is still largely conservative. What taboos do you think have yet to find their way into contemporary South African literature?
I don't know, we're dealing with all of it. You get straight novels like Niq Mhlongo's. He writes very realistically about being young and black in South Africa. But Sarah Lotz and her daughter writing together as Lily Herne in their *Deadlands* series (2011—2014), a series of zombie apocalypse novels, deal with corrective rape, which is not corrective at all. It's where you gang rape and murder a lesbian to teach her a lesson. It is a horrible thing they deal with in a young adult book. Crime fiction deals with our big crazy issues and I often hear the crime writers bitching about how they don't know how they're supposed to compete with reality because South Africa is so strange and the weirdest stuff happens and you can't make this stuff up; it's insane! It's the same with speculative fiction. It allows you a way into those issues that is more bearable.

I haven't had a chance to read Karen Jayes's *For the Mercy of Water* (2012), for which she won the Sunday Times prize two years ago. It's about rape and it's about this dystopian future where water is the most precious resource. Thando Mgqolozana and Siphiwo Mahala both wrote about male circumcision, which is absolutely taboo to talk about with outsiders or women. It's incredibly brave and interesting. I'd love to see more international attention with that kind of writing as well.

In your opinion, what might be some of the new voices or perspectives that we can see developing in South African literature?
In speculative fiction, Charlie Human, Sam Wilson, Diane Awerbuck and Alex Latimer are collaborating on a sci-fi Western book. It's set in Kimberley. It sounds amazing! Sally Partridge is still doing really interesting work. She is just a machine, prolific and dedicated. There is Songeziwe Mahlangu, who just won the Etisalat Prize. And there is,

of course, Yewande Omotoso. Thando Mgqolozana is just going from strength to strength and he's not even 30 yet, or he's just turned 30.

Which different genres do you see becoming more prominent as an attempt to break away from realist conventions?
Speculative fiction is really becoming bigger and bigger, partly because of the success of *Zoo City* and *District 9*, which again shone a light on the fact that you could tell these kind of stories in South Africa. Although I knew that from watching South African theatre, from watching people like Andrew Buckland and Rob van Vuuren who did these incredible one- or two-men shows; all mime, no props, nothing, just becoming the new characters. A lot of it had to take place in the imagination. They had these crazy speculative stories and magic and politics with insects. It was phenomenal. So I knew that you could tell a South African story using these elements already from theatre. But now a lot of other people know it and it's really exciting to see that blowing up. And it's partly also because of champions like Sarah Lotz and Oliver Munson. And the website *Pornokitsch* is kind of a specific website and they put out compendiums of books.[12] They're using South African illustrators and South African writers, really championing us overseas. It makes a huge difference to have these champions, to have these people who are putting South Africans out there and who are trying to get big international deals for them and spotlight a kind of writing that is not what we traditionally think of as South African literature. You know, it's J.M. Coetzee and it's Nadine Gordimer and it's André Brink and maybe it's Es'kia Mphahlele. South African fiction is allowed more space to be whatever it wants to be now, and that's really cool.

What's next from Lauren Beukes?
I'm very excited that *The Shining Girls* has been optioned for television by MRC and Leonardo DiCaprio's Appian Way. I also got to work with

---

12. *Pornokitsch* is a British 'geek culture' blog edited by Anne C. Perry and Jared Shurin. The blog publishes reviews and news on speculative (and other genre) fiction. From 2009 to 2013, *Pornokitsch* organised the Kitschies, a literary prize for 'the year's most progressive, intelligent and entertaining works that contain elements of the speculative or the fantastic'. See http://www.pornokitsch.com (accessed on 6 May 2016). Lauren won the Kitschies Red Tentacle for best novel in 2010.

one of my favourite South African NGOs, Book Dash, where writers, illustrators and designers work together to make a children's book in twelve hours. The book I worked on, with Anja Venter and Nkosingiphile Mazibuko, *And Also!*, is available for free online. I joined an awesome team of writers to work on a Jessica Jones fiction and audiobook series, and I'm currently working on a pitch for a TV show. And I've been busy doing talks, and I got to judge the Shnit Short Film Festival in 2019, with John Kani. I'm going to be on the jury for the Sci-Fi London Film Challenge in 2020, and I got to mentor a bunch of young film writers for Electric South. I finally finished my new book, *Afterland*. It took me five years to write. I've already started researching and drafting the next one. As I've said before, being a successful writer is 10 per cent luck, 10 per cent talent and 80 per cent sheer bloody-minded determination.

References
Doctorow, Edgar L. 1975. *Ragtime*. New York: Random House.
Gaiman, Neil. 2001. *American Gods*. New York: William Morrow.
———. 2005. *Anansi Boys*. New York: William Morrow.
Herne, Lily. 2011. *Deadlands*. London: Constable & Robinson.
_____. 2013. *Death of a Saint*. London: Constable & Robinson.
_____. 2013. *The Army of the Lost*. London: Constable & Robinson.
_____. 2014. *Ash Remains*. London: Constable & Robinson.
Jayes, Karen. 2012. *For the Mercy of Water*. Johannesburg: Penguin Books.
Miller, Penny. 1979. *Myths and Legends of Southern Africa*. Cape Town: T.V. Bulpin Publications.
Nightingale, Carl H. 2012. *Segregation: A Global History of Divided Cities*. Chicago: University of Chicago Press.

Films/TV
Bill and Ted's Excellent Adventure. 1989. Directed by Stephen Herek. USA: Orion Pictures.
Bill and Ted's Bogus Journey. 1991. Directed by Pete Hewitt. USA: Orion Pictures.
District 9. 2009. Directed by Neill Blomkamp. USA: TriStar Pictures.

'I think we're in a phase now where South African writers are starting to feel that perhaps they can do outright fantasy without a sense of duty to the past.'

Charlie Human (photo: Olivier Moreillon)

Danyela Demir, Olivier Moreillon and Alan Muller

In Conversation with Charlie Human
(b. 1980)

We met Charlie Human at Lola's on Long Street in Cape Town. Charlie agreed to meet us during his lunch hour away from work on a sunny Monday afternoon. He is the author of *Apocalypse Now Now* (2013) and *Kill Baxter* (2014), and he has contributed short stories to *Pandemonium: Stories of the Apocalypse* (2011) and *Pwning Tomorrow: Short Fiction from the Electronic Frontier* (Electronic Frontier Foundation 2015). His debut novel, *Apocalypse Now Now*, has been optioned for film to be produced by Redlab Digital and XYZ Films with Terri Tatchell (*District 9* and *Chappie*) writing the screenplay.[1] The proof-of-concept short was released in 2017 and can be viewed online.[2] His novels have been translated into Afrikaans, Italian, Czech, Turkish, German and Japanese. He currently works in digital publishing and has worked for *Men's Health*, *FHM*, *Sport Illustrated*, *Shape* and *Women's Health* magazines.

About the writing process he says: 'I like the flash of the initial idea. The ideas phase is cool because you're like: "Wow! This is amazing, this is going to be great." And then you get stuck in, and you get about 10 000 words in, and then there's a bit of a wall because now you've realised, in order to properly realise what you want to realise in the story, there's a lot of hard work that has to be done.'

Most recently he had read a copy of Umberto Eco's *The Name of the Rose* (1983), which he picked up from a library-cum-bookshop near his

1. See https://news.avclub.com/district-9-screenwriter-terri-tatchell-to-adapt-novel-a-1798281958 (accessed 5 February 2020).
2. See https://www.theverge.com/2017/8/31/16225772/apocalypse-now-now-concept-film-terri-tatchell-ghostbusters-district-9-charlie-human (accessed 5 February 2020).

home in Muizenberg where 'a local leaves books on a ledge outside her house every Tuesday' and 'you can just take if it's something you like. When you're done, you can put it back, or not. They don't really care.' For his day job at *Men's Health* he has also recently read *The Brazilian Jiu Jitsu Globetrotter: The True Story about a Frantic, 140 Day Long, Around-the-World Trip to Train Brazilian Jiu Jitsu* (Graugart 2012).

Having grown up in Cape Town, Charlie has a close connection with the city and its surrounds. He finds it difficult to pinpoint a specific favourite spot because 'it's so diverse in terms of the actual natural spaces and also the cultural spaces'. He lives in Muizenberg, which he enjoys 'because of the beach and also there's a really awesome community'. Before moving to Muizenberg he enjoyed living in Observatory 'because there's a sense of something happening there, and a little more going on than in the suburbs'. The Cederberg is his favourite natural spot in the area.

❧

Works

———. 2013. *Apocalypse Now Now* (Umuzi)

Apocalypse Now Now follows 16-year-old Baxter Zevcenko as he navigates adolescence and all it has to offer. The problem, however, is that he is not just any old kid from Cape Town. After his girlfriend, Esmé, goes missing, he turns to supernatural bounty hunter Jacky Ronin for help. On top of this, Baxter must come to terms with his own supernatural genetics.

———. 2014. *Kill Baxter* (Umuzi)

This sequel follows Baxter as he is sent to Hexpoort, a magical training school that resembles Hogwarts without the training wheels. To add to Baxter's consternation, he comes to realise that he is no good at magic.

❧

What were your reasons for choosing speculative fiction as the genre to tell your stories?

How *Apocalypse Now Now* actually came about is a bit of a story in itself. I'd started the creative writing course, and I was really trying to write a serious book because I sort of felt that, doing a creative writing course, this is what's expected of me. I was like: 'No, I'm going to write something really serious that grapples with issues', and I'd written about 30 000 words of it. I had cleverly backed it up on discs and on a hard drive. I put it all in the same case and someone broke into my house and just took the case; it made it really easy for someone to steal. But, in a way, it was the best thing that could've happened because during that first attempt at a novel, I think I was just trying too hard. I really debated with myself whether I was even going to continue with the course or whether to cut my losses and do something else, but I thought: 'No, I've committed to this and I want to write a novel, so I'm going to do it.' But actually, at that point, I lost a lot of my sense of self-importance, and I was just like: 'If I'm going to do this, then I'm going to write whatever I want. I'm not going to censor myself. I'm not going to take my foot off the pedal. I'm just going to do whatever I want.' *Apocalypse Now Now* was the product of that; it was the product of me going: 'Hey, that's a cool idea, let's put that in as well. Hey, that's another cool idea', and it actually turned out to be the best thing because I enjoyed writing it. It was cool because I was giving in to the creative impulse and not constantly questioning myself and asking: 'Is this good enough to be a novel?'

Your novel appropriates elements of Rowling's *Harry Potter* series (1997—2007), and Tolkien's *The Lord of the Rings* ([1954/1955] 2009), to name but two of the most obvious and important intertexts. What were your reasons for drawing so blatantly on what are probably the two most prominent fantasy narratives of the last 60 years?
When I started out writing a fantasy book, I was hyper-aware of all these kinds of influences. The other thing I was thinking about was that I had read the *Harry Potter* books and that these teenagers are incredibly chaste for people at a co-ed boarding school. I think about my own teenage years and that really wasn't what it was like. There were drugs, there was sex, there was alcohol, there was graffiti, there was all sorts of shit going on. I thought: 'Is that really realistic?' So that's where some of Baxter's energy comes from. I wanted to make it a more accurate representation of teenage life, where everything is a little bit crazy and everything's happening at a much higher pitch and all that. That was some of what I wanted to capture, and also the fact that Cape

Town does have this slightly dark edge to it in some ways. Most cities probably do, but it often doesn't get depicted. It's got that suburban layer, but there's a little bit of an edge underneath.

Despite drawing on these two giants of fantasy, you've managed to craft novels that are original and unexpected. What aspects of dealing with these archetypal fantasy texts did you find particularly enriching, and/or problematic?

One of the things that I actively wanted to do was to use African mythology because *The Lord of the Rings* is very Nordic and Celtic. I wanted to make it specifically African. Obviously I'm drawing on parts like dwarves and all that, but a lot of the stuff just happens in the subconscious as well. Having been exposed to this type of mythology for a long time, having read that as a kid, some of it isn't necessarily conscious. Like you said, *Apocalypse Now Now* is very much just like grabbing stuff. In a way, I did that on purpose. One of the readers for my MA loved it and I got a first for it. One absolutely hated it and I barely passed, and she said that it reads like a whole lot of B-movies spliced together. That was my intention. I drew not only on classic works of fiction, but also on Jean-Claude van Damme movies, Steven Seagal movies and very much that cheesy kind of action-y eighties thriller.

There was a lot that I actively drew on, and I was taking from everywhere. I was actively using all of my influences. It is very much a novel where I was explicit about what I was drawing from. You can see it in the text. I wasn't trying to take from something and then hide it.

One of the chapter's titles is 'I Think You're Phony and I Like it a Lot'. That's like a mixture of *The Catcher in the Rye*'s (Salinger 1951) Holden Caulfield and Die Antwoord. So I threw in a lot of those little things, and I hope that people find it rewarding when they notice those little things and try to see some of the South African influences. It's interesting having an international audience too because South Africans will be able to get some of the in-jokes more than international readers. A lot of international readers want to know how much of it is real mythology and how much I just made up. There's a lot of stuff where I just riffed off mythology. A lot of the Boer mythology I've just taken as a starting point and taken it one step further. Siener van Rensburg was a real figure, but then he never had a brother who had his own take on mythology; that was just invented.

Keeping with mythology, both *Kill Baxter* and *Apocalypse Now Now* draw on a really broad spectrum of African myths and legends. How did this rich corpus contribute to your Baxter saga?

Well, one of the books I read and was really interested in was Credo Mutwa's *Indaba, My Children* (1964). Credo Mutwa is a Zulu shaman and a lot of the history that he tells is oral history that has been passed down. One thing I like about him as well is that there are moments when you're not quite sure whether it actually is oral history, or whether it's something he's made up. He has this connection with David Icke; the UFO kind of guy who's just got these insane theories about how the world works. I quite like that connection because he believes that the [British] Royal Family is a race of lizard people. I was reading Credo Mutwa's book and seeing all this stuff, and then I was seeing him talk to this guy who's clearly invented this insane UFO cult. It's just like this weird mix of mythologies; there are some indigenous mythologies, and they talk about lizard people and that kind of thing. David Icke (1999) has picked up on that, and he's spun it into this wild yarn about the Illuminati. It's like that idea of the imagination and reality; where does your imagination start and reality end? I just drew from a whole lot of stuff and I find it amusing and I like looking at these entire cosmologies that people have invented, and going: 'Shit, logistically, how does that work? If there is a race of alien lizards that are controlling the planet, how would that work?'

We'd like to come back to reality and the imagination a little later. But for now, let's stay with mythology. Which mythological figures have you not yet written about and still want to get to?

I want to do something with the idea of the ancestors and ancestor worship and the concept of people who have gone before still actively influencing life on earth. I like that part of African mythology. That's something that I'd still like to do perhaps in the third instalment of the Baxter series. Someone, not so long ago, was telling me that they'd gone on a trip up the coast and they'd come into contact with this strange sex cult. I'm really interested in cults, religious groups and that sort of thing. I think the way people interpret the world around them is interesting, and not at all from a judgemental point of view; almost the opposite. I think whatever people are into is cool. Everyone's just making it up as they go along.

Your novels have a wide array of characters, many of whom have an auxiliary function, but are nevertheless both instrumental and fleshed out. How much research went into crafting both plot and characters?

In some ways, plot is always a function of characters and their motivations. Sometimes it is convenient to put a character in a particular place just to serve a function. I try not to do that, but, particularly in *Apocalypse Now Now*, there were certain points when characters existed purely to drive the plot forward. I've tried to take a more nuanced approach to creating characters now. In terms of how much research I do, I read widely. I'm very aware of how I write. Analysis paralysis is a real thing for me. If I read too much about something, or I research too much, I find it very difficult to write.

I made a conscious decision not to be constrained by facts in my books. I think a lot of people, and certainly a lot of people that I did my MA with, particularly journalists, found research a very constricting thing. They found that it actually stopped them from doing what they wanted to do because if suddenly they found out something entirely contradictory to the story that they wanted to tell, they couldn't get past that point. They felt they had to go research something else. If, for me, a fact got in the way of me telling the story, I just omitted that fact [*laughter*]. That's why writing's great. I'm not writing a non-fiction book and I don't feel like facts should constrain the story. I think some people will have a problem with that and will say: 'You talk about sangomas but that's not how sangomas operate', but it's all functioning within the confines of my story. That's what I always say to people who ask me for writing advice. Research enough to give you inspiration, but not so much that you feel that you have to give so much information that it becomes a non-fiction book. In books that operate in a fantasy setting, exposition is often a very difficult part because you have to explain the world in which all of this is happening. So in some sense there are information dumps, where you just say: 'This is the world where this is happening, these are the rules that govern magic, and these are the rules that govern how society deals with these mythological characters or monsters.' In some senses, you do have to have a character that just goes: 'This is how this operates.' In *Apocalypse Now Now* it was Dr Pat; she explained to Baxter the rules of this other world. He had just been initiated into this world with meeting the elemental in a township, and he was freaked out. This was something new, and she filled the information gap for him. You need that, but you have to try to be quite subtle about it. It can be difficult.

Your novels contain a huge number of characters. Which ones did you find more rewarding or taxing to write about?
I like Klipspringer, the bok-boy, just because he adds a lighter touch to the thing. In places the story can be quite dark, quite manic, and, like people always say, the pace is very fast. I think he adds a little bit of a comic touch; it lightens the story a bit, and he's certainly been the character that people have responded most to. A lot of people have come to me saying: 'Ah, he's my favourite character.' I liked writing him for that reason. He's got a manic energy of his own, but it takes away for a moment from that kind of breakneck speed where it's just stuff happening all the time.

Which one was particularly difficult to write?
I think the character of Katinka being a transgender character was difficult. I was very wary about writing her because I wanted her to be someone that was sensitive to the transgender community. I wanted her to be a rounder character on her own. She's also a character that I want to explore more of in the third book. I really enjoyed writing that, and I enjoyed writing the whole mythology of the flock, but I found her challenging. I wasn't sure if I was doing her justice.

By including the tale of Niklaas van Rensburg[3] as well as the British concentration camps[4] in the South African War, among others, your novels not only touch on histories that are commonly marginalised, but they also entangle them. What were some of the reasons for doing so?

---

3. Niklaas van Rensburg (1864–1926) was a Boer and considered to be a close confidant and adviser to General Koos de la Rey. A devout Christian, he reported hundreds of visions pertaining to the well-being of the Boers. For extended discussion of both Van Rensburg and his visions, see Raath (2011).
4. During the South African War, the British established concentration camps across the country. Emily Hobhouse would go on to document the abhorrent living conditions imposed on women and children. Her book is freely available at https://archive.org/details/bruntwarandwher01hobhgoog (accessed 4 February 2019). For a comprehensive discussion of both Hobhouse and the concentration camps, see Eales (2015). For more on the camps themselves and their inhabitants, see https://www2.lib.uct.ac.za/mss/bccd/ (accessed 4 February 2019).

I think Afrikaner history is incredibly interesting. I wanted my story to include a mix of South African history because South Africa, and particularly Cape Town, is such a mix of cultures. I wanted to include that, and also because no one else has done that; no one else has included Afrikaner history and it seems a natural fit. If I was going to include African magic, I wanted to include a whole spectrum of South African magic. In *Kill Baxter*, Hexpoort, the school, also brings up the idea of the colonial history and the melting pot of colonial and indigenous histories. I wanted it to be that. I wanted it to reflect the complete mix and not just show one particular aspect of South African history.

Apocalypse Now Now is set predominantly in Cape Town and contains many identifiable place markers. How important is the representation of place in your writing?

I think, historically, nature and place have always been strong themes in South African writing, and I was conscious of that. I was conscious of how South Africans write about South Africa and about the natural world. Living in a very cosmopolitan city like Cape Town, I wanted to include some of that in my writing, but apply it to the city. I've lived in a lot of different places in Cape Town, and each of them holds a specific meaning for me, a specific group of memories. It's like memories are anchored to that place. I think a lot of my own personal memories and my own personal understanding have come through in my relationship to place. I've taken public transport for a long time, so a lot of that also came through. Liesbeek River was also quite an important kind of anchor place for me. In the beginning of *Apocalypse Now Now*, Baxter talks about the river, walking along the river and noticing the darkness beneath the Botox of the suburbs. When I was a kid, I lived in Mowbray and we always used to go to Observatory to watch bands and then walk home along the Liesbeek River and it was always quite an interesting thing because there were people living in the river; people setting up their houses and it was also quite a dangerous place. We got mugged. That river had a lot of meaning for me. It was almost like the suburbs were right there, but there was something else happening right on the doorstep that a lot of people weren't aware of, which I noticed because we were truant teenagers.

In your second novel, Baxter is forced to explore his subconscious in an attempt to find his true self. To what extent does your fiction explore the boundaries between mind and body or imagination and reality? There seems to be a lot of blurring.

In the first one, it's Baxter grappling with questions of: is this really happening or am I just insane? In the second one, it's almost like that idea was extended to his inner realm, his psychic realm. I think it comes back to that idea of belief and what people choose to centre their lives around. It was almost an exploration of the psyche, using some tropes of psychological literature. There's the Freudian idea of psychosexual development, but also the mythological element. In psychological literature there's the idea of the Dark Triad, which are the three character traits that make up a destructive individual: Machiavellianism, narcissism and psychopathy. Baxter, in a way, was an exploration of that Dark Triad. Psychological theories and literature, I feel, did inform a lot of Baxter's character. *Kill Baxter* was taking it just one step further.

In what ways does that link to aspects of belonging and community in the novel?

At the beginning of *Apocalypse Now Now*, when Baxter is talking to the Afrikaans kid that he's doing a porn deal with, he says that being an English-speaking white South African is weird because, in a sense, we have no culture of our own. It's almost like everybody else in South Africa has a very distinct culture. Afrikaans people have a very strong cultural sense, but English-speaking white South Africans don't. It's a weird mix of European influences, or American influences that we get from the media, but I don't know if there is a particular culture. That idea of being rootless in a cultural sense is very much part of Baxter's character, and is almost an exploration of my own sense of being an English-speaking white South African. The idea of being in South Africa but not being part of a strong cultural group or having a strong cultural identity is a large part of what makes Baxter who he is.

While your novels deal with a number of current South African social issues, they do so with a particular brand of dark humour. How important a role do you ascribe to humour in your work?

Both the books have an edge of satire to them. Whether it's like you say, approaching young adult fiction like *Harry Potter* or approaching

South African social issues, it's always with an edge of satire. It is an important part of what I've done with these books and for my writing as a whole. I think I'm still trying to explore whether that's my style, or whether that's just what I'm doing with these books. I would also like to write something other than that, but I'm not sure what that's going to look like. I really enjoy writing like that though; it makes it fun for me. Having those one-liners in a book is enjoyable to write and that's what a lot of people respond to. I don't always know what people are going to respond to. Some lines that I've almost taken out have been some of the ones that people have found the most funny. It's difficult to know with humour; it's difficult to know what's going to work and what isn't. You almost have to just try it and see. I suppose that's why the rapid-fire approach is quite good; you put enough material out there and people are going to respond to some of it.

South African fiction of the last, let's say, 60-odd years has been characterised by a particular heaviness for obvious historical and political reasons. What role do you see humour playing in future South African fiction?

Well, I'd like to see more of it. I think there are a lot of funny South African books. Some of them don't have the obvious humorous element that *Apocalypse Now Now* does, where some of the set-ups and some of the characters are purely for humorous effect. I think we're in a phase now where South African writers are starting to feel that perhaps they can do outright humour, they can do outright fantasy without a sense of duty to the past. I think, being South African, there is always this kind of way of including social issues in what we write. I think it's just a natural part of what we do and what we experience, but the way that we do it, I think can change. It doesn't have to be a head-on approach where you're actively grappling with issues, and I think the more we do it, the more the local market will respond because people are reading overseas fiction and watching series from the UK and the US. They don't necessarily want to grapple with social issues in an overt way. I think the more writers feel free to do what they want, the better for writing in South Africa, for writers in South Africa and also for the local market.

Keeping with the local market, while we're aware that very few writers write with a target market in mind, your novels are commonly found in the young adult section. Without attempting to pigeonhole your novels into a specific genre or to a specific readership, where would you ideally see your novels positioned in the local literary landscape?

I think one thing that a lot of writers get frustrated with is that, often, their novels end up in the South African section, like, South African fiction. If you go to a lot of bookshops, the South African section is at the back and it's a wide variety of writers. If you're the type of person looking specifically for South African fiction, you're not necessarily going to be looking for fantasy or sci-fi, or crime or anything like that. I'd like to see mine just put in the fantasy and sci-fi section. It's really as easy as that, and I think a lot of writers feel the same frustration because they're like: 'Okay, it's not only South African fiction writing.' It has a broader appeal. In a way, it doesn't really make sense for *Apocalypse Now Now* to be there with a lot of the luminaries of South African writing; serious South African fiction. It doesn't really make sense because the person who's going to buy J.M. Coetzee is probably not going to buy *Apocalypse Now Now*, but someone browsing in the fantasy and sci-fi section might say: 'Oh, that looks interesting.' The young adult label is a bit of a weird label because I think more adults read young adult fiction. A lot of adults read books that are pitched at young people, so it is a bit of a strange tag to have.

The community of South African writers who work within the genre of speculative fiction seems to be particularly close and cooperative. Frequently, one finds recurring names in the acknowledgments, like Sarah Lotz and Lauren Beukes, among others. How does this community function and to what extent do the writers of this community work together to further the cause of speculative fiction?

It's cooperative in the sense that the community is so small. There are probably only a few people that I interact with: Lauren Beukes, Sarah Lotz and Sam Wilson. Those are the guys that I probably interact with the most. Lauren was my supervisor and she's been incredibly good to me in terms of opportunities or doors that she's opened for me. Sarah Lotz is also a fantastic writer and a fantastic person. In a way, we operate more by osmosis than by anything else in the sense that there's no kind of active organisation on our part. We're all doing the same thing in the same space. Lauren and Sarah have obviously been the most successful of us. Lauren's just done fantastically well, so she's leading the charge in terms of the international scene; taking South African fiction to the international stage. But it is the kind of thing where, if someone wants a story for an anthology and Sarah can't do it, she'll pass it along to one of us. We all know how hard it is to make it as a writer, so in a sense it's kind of opening doors for each other wherever we can. I have a pay-it-forward mentality to the whole thing, to people that are writing speculative fiction in South Africa, because people have done so much for me. Sarah was an early reader of *Apocalypse Now Now*. I will help anybody that approaches me with wanting advice about getting an agent, or who to pitch to first, the publisher or an agent, and how publishers in South Africa and internationally work. It's good to know that there are other people that you can ask for advice. If there's a specific issue or a thing that you don't know or don't understand, it's good to have cooperative people that you can ask.

Would you say that the sense of camaraderie that you experience within this community is different within other writing communities?
I wonder! Perhaps there's not a sense of being an American writer or a European writer, whereas with us, there's very much the sense of being a South African writer. It is a strange thing because you get asked in interviews: 'What is it like being a South African writer?' People don't get asked what it's like being an American writer. In some sense, I think we all understand being tied to our nationality and telling South African stories on an international stage. You do get the sense that, with publishers, there's a certain number of South African stories that we can tell a year. If you set it in South Africa, you're limited in a way; there's a limited appeal. So I think the sense of camaraderie maybe comes from that.

The South African publishing industry is weird. In some ways it's hard because the market is so small, but, in some ways, it's easier because you can submit directly to a publisher. In other markets, you can't just easily send your manuscript in to a big publisher; that's not going to get you anywhere. You need to go through an agent, whereas in South Africa you don't need an agent to publish locally. You can literally email Penguin Random House and say: 'Here's my manuscript.' And they'll look at it. Getting past the 'slushed' pile is much easier in South Africa.

But then, obviously, they have to be very careful because the market is so small and they take chances. *Apocalypse Now Now* was published in Afrikaans (2013) in South Africa, and it didn't do well. I said on Twitter that, at this point, *Apocalypse Now Now* has been read more in Japanese than it's been read in Afrikaans. Afrikaans people in Cape Town and in urban centres, I found, tend to read in English. They've told me: 'I'll read your book, but I'll buy it in English because it was written in English.' So maybe the kind of urban Afrikaans-speaking person is more likely to read it in English just because they can speak English fluently and read English fluently. But then they'll read Afrikaans poetry in Afrikaans.

Although South Africa is recognised as having one of the most liberal constitutions in the world, its society is still largely conservative. What taboos do you think have yet to find their way into South African literature? What still needs to be written about?
I think there's so much that can be written about. I mean, I was a little worried that there would be a religious sort of backlash to some of the things. Just look at the cover of that [points to a copy of *Apocalypse Now Now*]. There's a little bit of a demonic vibe going on there. There's also a little bit of irreverence in terms of traditional religion. Some people have said, for the most ridiculous things, religious things, like throwaway lines that don't have anything to do with the main thrust of the story, that they have taken offence to them. I was worried because although I come from an atheist family, one side of my extended family is very religious, and I was worried that they would take offence. But they didn't.

My grandmother read a few pages, and she said: 'No, I couldn't read any further,' and I was a bit worried, but then I realised that she had been offended by just some of the swearing in the first few pages so I was like: 'Phew! She didn't even get to any of the porn parts [*laughter*] or anything like that.' I thought it's probably better. But then, her sister, who lives in the UK, read the whole thing and loved it. She phoned my grandmother and she was like: 'Oh, you know, stop being so conservative, stop being such a prude', so that was cool.

In terms of taboos that could be written about, I think there's a lot in South African culture that could be interrogated and looked at. I think there's a lot within gender studies that could be looked at. Violence against women is one thing that could be interrogated. Also transgender issues; I think it's still very difficult to be transgender in South Africa. There's a very conservative part of the population that is aggressively anti transgender people, and I think that that's something that needs to be changed.

In your opinion, what might be some of the new voices and perspectives that you see coming out in South African literature? Who are the people we need to be paying attention to?
I don't have much of a chance to read any of the newer stuff that has come out. I've heard good things about *The Reactive* (2014) by Masande Ntshanga. In terms of publishers, there's a small publisher called Fox and Raven who do speculative fiction.[5] That's really exciting because someone that's focusing entirely on speculative fiction is very cool. There's a book called *Fletcher* (2014) by David Horscroft that they put out. They're very small and don't have the same kind of clout as Penguin Random House. Umuzi, my publisher, the imprint of Penguin Random House, is always trying new things. Kudos to them for taking risks because it is difficult, and there's a lot of stuff that they put out because they like it, but it might be difficult finding an audience for because it's pretty niche stuff. I think they are taking chances, and they're trying to get new, fresh voices out there even though they may know that it might be a bit of a hard sell.

You spoke about how South Africa, for a long time, had this realist stance and serious writing. Which different genres do you see becoming more prominent in an attempt to break away from these realist conventions?
I'm not so sure it's genre as opposed to a type of story. I think more individual stories, individual experiences of South Africa; an approach that sees the individual journey as important as opposed to the country's. It's someone's story as opposed to a South African story that just happens to be set in South Africa. I think it's really important that people feel that they can tell those stories, and that stories can exist in relation to South Africa's history, but also as their own thing entirely, as individual

---

5. Fox and Raven Publishers closed its doors at the end of November 2015, leaving many of its previously published novels currently unavailable.

stories that don't only exist in relation to South African history. What builds strong literature, I think, is that people are telling the stories that they want to tell, rather than people feeling that they have a duty to tell stories, and I think, organically, a lot of the real experience will come through, rather than taking a studied realist approach to writing.

In conclusion, do you have current and future projects in the works? Is Baxter returning?

I'm in a bit of a difficult situation at the moment, my day job is quite demanding. I have a three-year-old daughter and I wanted to do something different as a third book, so not within the series. I've ended up writing a sci-fi action thriller called 'Ancestral Elevator Pitch': it's a female Zulu John Wick with aliens. Although it's in the same genre, it's quite a departure from *Apocalypse Now Now* in that I've steered away from the humour a little. I'm not quite sure whether that comic dark humour tone is where I'm heading, or whether I want to break away completely. I think it's quite easy to be pigeon-holed early in your career, to be 'the guy who does darkly humorous urban fantasy'. I'm still trying to figure out whether I want to be that guy, whether I want to be the urban fantasy guy, or if I want to be the near-future thriller guy, or whatever. But writing when you have a day job is not easy. You have to do it and it's the kind of thing where, if people complain about it or people say: 'Ah, I can't write a book because I've got a day job.' I say: 'Well, that's bullshit. You can do it because I did it.' But I also totally understand the pressures that are involved. I had probably three years of writing every weekend. It's hard not having weekends and it's hard writing in the evening. At the moment I'm trying to balance out my life a little bit, and go: 'Okay, I want to write, I also have to have a day job, and I also need to spend time with my family.' Who knows? It just has to be what it is, I will try to do it as I do it. We'll see how it goes.

References

Eales, Robert. 2015. *The Compassionate Englishwoman: Emily Hobhouse in the Boer War.* Cape Town: University of Cape Town Press.

Eco, Umberto. 1983. *The Name of the Rose*, translated by William Weaver. San Diego: Harcourt.

Electronic Frontier Foundation (ed.). 2015. *Pwning Tomorrow: Short Fiction from the Electronic Frontier*. San Francisco: Electronic Frontier Foundation.

Graugart, Christian. 2012. *The Brazilian Jiu Jitsu Globetrotter: The True Story about a Frantic, 140 Day Long, Around-the-World Trip to Train Brazilian Jiu Jitsu*. Scotts Valley, CA: CreateSpace Independent Publishing Platform.

Horscroft, David. 2014. *Fletcher*. Cape Town: Fox and Raven Publishers.

Human, Charlie. 2013. *Bokveld Binnekort*. Cape Town: Umuzi.

Icke, David V. 1999. *The Biggest Secret: The Book That Will Change the World*. Illford: Bridge of Love Publications.

Mutwa, Vusamazulu Credo. 1964. *Indaba, My Children*. New York: Grove Press.

Ntshanga, Masande. 2014. *The Reactive*. Cape Town: Umuzi.

Perry, Anne C. and Jared Shurin (eds). 2011. *Pandemonium: Stories of the Apocalypse*. London: Jurassic London.

Raath, Andries W.G. 2011. *Niklaas van Rensburg: Die Siener*. Pretoria: Lapa Uitgewers.

Rowling, J.K. 1997. *Harry Potter and the Philosopher's Stone*. London: Bloomsbury.

———. 1998. *Harry Potter and the Chamber of Secrets*. London: Bloomsbury.

———. 1999. *Harry Potter and the Prisoner of Askaban*. London: Bloomsbury.

———. 2000. *Harry Potter and the Goblet of Fire*. London: Bloomsbury.

———. 2003. *Harry Potter and the Order of the Phoenix*. London: Bloomsbury.

———. 2005. *Harry Potter and the Half-Blood Prince*. London: Bloomsbury.

———. 2007. *Harry Potter and the Deathly Hallows*. London: Bloomsbury.

Salinger, Jerome D. 1951. *The Catcher in the Rye*. New York: Little Brown and Company.

Tolkien, J.J.R. [1954/1955] 2009. *The Lord of the Rings: The Fellowship of the Ring, The Two Towers, The Return of the Kind*. New York: Harper Collins.

'It's important to look at what's wrong and to look at our shadows . . . because I think those are the scary things.'

Yewande Omotoso (photo: courtesy Yewande Omotoso, taken by Pelayo Omotoso)

Danyela Demir and Olivier Moreillon

In Conversation with Yewande Omotoso
(b. 1980)

We met architect and writer of fiction Yewande Omotoso at Doppio Zero in Sunninghill on a Tuesday morning. Yewande is the author of two novels, *Bom Boy* (2011) and *The Woman Next Door* (2016). Her debut novel won the 2012 South African Literary Awards First-Time Published Author Award and it was shortlisted for the Sunday Times Fiction Prize, the M-Net Literary Award of the same year, as well as the 2013 Etisalat Prize for Literature. Her second novel was longlisted for the 2017 Baileys Women's Prize for Fiction, and it was shortlisted for the 2017 University of Johannesburg Prize, the 2017 Barry Ronge Prize,[1] and the 2018 International Dublin Literary Award.

Yewande was born in Bridgetown, Barbados, and spent her childhood in Ile-Ife, Nigeria, before the family relocated to Cape Town in 1992. She studied architecture at the University of Cape Town and then gained work experience as an architect before opting for a Master's degree in Creative Writing at the same university. She has since relocated to Johannesburg, where she does all kinds of work, including freelancing for NGOs, running workshops, supervising Master's students and occasional architectural design and consultancy work.

Before our meeting, Yewande had just finished reading Nawal El Saadawi's *Woman at Point Zero* (1983). She read the book after meeting El Saadawi at the 2016 Africa Writes Festival in London, where El Saadawi was the guest speaker. About El Saadawi, Yewande says: 'She's a phenomenal presence, both physically and on the page; I was inspired. I'd never read her work. She's written over 60 novels. The fact that she writes in Arabic, but is hardly translated, attests to the

---

1. Formerly the Sunday Times Fiction Prize.

hegemony of English. She's not celebrated as much as she should be. The book is incredible!'

For her own writing, Yewande does not have to go in search of inspiration, telling us: 'I don't have a sense of where I find it. Life is inspiring. Everything is inspiring. You guys are inspiring. My problem is that too much is inspiring. I have too many books lined up in my head. I have to train my imagination and reign it in, which is a different challenge to having to stimulate it.' What makes her anxious about writing is the uncertainty, during the creative process, about how the book will turn out. However, she does say that the uncertainty can also be seen as a beneficial component of the writing experience since this is what, according to her, 'allows the work to simmer'. She says that she likes everything else about writing, an occupation that she regards as a blessing.

One of her favourite spots in Johannesburg is Atlas Studios, which she frequents for their monthly First Wednesday Film Club. She also enjoys Melville, which she discovered during a four-month residency at the Johannesburg Institute for Advanced Studies. Because she likes walking, Yewande likes the Pipe Track in Cape Town and any of the city's mountains. She also used to go to the Rhodes Memorial. Yewande says that she went there 'obviously not because I'm madly in love with Cecil John Rhodes, but because the view from that outcrop is political. The complexity of the space interests me. It's a difficult space. It's a problematic space, but I go to it. Ought we never to go to spaces that are problematic?'

❧

Works
———. 2011. *Bom Boy* (Modjaji Books)
Bom Boy tells the story of young Leke, who lives in the suburbs of Cape Town with his adoptive parents. After his adoptive mother's death, he moves out, which is when his family history catches up with him and he starts displaying strange behaviours, manifesting in the form of stalking, petty theft and hypochondria. This ultimately forces Leke to confront his own multi-layered identity and the complex family history of his biological parents.

————. 2016. *The Woman Next Door* (Chatto & Windus)
The Woman Next Door is the story of Hortensia James and Marion
Agostino, two elderly neighbours, both recently widowed, in Cape
Town's suburbia. Their hostile relationship, because Hortensia is black
and Marion is white, is a microcosm of Cape Town's racially loaded
topography, which is further complicated when unforeseen events force
the women into closer proximity.

಄

**Besides being a writer of fiction, you are also an architect. To what
extent do you consider yourself more one than the other, and how do
these two fields of work influence each other?**
I don't really consider myself more one than the other because I think
we're all fluid. We are all everything all the time, and nothing. Do you
know what I mean? I am Yewande and all of that and more. I spent
between six and eight years being trained to think like an architect, so
it's definitely a part of who I am. That's a chunk of my life. Before that,
from when I can remember, from age four or five, I spent a lot of time
and energy writing and reading. I have always been around writers;
my dad's a writer, surrounded by other writers, and my brothers were
writing. So these are things that are deeply embedded. Did I love writing
first? Probably. True, I wasn't drawing buildings when I was five; I
wasn't imagining that. Maybe writing is what I've done the longest, but
I see myself as both. My late mother was a city planner and I think that
counts for something too.

I love both writing and architecture. They exist in the same body
and I think they both bring something special to my experience of
life. I see more of an impact of the architecture on my writing because
architecture was my training, and when you study something, it's kind
of an indoctrination, year after year, bombarding your way of thinking.
As architects, the indoctrination was around space and place and how
to look, how to observe. Whereas writing is less studied for me, maybe
it's more from the subconscious, more innate, in a way, although I did
do a Master's. But I think that my training as an architect informs my
thinking and practice as a writer.

How important are aspects of space and place in your writing?
Consciously, I wouldn't have thought of it. When I was writing *Bom Boy*, for instance, I was very much feeling my way through and I wrote what came to me. But looking back at it, I can see that space and place are important, and, if I look at everything I write, I can see that they will always be. We're always somewhere as human beings, so how can our positioning and our experience of where we are *not* be relevant as we tell stories about ourselves? Our experience of the city, a home, a room, or a chair. These are all spaces and places, just different scales of them.

What different aspects of home, belonging and community do you engage with in your fiction?
I'm interested in belonging. My own sense of belonging has always been complicated, firstly because my parents are of two cultures. My dad is Nigerian and my late mother Barbadian. I was born in Barbados, but I grew up in Nigeria. When I say complicated, I don't mean there is any angst about the multiple identities, just that it's not a straight line. I'm not sure how aware I was of that as a child, for instance. I think a lot of the complexity started, really, when I came to South Africa. I'm black, but I'm not South African. I'm Nigerian, but I'm also of this other place, and in many ways this prompted me to think about belonging. When we arrived in South Africa when I was twelve years old, it seemed that people (often white people) exoticised black Africans who weren't South African, as different, as separate, by almost putting you on some platform, which is deeply problematic.

But the complexities and politics around belonging shouldn't just be relevant for someone like me. These thoughts should occupy a white South African born in Joburg, who lived there their whole life, went to a school where their identity was reflected back at them. I don't want to put these issues in a corner reserved for certain kinds of people. I suppose that's what I'll continue to try to do with my writing in terms of belonging, home and community. I don't believe in hammering these things into the story though, but to do it in discrete and not so obvious ways.

Both *Bom Boy* and *The Woman Next Door* engage with various complicated family constellations. How central are these family constellations with regard to questions of identity and history?

Very central! I am fascinated by the family as a kind of microcosm for *everything*. Families contain our first loves, the first people we meet, the people we need. In family is contained our hatred, our rage, our anger and disappointment. There's a writer who said that everything that's happened between the ages of one and seven is all she's needed for her stories. She writes from these years of her life. I think the family is a rich source and I'll always kind of mine it. Family is particularly interesting because of the chasm between the myth of family, and the reality that it is, for example, the myths of motherhood, beauty, love. And marriage, you can have a field day with that institution! These are things I think are too juicy not to use as the armature for a story, together with the impact that these dynamics have on us as human beings and the kind of lives we live.

Early on, in *The Woman Next Door*, Hortensia reminisces that 'memories were balls of fire sitting in the centre of each earlobe', before discovering that 'if she remembered while walking, the memories were bearable' (2016: 3). In what ways does your fiction deal with notions of memory? Memory, both the individual and the collective, is how we keep the past present, and how we make sense of the now. I'm interested in the pathologies around how we relate to what's happened already, to us or the people around us, as well as what didn't happen, and the impact on our psyche. I'm always linking the past and the present in my writing, and not necessarily in that order. I did it in *Bom Boy* and some people said that it confused them. I think memory and how we grapple with past events can be confusing; perhaps confusion was an appropriate response to reading about Leke's attempts to come to grips with his place in life.

In *The Woman Next Door* I'm dealing with people who are much older. The characters here are at the end of their lives and the role of memory is palpable – everything has happened already, the characters are haunted by the past. I'm interested in how we talk about our past, how we remember it, how we remember it differently, how we lie because memory and lies go together. Sometimes, we lie knowingly. Sometimes, we don't even realise that we are lying or rearranging and designing it. I think that's important with people like Marion and Hortensia and, perhaps, particularly Marion.

` In *Bom Boy*, Lerato says in the voice of the ancestors: 'You need to give back, Leke. Give back what was taken' (2011: 248). What different aspects of forgiveness, reconciliation and healing do you deal with in your fiction?

I might not use those exact words, but I would think of it as repair. Repair is very important to me, because I think the world and all of us are damaged to varying degrees and in need of repair or healing. I'm not interested in fantastical repair – as in a fairy tale – where it happens and people live happily ever after. This is why both *Bom Boy* and *The Woman Next Door* had to reflect how much work it requires, how much of it involves actually changing oneself, and how you are never done with it. There's always further to travel. My books hint at that, that there is a lot of work still ahead. Will Leke make it? Who knows? That's not the issue. And unless they die, Hortensia and Marion have a lot of work to do too. Maybe that'll be possible for them, maybe not. Shame [*laughter*]. The point is that it lies ahead. Hope is important, but there's work, the work of reconciliation as you say, or forgiveness, or what I think of as repair, is ahead. There's always still more. I don't think we can ever arrive and I don't particularly want my stories to end with people having arrived, because that's too easy.

Most of your female characters are passionate and driven by a desire for independence. How vital is it for you to create strong female characters in your fiction?

Somebody recently asked me whether my books fit into certain narratives that are happening in South Africa. I wasn't sure if that was actually true. He was asking how premeditated my writing is, and I said I didn't get the opportunity to be that strategic, because I do write a lot from my dreams, from a flow and an intuition. Later I come back and edit carefully but the initial material is from the gut. So, in that sense, I think these are just the characters I wrote. I don't spend too much time thinking: I ought to write powerful women because I'm a feminist and that's the right thing to do. If my feminism is deeply ingrained in my imagination, then what comes forth, one must trust, would be imbued with the things that matter to me. At the same time it's not a tract or a manifesto. As a woman, I should have all the room to be helpless. I should have lots of room to be a mess, to be in need of saving, while at the same time I can also be capable. I have to have access to all of that, and men need to have access to all of that too, because that is the full spectrum of what it is to be in the world and to be human.

How important are issues of race, racism and white privilege for your writing, and to what extent is your fiction a contribution to an ongoing debate around these issues within post-apartheid South Africa?
I think it remains to be seen whether there's anything people can draw from it. What's interesting for me about race and racism is that these are things I mostly met here as a twelve-year-old. I wouldn't necessarily have had extensive experience, first-hand experience, of those things in Nigeria. I didn't, really. But we travelled a bit. I remember instances of strange experiences in London.

I'm really glad I grew up here because it has allowed me to make some sense of the immense complexity of this country. I'm not saying I fully understand it, but having lived here, even in my lack of understanding, there is a lived experience that gives me some kind of insight into the many facets of this country. I have an insight into the sort of history it carries, what this means for everyone who lives here, and how it's lingered, how it's stayed. I won't say race and white privilege are key issues for me in my writing; rather I am generally intrigued by human beings and all the things that go wrong, but not because I'm a miserable person and I want to dwell on problems. Happiness is also important, and love, and I think I'll always write about those things too, but it's important to look at what's wrong, to look at our shadows and to look honestly at them, or as honestly as possible. Rumi said the light comes in from the wound.[2]

Let's move on to South African literature more broadly. Although South Africa is recognised as having one of the most liberal constitutions in the world, its society is still largely conservative. What taboos do you think have yet to find their way into contemporary South African fiction?
Let me talk about myself here and my own taboos and inhibitions. I'm writing more and more about sex and sexuality and I'm simultaneously exploring and learning how to write about it. It's difficult and involves my own personal concerns, even ones as domestic as being worried about my dad reading my books. My dad's a big fan of mine. He reads

2. The original quote is as follows: 'The wound is the place where the light enters you' (Barks 1995).

my books, buys ten copies and sends them to all his professor friends [*laughter*]. I can have an adult conversation with my dad and tell him not to buy this particular book for Professor So-and-so, or to tell him to skip pages 35 to 50! But you know, we need to make jokes about these things and laugh about them. Sex is a part of who we are; it's a part of why we're here [*laughs*]. This is something I've noticed that I want to write more about. Sometimes, we're aware of our inhibitions and blocks, sometimes we're not, so you'll discover it and muster up courage to work through it if you choose to. I tried to do it with *The Woman Next Door*. I wanted to write about someone racist and try to make her relatable in the end. That's a taboo, the relatable racist. Not everyone finds Marion relatable, but many did, and whenever I get that feedback from readers I am pleased. Deliberately Marion is not written as a horror and yet her racism is gruesome. It's dangerous to think gruesome always has to look gruesome, in other words, thinking that we're not gruesome because we look in the mirror and we look okay. People rationalise the violence they do to other people all the time. They are rational, but if they look at someone else committing their violence, they call that horrific. Look at colonisers. Look at Hitler. Look at terrorists. I wanted Marion to be someone quite sanitised, not evil, not a monster. If I made her into a monster, then people would read it and say: 'Ah, she's a monster, I'm not.' She's not killing or beating anybody but is still deeply violent and problematic. I think that we need to look at the polite offences because my thing with South Africa is nobody ever says they're racist. Men don't come up and say they're sexist. I don't declare myself a classist. In so many ways, we can't see ourselves; we can't see how much violence we perform in the world, physical and emotional. I really like the idea of writing more and more about the fact that we are those things and showing how blind we are to them.

In your opinion, what might be some of the new voices or perspectives that we can see developing in South African literature?
South Africa is an exciting space when it comes to new voices because, as we repair and right the wrongs of our past, we'll be hearing from people that were previously told to keep quiet, who were told their point doesn't matter. If you think of the voices that have arisen out of #FeesMustFall, #RhodesMustFall or #OpenStellenbosch, these are incredible voices. I'm really inspired by the movement. Once human beings are involved, whether they're involved with the revolution or

they're the slave-owners, it will be fallible because human beings are. We've seen some of the issues, including hetero-patriarchy on full display. Nonetheless, I'm really moved by the movement and the people in it. I'm moved by its existence, the way it came about. I'm in awe of these young people and their voices. That will continue and my role in that is to be a reader, to consume their works and engage with them.

Which different genres do you see becoming more prominent as an attempt to break away from the realist conventions of this country that we see?

I challenge the notion of a realist convention in the country. Certainly, what we know is that what gets published is simply that, versus a representation of the full spectrum of what is actually being written. And the publishing industry in any country, acts as a kind of sieve, where certain people decide what passes through the holes and what does not. When we start seeing different kinds of literatures and genres on the shelves of bookshops, it's not necessarily because people are writing differently, it's because certain kinds of readers are starting to be privileged over others, and new kinds of publishers and booksellers are beginning to emerge.

This is a time of discovery and permissions, writers giving themselves permission to explore whatever it is that obsesses them. Notwithstanding the 'sieve effect', which we will always have with us and which is often steered by commercial appetite, this is an interesting time in South African literature.

What are you currently working on? What can we expect from you?

I've just finished a new novel, by that I mean it's a manuscript. I've been working on it for some years and I now think I'm finished. It's a story about a family that deals with loss and death. A couple coming to terms with the death of their estranged daughter. And it's also about art, expression and desire.

References

Barks, Coleman. 1995. *The Essential Rumi*. San Francisco: Harper.

El Saadawi, Nawal. 1983. *Woman at Point Zero*, translated by Sherif Hetata. London: Zed Books.

'[In archaeology,] there's a great deal of speculation and storytelling.'

Andrew Salomon (photo: courtesy Andrew Salomon, taken by Fernando Badiali)

Danyela Demir, Olivier Moreillon and Alan Muller

In Conversation with Andrew Salomon
(b. 1973)

It was on a beautiful Saturday afternoon – we had arrived in Cape Town early that morning – that we made our way to the Company Gardens to meet Andrew Salomon. As the Company's Garden Restaurant was rather crowded for our intended literary chat with Andrew, we made our way to the Royale Eatery at the top of Long Street in order to settle down for our interview over a cup of coffee.

Andrew is the author of four novels: *The Chrysalis* (2013), *Tokoloshe Song* (2014), *The Equilibrist* (2017) and *Wonderbear* (2017). He has also written a volume of short stories titled *Dark Shenanigans* (2017). *Tokoloshe Song*, then titled 'Lun', was shortlisted for the 2011 Terry Pratchett First Novel Award. *The Chrysalis* was shortlisted for the 2013/2014 Sanlam Prize for Youth Literature. Andrew's short story 'Train 124' won the 2015 Short Sharp Stories Award, 'A Visit to Dr Mamba' won second prize in the 2009 PEN/Studinski Literary Award and 'The Entomologist's Dream' was shortlisted for the 2016 Commonwealth Short Story Prize.

Andrew grew up in Pretoria, where he eventually did his BA and Honours in Archaeology, before embarking on a Master's at the Institute for Archaeology at University College London. He now lives in Cape Town with his wife, children and dogs, where he works as a heritage officer at the South African Heritage Resources Agency.

Asked about his likes and dislikes about the writing process, he says that he loves writing novels, but dislikes the fact 'that it takes so long' to write one. He half-jokingly adds: 'I started off with short stories, but I don't want to say I graduated from short stories to novels because they're no easier, but they do take a lot less time, although with a short story you don't get to waffle at all.' His favourite part about writing is the editorial work that goes into it: 'I love when you've got the first draft

179

finished, and then you can start rewriting and polishing. I'm a complete subscriber to Hemingway's opinion that there are no great writers, only great rewriters.'

The last book Andrew had read before we met was David Mitchell's *The Bone Clocks* (2014), a book about which he was 'biased'. He says: 'I think he's fantastic. I didn't think it was his best novel. But I still think compared to most things out there, *The Bone Clocks* was absolutely fantastic. I love what he does, how he weaves all these different narratives together into one story. I really enjoyed it.' Before that he had read Joan Didion's *The White Album* (1979). Andrew admits: 'I really like good essay writing.' His favourite essayist is Geoff Dyer, whom he finds 'absolutely brilliant'.

His favourite spot in Cape Town is Windmill Beach, just outside Simon's Town, right next to Boulders Beach. According to Andrew: 'It's a wonderful place for snorkelling. There's two little bays protected by huge boulders, and a kelp forest. It's a protected marine area, so you can see lots of fish and octopuses and crabs and all kinds of marine life. I just love going snorkelling and swimming there.' He also likes the 'wonderful tidal pools' in Kalk Bay, St James and Muizenberg, all three of which also lend themselves to hiking with his two rescue dogs.

Works

———. 2013. *The Chrysalis* (Oxford University Press)

The Chrysalis, Andrew's first young adult novel, is a mixture of a murder mystery and a crime thriller. It tells the story of fifteen-year-old Michael Matambo, who has difficulties coming to terms with his father's death. At his grandmother's home in Cape Town, he finds out that his father's death was not caused by an accident, but that he was murdered. And then, all of a sudden, Michael finds himself the target of his father's killer.

———. 2014. *Tokoloshe Song* (Umuzi)

In *Tokoloshe Song*, Andrew's first novel for adults, Richard Nevis finds himself being chased by Cape Town's most infamous gangster. Together with Lun, whom he meets while doing voluntary work at a shelter for mistreated *tokoloshes*, and two most unusual midwives, Richard flees to the Karoo, where they need to find an ancient box that will be the key to saving their lives.

————. 2017. *The Equilibrist* (Amazon)

The Equilibrist centres on the life of Flynn Oakley, an up-and-coming tightrope acrobat at the Circus Basilisk, which is now camped outside the northern English town of Kirkholme. When Flynn is falsely accused of a crime, he finds himself chased by various magical creatures and finds shelter in a maze of underground tunnels and caves in the Bleaks, the nearby marshlands.

————. 2017. *Dark Shenanigans* (Amazon)

Dark Shenanigans is Andrew's first short story collection, which contains, among others, the 2009 PEN/Studinski Literary Award-winning story 'A Visit to Dr Mamba' and the 2015 Short Sharp Stories Award-winning story 'Train 124'.

————. 2017. *Wonderbear* (Amazon)

Wonderbear, Andrew's second young adult novel, is the story of Teresa (Tess) Davey. When her father falls seriously ill and travels to Canada for treatment, Tess and her brother are sent to their aunt's house in the Drakensberg. Soon after their arrival, Tess is taken hostage and forced to dive into a deep and secret mountain pool in order to retrieve treasures for her captors. Through her forced expeditions, Tess learns more about her connection to the underwater world – her only chance of escape.

~

What were your reasons for choosing speculative fiction as the genre to tell your stories?

I think it's because that's what I really like to read. Years ago, I came upon a bit of advice that said to write the kind of novel you'd love to read yourself, and I very much stick to that. Even when I try to write other genres, the speculative thing always sneaks in. There's this thing called the Short Sharp Stories Award, and the first one was for crime writing, and I had a story in there, and then the second one was erotic South African fiction, and I wrote one for that, and it ended up a spec fiction piece where this guy discovers that he has this amazing ability to have sex with spirits and this spawns a very niche profitable piece of Internet porn [*laughs*]. So I think spec fiction always just creeps in, whether I like it or not.

Besides being a novelist, you are also an archaeologist. How do the two professional fields influence each other?
Well, I think archaeology is a great thing to mine for fiction because through archaeology you are storytelling a bit as well. It's supposedly a science, but only on its best day, in a way. But that is not necessarily the best bit. A lot of archaeology is straight lab analysis, but there's a great deal of speculation and storytelling about what rock paintings and rock engravings, the two areas I specialised in, actually mean – some of it good, some of it not so good. So that feeds into it. There's just fascinating stuff you find in archaeology, and it joins up with Classics and mythology and legends, and a lot of rock art is connected to altered states of consciousness, where you have experiences in a spirit world that can be caused by either chemicals or chanting and fasting, so that fits wonderfully into kind of horror, spec, fantasy, sci-fi writing and also just by observing the human condition.

I used to take students to Mozambique for a month; pampered young people from Johannesburg who'd never been without electricity or water, and now they have to climb up mountains and down mountains, get bitten by spiders, and all that kind of thing, and you get to observe the human condition and yourself as well. You get to realise, maybe you're not as nice as you thought [*laughs*]. And that is really great to exploit in your writing.

The *tokoloshe* is undoubtedly the most famous figure in South African mythology. What were your reasons for using the *tokoloshe* as opposed to any other South African or even Western mythological figure?
Well, it came from the short story, 'A Visit to Dr Mamba'. It was one of the winners of the PEN Literary Awards for African Fiction and I got an incredibly positive response to the story. I had people at advertising agencies phoning me; I had directors phoning me, people meeting me and wanting to do film scripts. Most of those things just fall flat, but a very nice short film was made out of it, which they now are busy with the CGI [computer-generated imagery] for, and the music; and I just felt that this was something that resonated with people, and I thought, 'Well, if you can have a *tokoloshe* not as a terrifying thing but as kind

of an underdog, then that makes it really interesting.' And I decided to exploit that more.

I think the *tokoloshe*, by being small and by being an outsider, is a character that you can get a reader behind and to care about. Like in *District 9* (2009), the little baby alien, the baby prawn, which is as unhuman as you can possibly think, but you care about this little guy so much. I thought it was so well done, and I thought: 'Well, that's a good trick to pull off.' Also, I do like to do a lot of research, and I found that you get these kind of knee-high mythological creatures all over the world: You get them in the Congo. You get them in Australia. You get a lot of them in the Nordic myths as well. So it seemed to be something that resonates with people. I kind of like them, and at the time when I was writing the book, there were a lot of problems with xenophobic violence in the country, and I found that this issue actually found its way into the book. The *tokoloshe* could be a universally despised foreigner in people's minds.

What other mythological aspects do you engage with in your writing?
Well, I found that Africa is so rich in myths, and I can't believe more writers aren't engaging with it. Neil Gaiman, not that he's using African myths, but in *American Gods* (2001) he incorporated a lot of the Scandinavian Nordic gods and myths and brought them to America, which was very clever because it's still his bestseller, and I almost think his weakest book. But I found quite a few other things. My story 'Nkisi', which was published in *African Pens 2011* short story anthology (Coetzee 2011), incorporated something called *nkisi* (also called *nkishi*), which is a small wooden idol covered in nails, and it comes from the DRC and it's kind of an African jungle fetish. If you have a problem, or your family has a problem, you have *nkisi*. It's an extremely potent thing that can absorb trouble and problems and evil. So you take a metal nail, you imbue it with whatever is haunting you or bothering you, and you drive it into the *nkisi* and the *nkisi* takes it away from you. Stuff like this is just fantastic for fiction. You even get some with a little window in their belly and a little baby *nkisi* in there. That's just incredible!

What other figures do you still want to write about?
There are so many water spirit myths in Africa that are just fantastic to use. There's one that apparently lives in the Howick Falls in KwaZulu-

Natal. Africa's rich in myths and I plan to use a whole lot more [*laughs*]. So I definitely want to do a lot more with water spirits. Maybe something with *nyami nyami* in Lake Malawi, which is among Chewa-speaking people who you find in Mozambique, Malawi and Zambia. There's this very pervasive, very potent myth about this giant water creature that lives in Lake Malawi, which every now and then will surface and open its giant jaws and these billions of insects will come out and then it'll close them again. So ja, definitely something like that. No vampires or werewolves [*laughter*].

Also, African witchcraft is still very potent in Africa. I've been reading up about the things that witches can do, like employ spiders who will spin a web around all the door handles in a village, so whenever someone opens their door, the witch will know that you're coming in and out. Things like that, stuff that makes your skin crawl, I find really interesting and I'd like to exploit, to use. Steal [*laughter*]. Borrow.

The *tokoloshe* seems to be associated with rural conditions as opposed to the urban. To what extent do you play off the urban and the rural, and to what effect?
I think I do that a lot, and I think the reason I do is because of the archaeological fieldwork that I've done, especially in Mozambique and in Zambia, where we would always be in a very, very rural setting, where you'd never have running water, you'd never have electricity and you had to be totally self-sufficient, but self-sufficient in the sense that you had to rely on the kindness of the rural people in order for you to be able to survive. You always had to go and introduce yourself to the local chief, and you'd set up your camp within the local village, and you'd employ local people to carry water for you and cook for you, and it created a deep love of rural Africa in me. To me, there's nothing like making a fire under an African sky and drinking a cold beer after a hard day of exploring for archaeological sites. What I used to love, whenever we used to stay near small towns, is to go and walk around at night, walk past huts and cooking fires and the smell of woodsmoke and the sound of children playing and the sound of people talking, and almost be like a ghost, but a very happy ghost. I loved to be in this environment and just to absorb it, and you feel this kind of incredible, deep, ancient, persistent beauty and kindness of Africa in places like that, which you don't usually get in an African urban setting. Cape Town's a reasonably

friendly city, but you need to be able to afford that friendliness as well. Where you live very much depends on how friendly it is around you and how kind. I find large African metropolises to be very daunting, rough places. I've spent a lot of time in Maputo and it can be a hair-raising city. Same with Lusaka. So, I'm fascinated with African metropolises but I'm not fond of them, but I'm aware they exist and I want to incorporate them, but I think I do juxtapose them with the rural, which is no more real but is more real to me.

The first third of *Tokoloshe Song* is dedicated to introducing multiple narrative perspectives. How much research and planning went into this process and how did you go about crafting the plot and characters?
That's a good question. I'll answer it honestly. I was extremely pressed for time. I had about three-and-a-half months to write the whole thing. So, I realised that I had to plot as much as I could, but I had never plotted a novel before, so I just wrote down ideas, and as I was writing, I also realised I had to try to cannibalise whatever I already had. So a lot of short stories became chapters. 'Pit Bull Midwives' was a stand-alone short story, but that then became a chapter and characters in the novel. 'Doorway' was a stand-alone short story and then he made his way into the novel. Funnily enough, I've had a lot of calls for more Doorway, and what I would love to do is, like every novel I write now, I would like Doorway to have a little scene in it, like a recurring character.

Neal Stephenson, who has almost achieved god-like status with very iconic modern spec fiction. He wrote *Snow Crash* (1992) and *Cryptonomicon* (1999), but I think his earlier work's better. He has this recurring character, Enoch Root, who is an alchemist and doesn't die, and appears in several of his books. I really like that idea and I wouldn't mind emulating that a bit.

I realised that I have to plot out, really as much as I can. I think I got pretty good at plotting, and I realised that plotting doesn't have an adverse effect on your creativity. It's actually quite the other way around. I knew André Brink quite well, our wives are close friends, and I was on about 20 000 words and I said to him, 'I'm stuck. I'm not sure where to go now [*laughs*]. You know, it's only a quarter in and there's two months left!' He said, 'Ag, you know, just take a walk and have a bath, and then plot some more!' [*laughs*]. And it turned out to be really good advice. I found it to just be a craft project.

I also realised that you certainly don't need to write a novel in sequence. You can write whichever bit feels right to you on that day and make it fit later on. I do think with *Tokoloshe Song* there are too many characters that get introduced right at the start, but that's just the way it worked out. My main aim was getting to that bloody 80 000 word limit that entries for the Terry Pratchett First Novel Award had to be.

So, you've got this vast array of characters. Which ones did you find the easiest or the most difficult to write?
I found Doorway the easiest to write because he's not encumbered by conscience. He's probably the most relaxed character in the book. He's not worried about what he does, if it's right or wrong. It's right for him. When I wrote Doorway, I always thought like that: I'm doing what I feel is right. Don't subscribe to any kind of morality. I found Richard, the main character, almost to be the most difficult to write because I wanted him to be slightly nerdy and slightly out of place, but also to be caring and courageous at the same time. I also wanted him to grow throughout the novel and I found that to be quite difficult, whereas with Doorway, he arrives and leaves fully formed, that's quite easy [*laughs*]!

Many of your chapters start with a very detailed description of landscapes and/or the weather. In addition, these landscapes almost always contain identifiable place markers, that is, places you can pinpoint on a map. How important is the representation of place in your work?
I find in my writing it is very important. I'm not sure why, but I find that most things I write just work out that way. I think it's probably just a preference for what I like to read. I don't like long-winded descriptions of places, but I like to feel very centred within a scene. That's when I feel I can inhabit it when I'm reading, and I like to lead my reader along the same route through my own writing. I just find it easier to write about places where I've actually been.

Cape Town serves as a confluence of a great many global aspects and several of your characters seem to be in varying states of motion. How important are different aspects of movement in your work?
I think it's very important for me. A lot of my work has to do with a journey and a quest, and I think it's because I love travelling myself, and have done so ever since I could. I finished school. I went to the military for a year – back then there was still conscription. Then I got

out of the military. I had no idea what I wanted to do. I knew I wanted to study, and then I went travelling. I went backpacking around Europe and doing odd jobs and all that kind of thing. Then I came back, started studying, and then started hitch-hiking across Africa, and at the end of my first year, myself and eleven other people hitch-hiked from Pretoria to Zanzibar and back. We didn't know it, but no one had done that before. Well, no one from the University of Pretoria anyway. You know, there were articles about this in newspapers and magazines and we were just naive, and so it worked, and the travel bug really, really got me then. And it's never left me. So I love the whole idea of a journey. I love travelling somewhere, you have no idea where you're going to sleep that night, but it doesn't matter. I love that feeling. To me that's the definition of being free and I think that finds its way into my fiction. I love the idea of a journey and growing through it. Just discovery, exploring and discovery. To me that's the spice of life.

The character Doorway, for example, is in Mumbai at the beginning of the novel. Then he's in London and ends up in Cape Town. How does your fiction engage with positioning South Africa within a more global context?

Well, I don't think that I'm trying to do so consciously, but I am very aware that South Africa, even in the global village, is a very isolated place, just geographically, and Cape Town very much so as well. I really think that anything set here can be as good as anything set anywhere else in the world, and I think that Africa is almost more interesting because it's been written about less. I find the idea of writing African fiction that is a thriller or a horror, or something that you read more just for the pleasure of reading, than to actually come to some kind of great socio-economic or socio-political realisation, very interesting. I think there are a lot of people writing really good serious literature that's set in Africa, and that's good and fine. But it's not something I necessarily aspire to, or even enjoy reading, to be honest. I am also very much aware that if you set something in Africa, or in South Africa, your chances of getting an international publisher reduce exponentially. Whether that's right or wrong, I'm not really concerned with, but that's just the reality of it. The South African writers I know, who have had success to the degree that they can actually write full-time, for them it's all happened once they started setting their stories somewhere outside of South Africa.

Which aspects of home, belonging and community do you engage with in your fiction?

Oh, that's an interesting one. I think I'm quite a nomadic type, so it took me a long time to think of South Africa as my home. I grew up in Pretoria and it never felt quite right to me. I went to a very conservative Afrikaans boys' school, which I hated, and which I just didn't fit into at all. I went to the military, which was the most bizarre experience, one which I don't regret, but if I think back to it, it's like someone else's life that I look at. And the whole way the country was before 1994 – you can list the usual suspects of apartheid and racism and everything, but it's also just the incredible narrow-mindedness of the place that just never resonated with me and that I didn't want to be associated with. So when I went abroad the first time, I thought I'd probably want to stay in Europe, I wouldn't want to come back to this place where I've never really felt at home. Even to this day, I'm not really sure. I'm a transplant to Cape Town as well. I like living here, but I don't need to feel that a place has to be home. It's just kind of a happy place. If my wife, my children and my dogs are happy, then I'm quite happy to be here, but I think I could be happy somewhere else too.

Community's an interesting one because I think in South Africa we've mostly lost a sense of community. The closest thing to community that I experience here is our road. We have a WhatsApp group [*laughs*] and everyone in the road is on the same group, and in a South African sense that's huge for community. A lot of people don't know their neighbours at all, and I suppose that's what I enjoy about a countryside setting – places like Nieu Bethesda, a place like Prince Albert in the Karoo – smaller towns where it's kind of just easier and more the done thing to actually get to know people, but I'm also a very independent person. In contrast, I have Brazilian friends, and for them not to have a sense of community would be like a death sentence, whereas I don't share that.

Richard, the protagonist of *Tokoloshe Song*, has a noticeable preoccupation with boats and the sea. How important is water and the concept of fluidity in *Tokoloshe Song*?

Oh, I think so much of it is connected with water. The book's climactic scene, for example, is connected with water, and in the very last scene of the book, they're actually on the beach, I realise now as well. I think it goes back to my childhood and growing up in Pretoria, where you are six hours from the nearest beach or sea, and so the most I would ever see the sea would be once a year, if that, on a family holiday. To me, the sea has always had this incredible attraction and mystery, and to this day that feeling still persists with anything aquatic. I think something in me just resonates very deeply with water. I love being in water and I think that just finds its way into the story. With *Tokoloshe Song* being set in Cape Town, or along the coast, it was just easy. It worked. I hadn't realised how much of it was set on or close to water until you mentioned it.

What about the importance of water and aspects of fluidity in your other works?
Now that you make me think of it, water does feature prominently in a lot of my other work. I think it has to do with a deep love I have of being submerged; as a child I swam underwater well before I swam on the surface. Being in a silent world, surrounded by a different element allows you freedoms that air and harsher gravity do not. Added to that is the sense of mystery, of there being unknown things under the surface. I think I feel very much the same about caves as well.

There are a lot of parallels between you, or your writing, and that of Olive Schreiner and the way that she depicts the Karoo. To what extent is your depiction of the Karoo influenced by her?
Well, that's very kind of you. I'm not sure how much of it is. I know she spent a lot of time there. She wrote *The Story of an African Farm* (1883) there. I think it's very easy to be influenced by the Karoo, if you're a writer. There's something about these wide, open spaces that kind of whisper to you all the time, but you don't know what they are whispering, and through the writing you'd like to find out. There really is something extremely, extremely quiet about the Karoo, but it's a silence that is very, very much alive. To me there's something about the geology, and I think there's something about the earth that spoke to her about the Karoo, and I think it's just those rocks, they're among some of the oldest rocks in the world.

The community of South African writers who work within the genre of speculative fiction seem to be particularly close and cooperative. Frequently one finds recurring names in the acknowledgments, such as Sarah Lotz and Lauren Beukes, among others, and your novel is no

exception. **How does this community function, and to what extent do the writers of this community work together to further the cause of the genre?**

I think we're extremely fortunate. The community's small but very, very supportive. Sarah Lotz is absolutely fantastic. She actually introduced my wife and me, so she's very special to us! And Lauren is the same. Lauren's always kind of carrying the flag for South African fantasy and horror and sci-fi, and she was already that way before she had massive success. It's not a new thing, and that's one thing I really respect about Lauren. We're all in touch via email and Facebook. We'll all give each other props during interviews.

I've found, especially in Cape Town, people who have been previously published have been extremely supportive: with advice about agents, advice about publishers, being willing to read the first three chapters of novels before you submit, and so on. My wife, Alex Smith, is a writer, and it's fantastic having someone who you can trust to be honest but kind, and I think it's the same with Sarah Lotz, with Lauren Beukes, with Charlie Human, Louis Greenberg and everybody else. Also, I think the community's really small, so you don't want to be an arsehole either [*laughs*].

Would you say, then, that the sense of camaraderie is different in other writing communities?

I think so, because it's a small bunch of people, and I think because it's still small, it's open and welcoming to new members. I'm purely speculating, but I think if I were to start writing purely crime, it might be a very different experience, whereas I think with South African speculative fiction, it's still something that's evolving and growing. The doors have now been opened by Lauren Beukes and by Sarah Lotz. They've done a lot of the hard work already, which is great for the rest of us.

Although South Africa is recognised as having one' of the most liberal constitutions in the world, its society is still largely conservative. What taboos do you think have yet to find their way into contemporary South African literature?

I think there's very few taboos that haven't been broken, but I think there are definitely one or two. I'm thinking about Geoff Dyer at the

Open Book Festival one year, where there was the launch of a book about Mandela. I'm not sure if it was *Good Morning Mr Mandela* (La Grange 2014), or something else, and he actually asked the question, when will it start turning and when will somebody actually start writing stuff that is not complimentary about Mandela? And he was crucified by the audience. Not that I feel you have to write something that's critical about Mandela, but I'm sure somebody could, and maybe somebody should, just to have a little bit of a counterweight. But I'm not sure if there are all that many taboos that haven't been addressed. Maybe that's more of a thing for so-called serious fiction [*laughter*] to concern itself with.

In your opinion, what might be some of the new voices or perspectives we can see developing in South African literature?
Well, I think South African fantasy, sci-fi and horror are definitely a place where a lot of the new and interesting things are going to come out. I think a lot of writing from the born-free generation, anyone born post-1994, is going to get very, very interesting. I wouldn't be able to say what genre, but I think definitely from South Africa's born-free generation we're going to find innovative writing that we probably can't even anticipate at the moment. But it's exciting.

Which different genres do you see becoming more prominent as an attempt to break away from realist conventions?
Well, yes, as I mentioned before, fantasy, sci-fi and horror, but I think crime, too. I think we're going to start seeing a lot more innovative crime writing from South Africa than what we've had. It hasn't been bad necessarily, but it's followed a very set formula, and I think we're going to find a lot of cross-pollination as well. I think we are going to find more kind of crime-fantasy, or fantasy-crime, hopefully some really good and innovative horror, that's what I'm hoping for. And I would love to see comedy writing; I'd like to see the South African Terry Pratchett almost come out, something that's really clever but that's funny at the same time, which I think we've sorely been lacking for all kinds of good reasons, but maybe the time is right now.

What are your current/future projects?
I recently completed a couple of short stories, one of which, titled 'Where the Wild Things Are', was chosen as the opening story for the Africa

edition of the flash fiction site *Flash Frontier*.[1] It was a real pleasure working with their editorial staff. And I am currently doing research for a novel set on an Icelandic island, a kind of post-apocalyptic murder mystery. With two small children, a day job, and an after-hours tutoring gig, it's going a bit slow.

❧

References

Coetzee, J.M. (ed.). 2011. *African Pens 2011: New Writing from Southern Africa*. Johannesburg: Jacana Media.
Didion, Joan. 1979. *The White Album*. New York: Simon & Schuster.
Gaiman, Neil. 2001. *American Gods*. New York: William Morrow.
La Grange, Zelda. 2014. *Good Morning, Mr Mandela*. London: Penguin.
Mitchell, David. 2014. *The Bone Clocks*. London: Sceptre.
Schreiner, Olive. 1883. *The Story of an African Farm*. London: Chapman & Hall.
Stephenson, Neal. 1992. *Snow Crash*. New York: Bantam Books.
———. 1999. *Cryptonomicon*. New York: Avon Publications.

Film
District 9. 2009. Directed by Neill Blomkamp. USA: TriStar Pictures.

---

1. See http://www.flash-frontier.com/2018/11/08/story-andrew-salomon-where-the-wild-things-are-cape-town-south-africa/ (accessed 4 February 2019).

'South Africa's history after 1994, certainly up to 2000, made a lot of people feel [betrayed] about what they invested in.'

Imraan Coovadia (photo: courtesy Gerhard Müller)

Danyela Demir, Olivier Moreillon and Alan Muller

In Conversation with Imraan Coovadia
(b. 1970)

We met with Imraan Coovadia at his parents' home in La Lucia, north of Durban. He had come to his hometown to attend the eighteenth annual Time of the Writer Festival, hosted by the University of KwaZulu-Natal. After a 30-minute drive on a sweltering Thursday afternoon, we were welcomed by Imraan and, after navigating a minefield of toys (belonging to his son), installed on a couch with a view of the sunny Indian Ocean.

Imraan is the author of six novels, *The Wedding* (2001), *Green-Eyed Thieves* (2006), *High Low In-Between* (2009), *The Institute for Taxi Poetry* (2012), *Tales of the Metric System* (2014) and *A Spy in Time* (2018). He has also authored a collection of essays, *Transformations* (2012), and two scholarly monographs, titled *Authority and Authorship in V.S. Naipaul* (2009) and *Revolution and Non-Violence in Tolstoy, Gandhi, and Mandela* (2020).

His debut novel, *The Wedding*, is part of a body of literature by a group of South African Indian writers, the so-called 'Grey Street writers', whose work forms the basis of the KwaZulu-Natal Grey Street Literary Trail.[1] Included in the trail are a number of non-fiction writers, such as Phyllis Naidoo, Dr Goonam, Fatima Meer and Ravi Govender, as well as writers of fiction, such as Aziz Hassim and Mariam Akabor. Tourists can visit a number of landmarks that feature in these authors' works (Stiebel 2010; McNulty and Stiebel 2017).

Imraan was educated at the KwaZulu-Natal private boarding schools of Highbury Preparatory School and Hilton College, in Hillcrest and

---

1. See http://www.literarytourism.co.za/index.php?option=com_content&view=article&id=68:grey-street-writers-trail&catid=16:trails&Itemid=30 (accessed 15 April 2018).

Hilton respectively. After completing high school at Hilton College, he read for a Bachelor's degree at Harvard University, graduating in 1993, and he obtained an MFA at Cornell University and then a PhD from Yale University in 2001. His debut novel, *The Wedding*, received wide critical acclaim and was shortlisted for the 2002 Sunday Times Fiction Award, the 2003 Ama-Boeke Prize and the 2005 Dublin International Literary Award. *High Low In-Between*, Imraan's third novel, has been his most acclaimed work to date, winning both the 2009 University of Johannesburg Prize and the 2010 Sunday Times Fiction Prize. *The Institute for Taxi Poetry* and a collection of essays titled *Transformations* were both shortlisted for the 2013 University of Johannesburg Prize for best creative work in English. *A Spy in Time*, Imraan's most recent novel, was shortlisted for the 2019 University of Johannesburg Prize. Both *High Low In-Between* and *Tales of the Metric System* were translated into German by Verlag das Wunderhorn.

Imraan is currently associate professor at the University of Cape Town and director of the Creative Writing programme. When asked how his academic background influences his fictional writing he says: 'I think it probably does in lots of bad ways, in the sense that, as a good writer, you have to be kind of innocent about writing, and it's not really clear that being an academic is a good way to keep that innocence.' Having written prolifically, both academically and creatively, for over fifteen years, he is indifferent about the writing process, explaining: 'I think when you've been doing something a really long time, you stop thinking about what you like and don't like about it; it's more like just something that happens every day.'

Against Affective Formalism: Matisse, Bergson, Modernism (2013), by art historian Todd Cronan, was Imraan's most recent read before our conversation. He found it interesting because it is an argument against the view that 'as a writer, you have to think about what happens in readers' heads and predict people's responses to things as you're writing'.

He admits to not going out very much when he is in Durban since his parents 'live by the ocean' but does 'really like Umhlanga Beach'. He doesn't have a favourite spot in Cape Town, but explains that he likes 'the fact that it's the one South African city where you can spend a lot of time walking. I can get through days and days without having to drive a car, you know, and that makes everything kind of an interesting spot.'

ॐ

Works

————. 2001. *The Wedding* (Picador)

The novel follows Ismet Nassin and his unwilling bride, Khateja, as they leave India for Durban, South Africa, at the end of the nineteenth century. Both comical and critically insightful, the novel focuses on the first-generation South African Indian experience.

————. 2006. *Green-Eyed Thieves* (Umuzi)

This transcontinental crime story is told from the perspective of Firoze Peer. Born into a family where crime is a constant, it is not long before they pull off a heist at the Sun City leisure complex. Firoze's twin brother, Ashraf, a skilled artist, begins producing counterfeit licences and identity documents, a trade that results in the brothers frequently changing their identities as they travel across the globe.

————. 2009. *High Low In-Between* (Umuzi)

Set in Durban, Imraan's third novel follows Nafisa as she renegotiates her relationship with contemporary South Africa and the people around her, all the while trying to solve her husband's murder. The novel blurs the boundaries between a moral 'overworld' and an underworld characterised by illegal organ trafficking.

————. 2012. *The Institute for Taxi Poetry* (Umuzi)

Imraan's fourth novel follows ex-taxi poet turned lecturer Adam Ravens as he tries to make sense of the death of his poetry mentor, Solly Greenfields. Divided into five chapters, the novel is set over the course of a week, during which Ravens tries to uncover the reason for his son's unusual behaviour and simultaneously unravel Solly's murder.

————. 2012. *Transformations* (Umuzi)

This collection of essays covers a range of topics, from Thabo Mbeki's 'Letters to the Nation' to Vladimir Nabokov's novel *Lolita* and J.M. Coetzee.

————. 2014. *Tales of the Metric System* (Umuzi)

Imraan's fifth novel consists of a set of interconnected stories that span the years from the 1970s to 2010. The text traces individual narratives, along with South Africa's narrative of transition from apartheid to democracy, over 40 years.

————. 2018. *A Spy in Time* (Umuzi)
Imraan's sixth novel follows Enver Eleven, a 25-year-old time traveller and spy for the Agency. Setting off from his hometown of a post-apocalyptic Johannesburg, Enver is sent on a mission through space and time to prevent the apocalypse from happening and to preserve the existence of humankind. However, his task is complicated by the fact that his fellow time traveller and head of the expedition, Shanumi Six, is kidnapped.

————. 2020. *Revolution and Non-Violence in Tolstoy, Gandhi, and Mandela* (Oxford University Press)
This monograph is concerned with twentieth-century histories of resistance by tracing the lives and intersections of Leo Tolstoy, Mohandas Gandhi and Nelson Mandela. The book explores the possibilities of resistance through non-violence and the limits thereof.

❧

You have written about all three major South African cities: Johannesburg, Cape Town and Durban. How important are aspects of place in your writing?
I think it helps you to reset stuff. If you set a book in a city, it clears up a lot of the stuff you've been thinking and lets you try a bunch of new things out. So I think that's pretty useful. I often don't know places very well. I wrote about Joburg, but I'd never been to the place I wrote about. I've only once been to Fordsburg. Other places I feel I know better, but I sometimes think that if you know a place well, it's not necessarily all that great either. I think sometimes it's just an internal thing that lets you cut up what you think, or divide what you think, into useful spaces or compartmentalise them. Also, each city in South Africa has a very different feeling or has a different dynamic or demographic, and I think it's quite useful to be able to use them as backdrops in different ways.

Which of these cities did you find most rewarding to write about or to (re-)construct in your fiction?
It's probably always whatever city you grew up in that is the easiest one to write about. I think Durban, for me, is the easiest because I

assume that I know it, without worrying whether I know it or not or trying to show that I know it. I think it's most useful for me that way. But it's changed so much since I lived here permanently that it's quite a strange place to me as well. I don't really know how it runs now, or where people go, or even where people live in the city, but I think it's an interesting topic. I also like the fact that it's hardly been used. Barbara Trapido used it,[2] and yet it's this huge place with all these people. So I think that's quite useful, but it's probably more internal than anything to do with Durban.

Let's speak about the city that you come from. What aspects of home, belonging and community do you engage with in your fiction?
It's hard to say. I think at different times you need that. I think, certainly as a writer, you start writing from there, but I think, more recently, I've been trying to see: Can I use that sense of confidence in writing about one group or set of people? Can I extend that to other people that I didn't grow up with? So, can I feel at home with other kinds of situations? It's quite a hard thing to do, and I'm interested in doing it, or trying it.

Many of your characters seem to be in varying states of motion. How important are different aspects of movement in your work?
Look, if two characters have a conversation and they're just sitting around, they're kind of dull. And if they're moving, or if they're in a car, it makes it more interesting. So, technically, as a writer, you're always looking for ways for conversation to happen around action and happen around different scenery. After a while, the scenery becomes part of the situation and I think it's probably how most conversations work. People don't sit down to have intense interactions or conversations. They seem to happen around other things. So I think it's important for talking characters to move as much as possible, to keep them healthy, imaginatively. A lot of individual characters move and that's just

---

2. Barbara Trapido (b. 1941) is a South African-born novelist currently living in England. Her novels *Frankie and Stankie* (2003) and *Sex and Stravinsky* (2010) are both set in Durban. *Frankie and Stankie* was shortlisted for the 2003 Whitbread Award and longlisted for the Booker Prize that same year.

storytelling. It's really about moving in a different way. If your characters stay still, it's quite hard to know what to do with them. They can only put their hands in their pockets and take them out again so many times.

In contrast to works by many other contemporary South African authors, yours seems to be characterised by global movement – a lot of travelling. How important is global movement in your fiction?
I don't know. I feel very unglobal, personally. I don't like moving at all. I like jogging, but I don't like travelling or flying. I like other countries, if I could just teleport there, but I really don't like going into aeroplanes. I almost never go on holiday. I have been more recently, but I've never been a holiday person. I think, inherently, I'm not a moving person. In terms of the global thing, I think most South African writers think it's quite hard to write about just this country; that a lot of writing has to connect things here to other places, and seeing what happens here as the product of other places. I think that's something that a lot of people share, which I don't.

While your first two novels, *The Wedding* and *Green-Eyed Thieves*, were very humorous, and, to a certain extent, this is also true for your fourth novel, *The Institute for Taxi Poetry*, your other novels are more serious in their tone. What are the reasons for this elliptical employment of humour in your fiction?
Look, I think certain types of novels you write, and they inherently allow humour, in a way. In Bakhtin's theory of the novel, it's a compendium, an anthology.[3] You can put anything in the novel form and it's fine. But as a writer, you can't stretch it very far. It's quite hard to put certain kinds of things in a comic novel and it's quite hard to have stretches of comedy in a serious novel. In a play you can do it, but I think novels have more

---

3. Mikhail Mikhailovich Bakhtin (1895–1975) wrote an essay 'The Epic and the Novel: Towards a Methodology for the Study of the Novel' in *The Dialogic Imagination* ([1975] 1982). Bakhtin suggests that the novel as an art form is best described and understood as being heteroglossic and dialogic in nature – existing as a collection of languages, voices and genres. Bakhtin, through heteroglossia, looks at the dialogue between not only the characters, but also the authorial self. The central conflict resides in the speech, languages and voices that make up the novel in its entirety.

consistent tones, require more consistent tones, certainly nowadays. So I think some of it is just the structural quality of that novel: what kind of thing is it? Does it make sense? Would it be appropriate to have humour in certain parts? I think, inevitably, if you write long enough, something funny or strange will happen, but I think humour is quite disruptive for a lot of other things. It's quite disruptive for sympathy, or other kinds of tragic feelings, so to some extent you exclude it.

How much research and planning went into your novels in general and into *Tales of the Metric System* in particular? And how did you go about crafting plot and characters?

I think in the same amateur ways that you can imagine. Google, and reading old newspapers and reading books set in the seventies. If you go to the library, you get a book called *The Seventies*, or *The Eighties*, and you work out what people were listening to in the eighties. Then, also just trying to get a feel for the moods that people were in. The seventies were very policed and people felt a lot of fear. Where you went was quite tightly controlled. So, trying to reconstruct that was interesting. I also could remember most of it; so I had some sense of it that way. But then I think, tactically or strategically, you use what information you find in ways to make it feel as if you understand that era, and you define the situations narrowly, so that it's not obvious how much you don't know about what went on.

What is easier for you to construct? Is it the plot, the dialogue or the characters?

Characters come much more easily because you meet characters in real life whereas you don't really meet plots very often [*laughter*]. Sometimes, you see them in newspapers. I think Athol Fugard saw a story about someone being knocked over by a train and turning into the train driver. But I think plots are quite rare, actually. I don't think you come up with that many in a lifetime, so I think they're much harder. And more valuable.

***Tales of the Metric System*, in particular, but also *High Low In-Between*, deal with the anti-apartheid movement. In which ways do you see the themes of betrayal and responsibility linked to this topic of the struggle?**

Good question. I don't know. I guess anything that asks for your loyalty, and promises something, is going to lend itself to betrayal. South

Africa's history after 1994, certainly up to 2000, made a lot of people feel that way about what they invested in. They're just classic themes of melodrama, so you use them. I'm not sure I have much more insight into it though. I probably overuse those kinds of themes or situations.

Staying with the theme of betrayal, the topic of political betrayal has flourished within the last couple of years or so, in literature specifically. We're thinking of novels such as C.A. Davids's *The Blacks of Cape Town* (2014), Niq Mhlongo's *Way Back Home* (2013) and Mandla Langa's *The Texture of Shadows* (2014), among others. Why do you think political betrayal has suddenly come to the fore?
I think it's probably because of the way people feel about the ANC [African National Congress], certainly after 2000. It became clear that what happened in 2008 actually didn't change anything and even made everything worse. I think it's clearly how people felt. It's kind of the breakup of those forms of loyalty. I also think there's continuity between the world before 1990 and the world afterwards, in the sense that we were trained to love inequality before 1990. In a way, that was preserved; it just became a larger group of people who could be unequal to another, an even larger group. That seemed to be a constant thing. I think, in a way, that the world of espionage and betrayal became the world of politics and the world of institutions. One of the things about being an academic is that you work in an institution, and it's amazing how badly they function, and how badly South Africans behave in institutional structures. You know, it's across race; it's across politics, across whatever. And I think that lends itself to that sort of analogy of betrayal even though it may be too simplistic. That's probably part of what's behind it.

To what extent have *High Low In-Between* and *The Institute for Taxi Poetry* been influenced by elements of crime fiction?
Probably quite a lot. When I was looking for a plot, you think about crime, murder, criminal enterprise. I was also thinking about how closely all the legitimate enterprises in South Africa are to criminal enterprises, or how the underworld is inseparable from the overworld, just economically: from illegal miners to the way the mining companies pay, or taxi companies and the way that they take over areas, and so on. I think there is probably that sense of the inseparability of those worlds;

how closely they work with each other and how much they're just the same, seamless thing from politics to economics.

Although South Africa is recognised as having one of the most liberal constitutions in the world, its society is largely still conservative. What taboos do you think have yet to find their way into contemporary South African literature?

I don't know, there must be some because we live in a world of the Internet. People who are never exposed to challenges are now exposed to challenges all the time, and they find different ways of preserving their taboos of different kinds. I don't know if it's a question of taboos, though. Generally, it's more that, in our society, people tend to form quite small, closed circles, or they behave in very closed ways, so that most institutions are most open to this set of people; or most political parties have a sense of this network, rather than that one. In the old days, the dream of the South African would be to have his own Mercedes dealership; and then the point was that nobody else would be able to sell Mercedes within 50 kilometres of that Mercedes dealership. I think that quality of wanting a monopoly and not wanting to compete, that's kind of at the base of a whole lot of stuff in our country and I'm not sure it's a taboo, but it's a hard structure to fix or to bring attention to.

In your opinion, what might be some of the new voices or perspectives that we can see developing right now?

You know, it's quite hard to tell. I think probably people in their twenties or thirties are doing stuff that's totally different to what any of us, who are older, are doing. I happened to teach Masande Ntshanga and I think his book, *The Reactive* (2014), is really interesting, and I think he'll do all sorts of interesting work. And I think there are probably some playwrights who are doing interesting work. I haven't read C.A. Davids's *The Blacks of Cape Town* (2014), but I've heard it's very good. More surprising about South Africa is how pro-geriatric it is, and how much we still write for people who are in their fifties, sixties and seventies. It's very weighted towards the elderly. I think that's actually a bad thing about our culture; it takes decades for a young South African writer to become established in any way. Obviously, there are a lot of writers writing horror fiction, science fiction, serial killer fiction. I don't know much about it because I can't read it, but I assume there's some interest there.

When you say you can't read it, is it just a lack of interest?
I think it's just a paradox. These are the things that millions of people read; and they must find them easy to read. I actually find it quite hard to read a lot of schlocky writing. I don't know what it is that pushes me away, but I find I actually can't concentrate after two or three pages. I think it just seems so disorganised on the page, and, I don't know, the tone seems off, or whatever it is. I feel like I need writing to be quite clear, and it really needs to guide me, or guide a reader. I feel a lot of the schlocky stuff is about sensations, which I'm not that interested in – certain kinds of bloody thrills or whatever it is. Since they don't work on me, it's hard to keep reading.

What genres do you see becoming more prominent in an attempt to break away from the prevailing realist convention within South African literature?
Well, I think definitely airport-type novels, things that people would read on an aeroplane; sensationalistic novels, science fiction. Maybe Afro-science fiction would be interesting. Perhaps Teju Cole's strange blend of the essay, and other things. There's bound to be more stuff like that. What was I just reading that was really good? I was just reading *Sefarad* (2001), by a Spanish writer called Antonio Muñoz Molina, and there's a book called *Danube: A Sentimental Journey from the Source to the Black Sea* (1986), by Claudio Magris. I don't know if you've read it, but it's a similar kind of really dense, interesting essayistic travel writing about a river, or just about an area, but it's full of cultural and historical thought and imagination. I think there's probably quite a lot of scope for that, but also South Africans love junk. We love junk. Junk of all kinds, and, I think, overwhelmingly, what will publish will be junk of various descriptions.

You mentioned a lot of junk and that perhaps airport novels are, or will become, very popular. Which South African voices do you consider worth looking at specifically?
Look, I think I'll read anything that comes my way, and there's often interesting stuff to be found in it. I really liked Damon Galgut's *Arctic Summer* (2014). I thought it was really good. I thought it was really unexpected. I don't always like what Damon writes, but that book was really unusual. I thought Masande's book was quite good. Nadia

David's first book had a lot of possibility. I'll read what Ivan Vladislavić writes. Sometimes I find that interesting. Sometimes I find it uneven, you know? But I'll read it. I read Mark Gevisser's book, *Lost and Found in Johannesburg* (2014), and I think there are bits of it that are really good. You know when you read a book and bits of it, or pages, seem excellent, and the structure doesn't quite seem fixed, or sometimes it's the other way around.

What are your current and future projects?
Nothing. I can't think of anything to write. I thought I might write about superheroes but I don't know. I wrote a piece about dogs, South African dogs, titled 'Best Friends and Worst Enemies: Years of the Dog in South Africa'. It's on the Web, I think it's the *Los Angeles Review of Books*.[4] And then I wrote some other piece, I think. I feel like I don't want to write a book just for the sake of writing a book. I feel like I'll write something if I make some discovery, or if there's something I understand now that I couldn't figure out five years ago. Right now, there's nothing I really understand more than I did a few years ago.

References

Bakhtin, Mikhail. [1975] 1982. *The Dialogic Imagination: Chronotope and Heterolglossia*. Austin, TX: University of Texas Press.

Cronan, Todd. 2013. *Against Affective Formalism: Matisse, Bergson, Modernism*. Minneapolis: University of Minnesota Press.

Davids, C.A. 2014. *The Blacks of Cape Town*. Cape Town: Modjaji Books.

Galgut, Damon. 2014. *Arctic Summer*. Cape Town: Umuzi.

Gevisser, Mark. 2014. *Lost and Found in Johannesburg: A Memoir*. Cape Town: Jonathan Ball.

Langa, Mandla. 2014. *The Texture of Shadows*. Johannesburg: Picador Africa.

Magris, Claudio. 1986. *Danube: A Sentimental Journey from the Source to the Black Sea*, translated by Patrick Creagh. New York: Farrar, Straus and Giroux.

McNulty, Niall and Lindy Stiebel. 2017. *A Literary Guide to KwaZulu-Natal*. Pietermaritzburg: University of KwaZulu-Natal Press.

Mhlongo, Niq. 2013. *Way Back Home*. Cape Town: Kwela Books.

---

4. See https://lareviewofbooks.org/article/best-friends-worst-enemies-years-dog-south-africa/ (accessed 15 April 2015).

Molina, Antonio Muñoz. [2001] 2003. *Sefarad*, translated by Margaret Sayers Peden. San Diego: Harcourt.

Ntshanga, Masande. 2014. *The Reactive*. Cape Town: Umuzi.

Stiebel, Lindy. 2010. 'Last Stop "Little Gujarat": Tracking South African Indian Writers on the Grey Street Writers' Trail in Durban'. *Current Writing: Text and Reception in Southern Africa* 22(1): 1–20.

Trapido, Barbara. 2003. *Frankie and Stankie*. London: Bloomsbury.

———. 2010. *Sex and Stravinsky*. London: Bloomsbury

'Perhaps one day we'll find more room to breathe, to detach from the trending antics of the moment and daydream ahead of us with greater imagination, curiosity, creativity and even hope.'

Fred Strydom (photo: Olivier Moreillon)

Danyela Demir and Olivier Moreillon

In Conversation with Fred Strydom
(b. 1982)

Fred Strydom generously took time to chat to us during his lunch break on a sunny Monday in Johannesburg. Fred is the author of two books: *The Raft* (2015) and *The Inside-Out Man* (2017). The latter was shortlisted for the 2018 University of Johannesburg Prize for South African Writing in English and has been optioned for a movie by three producers.

Fred was born in Cape Town and studied Film and Media at the University of Cape Town. He currently works as a film producer in Johannesburg, where he lives with his wife and two children.

What he enjoys most about the writing process is 'not even the writing, but when I do something completely arbitrary, and then things start to click. *The Raft* came together during several road trips from Cape Town to Joburg without the radio on.' He also enjoys the phase when he does not know 'what exactly is going to happen throughout the story', and when he is 'getting to know the characters'. He does struggle at points where it is crucial to unpack the plot, though, which he finds 'dull'. He prefers 'segueing between it'.

The last book Fred had read before our interview was *The Season of Glass* (2018) by Rahla Xenopoulos, which he thought was fantastic. He says that it is a powerful novel, which 'blends mysticism, spiritualism and science, which is up my alley. It is really a magical book.'

While he lived in many places in Cape Town, Fred says that if he and his family were to return there, they would probably live in the Southern Peninsula. He enjoys surfing and his wife loves horses, so it would be ideal for them to live in a quiet place, by the beach. In Johannesburg, the family lives in North Riding.

⌘

Works

———. 2015. *The Raft* (Umuzi)

The Raft is largely set in a commune on the beach, in an unspecified country. It follows the life of Kayle Jenner, who attempts to find his son, Andy, after Day Zero, when the entire population on earth loses its memory. An organisation referred to as The Body controls communes all over the world, ensuring that people conform to certain rules and regulations. Kayle eventually sets off on the quest to find Andy, a boy who may or may not be his son.

———. 2017. *The Inside-Out Man* (Umuzi)

The novel focuses on the jazz musician Bent who plays the piano in Cape Town's dingy bars. His life is spiralling downwards until millionaire Leonard Fry makes him a seemingly irresistible offer: Bent can live in his house and use all of Leonard's possessions and money while the latter locks himself inside one room for a year. All Bent has to do is to provide three meals every day for the millionaire. However, this seductive lifestyle soon turns into a nightmare of doublings and life-threatening encounters for Bent.

What were your reasons for choosing speculative fiction as the genre to tell your stories?

I think that the obvious reason is that when I was growing up, it was the genre that entertained me the most, the one that I found most engaging. I didn't really give much thought as to why that was. I also don't like all speculative fiction. It's such a broad term. I think people throw it and then they expect you to be part of some kind of club. Speculative fiction is simply a broader toolkit for saying things that maybe you feel you can't say outright, or that are difficult to explain about the world as you see it. I find certain genres quite difficult to read or get behind because of how linear they are. I struggle with crime fiction, I really do. I've read a lot of crime fiction, but I struggle with being in that world all the time. But that's an example of a very specific genre. I feel like speculative encompasses so much more. You can get everything; from Gabriel García Márquez to Rushdie to David Mitchell to Stephen King! It's just so wide. I also have a sense, in my everyday life, that things aren't the way they appear to be. And the more I read into science and quantum mechanics and string theory, and the more I read into esoteric cosmology and spiritualism, the more bizarre overlaps I come across. I think that's something worth exploring. Also, it's just an incredibly underrepresented genre. Its contribution to the world is often really not recognised, although it may make the most significant impact on the world as we know it. From Arthur C. Clarke to Aldous Huxley to Philip K. Dick, reality today echoes so many of these writers' ideas, concerns and even predictions. I just don't think we'd be the world we are today without it.

Besides being a writer of fiction, you are also a television writer and producer. How do these different fields of interest influence each other?
That's a really cool question because I had a discussion about it with my wife recently. There's something liberating about both of them. There's something about the freedom of writing a novel and how all those standard, populist conventions don't necessarily need to apply. You really are free to build a world any way that you want. You are the cinematographer, you are the cameraman, you are the set designer. There's also something really satisfying about writing stretches of meaty prose, like a hearty meal, perhaps.

What I like about screenwriting, however, is that it refines the technical aspects of my writing a lot more. It teaches me to be more economical. You have to tell your story through dialogue and you have to tell it through what can be seen. And my dialogue gets better because now I'm really focusing on how people are communicating, rather than all the leeway for narrative exposition that novels afford you. I'm also a big lover of film, and I think it's nice to know that you're writing something that's designed to be seen and told at once. It's also highly collaborative. I think that's good for me too, learning to trust someone else and just go: 'This is the vision, here it is, make it your own.' There's something humbling about that too.

In what ways do your novels deal with aspects of identity, memory and history?
[*Chuckles*] You must be relating specifically to my books because that's pretty much all they're about. I think they just come down to the idea that all stories are about the same thing: 'Who am I?' In every story ever told, it doesn't matter which story you start with, there's always a character who knows a certain amount and goes through a journey and

then learns more about it. It's easy to say that the subject of identity in my novels has to do with the socio-political aspects of South Africa, a past we're naturally inclined to write about, but I don't see it as such. I see it as a very humanistic question and I tackle it in as broad a manner as possible. With both *The Raft* and *Inside-Out Man,* I'm not terribly obsessed with hyper-localisation of my stories for the sake of some kind of socio-political context. I find it limiting. I find it far more inclusive to tell stories that are just human stories. I don't think we live in a hyper-localised world anymore. I think we're so affected by the rest of the world and it's so affected by us, whether it admits it or not, that we just have to figure out who we are as people, generally. And we've all got a different entry point, and a different background, and that's fine and all, but at the end of the day the questions are always the same.

As for memory, well, I specifically wrote a book about people losing their memories. It comes down to the fact that we are probably just the stories that we tell ourselves, of ourselves. And it really is one of the central pillars of identity. I often wonder how much of that is choice. How much we choose who we are, and how much who we are is dictated by the events that happen to us. And that really, really mystical power we have to decide for ourselves. So I guess that's it.

And what was the other one? Identity, memory and . . . oh yeah, history. We just have this weird relationship with it. It's all lumped together into this one big thing called 'history', often trying to understand ourselves, based on the cyclic megatrends of what's happened before, rather than the personal takes on it. That can be very conflicting for many to accept. Of course, we can learn a lot from the big overarching narratives, and see how they repeat. I see a reversion to tribalism happening in the States, for example. I see that insecurity and hunger for power are the most common causes of the very worst of our historical selves, and the very worst of our present selves, but we often negate the experience of the individual. For instance, my experience of being a non-white person is complicated and personal and challenging, in my own uniquely personal way. Everyone talks about apartheid as a grand machine, with good on one side, evil on the other and clearly drawn lines between oppressor and victim. That's all certainly true, but for me it was just, you know, one minute I was in one school and the next minute I was allowed to go to another school. And then I lived in a Coloured – so-called Coloured – area in Cape Town while attending a white school during the day. This meant I was suddenly listening to white kids' music as a little kid, and then coming home and playing it at home, and then the other kids in my street not knowing why I was playing this kind of music. And just being a normal little kid, trying to figure out why his friends at school and his friends on the street didn't really have the same interests. You're just a normal kid. It's not the whole of apartheid that knocks on your door, it's just these little daily things that you deal with. In this regard, it's very controversial to get down to that anecdotal level on the subject because it interferes with the larger narrative. I'll give you an example. My grandfather was non-white. He was a guy who said things that may surprise some liberally inclined people, but he was just a person with a story of his own. He'd say things like: 'Things were better during apartheid!' I've told people that, and people shudder to hear it. But what he was really saying, in his own blunt way, was that when the Cape Coloured community got segregated, and moved into their designated areas, my grandfather was able to run a fruit-and-veg shop for 40 years in a community that he knew and understood. People would come in and come out, and he knew his life. Even though they were segregated, they created their own little world. When apartheid ended, that stability in his life was shattered. Everybody split up. His neighbours left the area. New people came in, people he didn't know. He lost his business. The real devastation of apartheid was that it really messed around with who people were, on the most fundamentally existential level. It wasn't just a political movement from right to left. It disrupted reality on levels most people can't comprehend. But people prefer the Tolkienesque approach to understanding history – goodies on one side, baddies on the other – with everything working out for the best for everyone when the oppressor was finally vanquished. In larger terms, yes, of course! It had to end! There's no argument there. On personal terms – well, everyone has a story of their own – it takes a certain type of open-mindedness to empathise with people's experiences on all levels. I think those are the kinds of ideas I prefer to explore.

How important is the representation of place in your writing?
Not very. You know *Inside-Out Man* takes place in Cape Town, but Cape Town's never mentioned once. If I say Cape Town, you've all got your own picture. It's like mountain, ocean, beach, whatever you want to say. I didn't want that. I also wanted to write a story in which the world is only what it is because of the way you see it. I wanted to create

an almost Lovecraftian[1] version of Cape Town not often associated with the city – unless you lived where Bent lived and lived the way he lived and saw the world through his lens. That just interests me more. And the same thing goes for *The Raft*: it alludes to being here in South Africa, but I think one of the pleasures, one of the privileges of writing a book in which the entire world has lost its memory, is that you can get rid of all that stuff, right off the bat. The other thing is, as soon as you take away the names of places, it becomes a bigger place. When I wrote *The Raft,* one of the ways in which I figured I could make this world feel bigger and broader was that I just took away that simple thing of knowing where it was. We live in a world where we think of Cape Town, Dubai or London as being places separated by ten to twelve hours. It's insane that we've just shrunk it down to a village. However, I think, with no technology, no memory of the earth, the world would go back to feeling big. You've got to really travel to get places.

Apart from very few allusions to real places, which link the novel (to a certain extent) to South Africa, *The Raft* seems to be of a more universal nature as it is mainly situated in a fictionalised world. To what extent do you see this as a contribution to positioning South Africa in a more global and integrated context?
I don't know if I'm actively trying to break through, or if I'm just doing it because that is the book I want to write. There's a part of me that keeps a little bit of the South Africanness in there. Whether it's a little bit of Afrikaans, or a little bit of something that is really not intended to do anything but casually introduce ourselves. Not to bludgeon anyone, but just to say: 'If you happen to have a question about what this Afrikaans line is, there is a world, or there is a country, in which this makes sense.' That's the extent to which I'm willing to spoon-feed. At the same time, I also feel – this comes out a lot, especially when I speak at schools or on panels – that we aren't constantly providing a state-of-the-nation approach to everything. We can look further, ask more philosophical questions about life in general. If we look at where science fiction and

---

1. Howard Phillips Lovecraft (1890–1937) was an American short story writer, novelist and poet. He is one of the most significant writers of weird and horror fiction of the twentieth century.

speculative fiction thrives, we need look no further than the States or the UK or Japan. It's no coincidence these genres thrive in First World countries. When you're not focusing on survival, on a daily basis, you can appreciate creative speculation, instead of resigning yourself to simply retrospection and introspection. I think in South Africa we get our comedy and tragedy from politics; we get our action from sport [*chuckles*]. We're pragmatic in that way because it's all about surviving the immediate present. I understand the need for it, but it's also sad. Perhaps one day we'll find more room to breathe, to detach from the trending antics of the moment and daydream with greater imagination, curiosity, creativity and even hope.

In what ways is your writing concerned with aspects of home, belonging and community?
You see, this is kind of interesting. You wonder how much you're willing to say, but I have generally quite conservative ideas about things. One of the things about *The Raft* is that it's about the danger of extremism itself. Whether it's leftist extremism or totalitarian right extremism, just extremism itself. I'm conservative in the way that I don't side too much with the far leftist idea that a government should be our first point of call for the problems in our lives. I'm not the first one to run out and yell to the state that the state should do something differently. I know it's complex. I know it's not black and white. What I essentially believe is that, yes, there are victims, there are oppressors, there are all kinds of things. But, as a person, just as a person, I think it would be wise not to wake up in the morning and see yourself as a victim first. It doesn't mean you aren't, I'm simply wary of the dangers of primarily identifying yourself as such. I also think it's easy for a culture of victimhood to be manipulated by certain leftist groups – a means of manipulating the dispossessed and encouraging victimhood for power-hungry ends. Basically, in this regard, I think it's good to take care of yourself. When you do that, you're in a better position to empower and help your family. And when your family as a whole are more empowered, they're more empowered to help their street, and so on and so on. I believe in community, and I believe in people taking care of each other, and I believe the more people do that, the more responsible and empowered they'll be for themselves and for others. Like I said at the beginning, it's a tricky conversation to have, but that's what I believe.

In both your novels, the characters seem to be in varying states of motion. How important are different aspects of movement in your work?
In motion? Like literal movement? That's interesting, only in relation to the two books that I've written so far. The first book is very much an Odyssean story that relies on literal movement as a form of philosophical journeying. When the time came to write a second book, I think a lot of people were starting to ask: 'How are you going to write a bigger book? Are you going to write a wilder book?' The idea for the second one was: 'What if I did the complete opposite? What if I wrote a book that had minimal characters, characters literally incapable of moving from their situation, and incapable of escaping one very finite area?'

In *The Inside-Out Man*, the intersection of music and writing comes to the fore. Where do you see crossovers between music and writing in general, and in your writing in particular?
That's a cool question. So, one of the things that I wanted to do with *The Inside-Out Man*, and it's maybe even a silly thing to do, was write the book with a kind of jazzy rhythm to it. When I say jazzy, I wanted the writing to feel jazzy – and dark jazz, you know? I wanted the whole book to work like a weird piece of music. One part of you feels like it's being made up as you go along, and another part must feel that you can only make it up as you go along, if you have some real understanding of how the fundamental notes work [*chuckles*]. So there was definitely that element to it; and it was a very conscious element. In a very literal way, music forms a big part of my writing process. I tend to make a playlist that I use when I write. Definitely music without lyrics, and I often use music when I'm struggling. I often use that tactic when I'm struggling to remember why the heck I'm writing this book. That's the biggest challenge of writing a book. It's just trying to remember what was so great about this idea you had six months ago. And for this new book I've been listening to a lot of God is an Astronaut,[2] and Mogwai,[3] and Godspeed You! Black Emperor,[4] and a lot of very, very cerebral post-rock. And it stands me in good stead. For *The Inside-Out Man*, I

---

2. See https://godisanastronaut.com (accessed 17 April 2019).
3. See http://www.mogwai.co.uk (accessed 17 April 2019).
4. See https://www.allmusic.com/artist/mn0000665945 (accessed 17 April 2019).

listened to a lot of jazz; and I watched a lot of jazz documentaries. Not that I was going to use any of it, but just so that I was filled with it, so that it was in me. For *The Raft*, there wasn't any musicality to it. *The Raft* was very much the segueing of one fairy tale to the next. Each story is my take on a fairy tale. What I wanted *The Raft* to be was a very bizarre, round-the-campfire storytelling thing that was virtually devoid of pop-cultural influences and what-not.

The community of South African writers who work within the genre of speculative fiction seems to be particularly close and cooperative. Frequently, one finds recurring names in the acknowledgements, such as Sarah Lotz and Lauren Beukes, among others. How does this community function and to what extent do the writers of this community work together to further the cause of the genre?
I think yes, we are a very close-knit community. I think that we could be probably a little bit harder on each other. I think we're a little bit too tolerant of each other [*chuckles*]. There's nothing wrong with saying outright that maybe we feel that something could be different or better. It's an intrinsically South African thing. We want to be really supportive, but support is what you do when you go on a machine [*laughs*], just before you die! I don't tend to like using the phrase 'supporting South African fiction'. The intention is good, but it rings false. I think we must help each other in honest ways. I don't think the arts need to be competitive or anything, but I want people to read South African novels because they're great, because they're different, refreshing, even earth-shattering. Maybe the 'support' thing is the right start, I don't know, but we can't run on that campaign indefinitely. People will read what captivates them. I think we just need to broaden our range, take creative chances, keep hammering at it, and people will gravitate towards our voices. I've certainly seen an upward trend recently. It's definitely getting more exciting out there. I'm also not a fan of stacking all the South African books on some 'General Africana' shelf at the store. It doesn't do anybody any favours. If you want horror, go to the horror section and peruse. Don't stick your South African horror novel between Nadine Gordimer and Deon Meyer on the Africana shelf, simply because we live in a similar geographical region, and decide that's what matters most about what we as writers are trying to do. It's kind of absurd.

Would you say that the sense of camaraderie is different within the speculative fiction group in comparison to other writing communities?
That's hard to say because I'm not in the other writing communities, but I think to a degree, yes. It feels as if it may be the strongest community of writers at the moment. We have a small pie of readers in South Africa: take away people who can't read, then the people who can't afford to read, then the people who need to find your book out of all these other books – it's minuscule. Therefore, I think when you're on the fringe with an underappreciated 'genre', you're always just a little bit closer to each other.

Although South Africa is recognised as having one of the most liberal constitutions in the world, in many ways you can say that South African society is still largely conservative. What taboos do you think have yet to find their way into contemporary South African literature?
That's quite tricky. I think in South Africa we're pretty ahead in terms of the rest of the world, in terms of certain socio-political issues. You see what happens in the States. You see the rise of the right in Europe. You see these kinds of things happening. I think a lot of it we've dealt with. We've been there. We've done that. I don't know that there's any subject we can't tackle in South Africa. I think we do have the capacity to be collectively brutal when somebody gets out of line – like some of these viral videos that go about – but that's just people against idiots. Generally, I think we have it within us to be far more honestly expressive than almost any other country out there because we've endured what few others have. Other countries are worried about what happens when the far right takes over. We had it here less than 30 years ago. On a significant level, we beat it – without civil war. We've got many, many problems today, but here we are. We're still going – and that should entitle us to say what many countries can't yet say, about virtually any subject under the African sun.

In your opinion, what might be some of the new voices or perspectives that we can see developing in South African literature?
That's a tough one for me because I'm struggling to follow them. I'm not going to come up with any groundbreaking new person that's going to blow your mind. What I like seeing is how current writers, or established writers who are in the spotlight, are exploring more. I like

seeing Deon Meyer write a post-apocalyptic fiction novel. He's clicked onto something. I like seeing that. I like that Rahla Xenopoulos wrote *The Season of Glass* – this multi-generational, kind of esoteric novel – after writing two very personal memoirs. I look at somebody like Lauren Beukes, and I'm endlessly appreciative about what she's been able to do, to really smash down a lot of those walls. I like what's happening in terms of Afrofuturist fiction from central African countries, and what's coming out, not just in fiction, but in music. I'm really pleased that there are publishing houses now that are taking big chances, like Umuzi and Penguin Random House. That's also a really big thing.

Which different genres do you see becoming more prominent as an attempt to break away from realist conventions?
I guess it comes back down to the question of genre, and whether something like speculative fiction is a genre, or just a closet we stuff things into that fall out [*chuckles*]. What's more interesting to me than the genre thing is how difficult it is to tell these stories sometimes. I look at what somebody like David Mitchell does and I think that that's the key.

It's great to be into hardcore science fiction. I spoke at Science Fiction and Fantasy South Africa. They were all hardcore and that's great. It's great to be part of a group. It's great to see that purist fandom develop. But I think the most interesting thing is the bending of genres – slipstream fiction, New Weird, etc. You see Imraan Coovadia doing it. I always like to write books that teach the reader how to read them as they're being read. We should do the same thing. We should teach people how to think differently. Not in any dictatorial way, but by introducing them, piece by piece. We should also show that all things are connected, that crime fiction and romance and spiritual books and science books are not part of different worlds. They're all funhouse mirrors of life, imagined and real and everything in between.

What's next from Fred Strydom?
I've just wrapped up the first draft of a book called 'Foreign Bodies'. I've not spoken to anyone about it, so I will give it to you first [*chuckles*]. I guess it's kind of a metaphysical love story between a female photographer, a male Hindu professor and [*chuckles*] a disembodied consciousness. It's a book about what it means to just be a person. That

sounds really pretentious, every book is about that. But I think I've actively tried to work out whether our total craziness as human beings is something of value. Who are we? Why are we the way we are? And what is it that we find interesting about ourselves and the world, and stuff like that? It is a love story. It's not as thick as *The Raft* and not as thin as *The Inside-Out Man*. It's smack bang in the middle. It's not as wild, not as science-y as *The Raft*, and not as much of a psychological thriller as *The Inside-Out Man*. It's also a book that has been very much inspired by the fact that I have a family of my own now. So, there's a lot about relationships in there. When I say 'love story', it's not a love story necessarily between these main characters, but parent love and general human love, and self-love and all kinds of things. So, yeah, I guess you could say it's a love story.

References

Xenopoulos, Rahla. 2018. *The Season of Glass*. Johannesburg: Penguin Random House.

Some Closing Remarks on World-Literature and the Broadening of 'South Africanness' in (Post)Apartheid Literature beyond 2000

In September 2014, we attended the summer school 'World Literature: Theories, Practice, Pedagogies' at the University of Warwick. Maria Elisa Cevasco's opening keynote address 'World Literature: Can We Not Want It?' initially left us with more questions than answers as to how we could apply the concept of world-literature to the field of South African literary studies. At one point during the four-day summer school, we found ourselves in conversation with Neil Lazarus, expressing our doubts as to the possibilities of world-literature for South African literary studies. The answer we received, a simple question, was to accompany us for the entire duration of the project that was to become this book: 'What makes South African literature South African?' Six years and many deliberations later, we must answer Cevasco's question with a decisive 'No', we cannot *not* want world-literature. Within the broader field of postcolonial studies and, by extension, the South African context, Franco Moretti's and the Warwick Research Collective's (WReC's) (re-) conception of literary studies is particularly productive as it offers a unifying theoretical framework to heed Lazarus' advice.

In summary, the WReC's theorisation of world-literature has three pillars:

- Following and elaborating on Moretti, the WReC firstly conceives of literature as the literature of the capitalist world-system.
- Secondly, they highlight that the capitalist world-system is to be seen as 'one, but unequal'.
- Thirdly, taking Fredric Jameson's theorisation of a singular modernity as a starting point, the WReC seeks a 'reconceptualisa-

tion of the notion of modernity, which involves de-linking it from the idea of the "west" and yoking it to that of the capitalist world-system' (WReC 2015: 15). Modernity, whose origins they see at the beginning of the nineteenth century and whose development is 'combined and uneven' across the world-system, is the onset of the capitalist world-system and, as a consequence, the central subject and form of world-literature.

Based on these presuppositions, the novel is seen as the paradigmatic literary form of modernity and the registration of the socio-economic and socio-cultural developments of the capitalist world-system. The WReC argues: 'The peculiar plasticity and hybridity of the novel form enables it to incorporate not only multiple literary levels, genres and modes, but also other non-literary and archaic cultural forms . . . in order to register a bifurcated or ruptured sensorium of space-time' (2015: 16). Arguably, the city, *the* cultural and economic hub of modernity and its representation in literary texts, then becomes a repository for the WReC's suggestion for analysing the 'combined and uneven development' of the modern capitalist world-system.

Anglophone South African literature may have had its initial focus on the countryside, if one follows the general acceptance of Olive Schreiner's *The Story of an African Farm* (1883) as its founding text (see, for example, Heywood 2004). There is, however, a clear continuity in the city's importance for, and influence on, the country's economic and social development and, as a result, its literary imaginary. Three threshold moments in South Africa's history are enough to illustrate this claim. South Africa's urbanisation saw a sudden surge during the 'mineral revolution' in the late nineteenth century. Before that, none of the country's three major metropolises were of any considerable size. Then, during apartheid, the country's urban influx was heavily controlled. After the end of apartheid, the country saw another wave of urban growth as racial segregation was lifted and the movement from, to as well as within South Africa's cities was no longer restricted. In literature, these developments found expression in the 'Jim Comes to Joburg' trope, the works of the *Drum* writers, the Black Consciousness poetry of the seventies or the literature of the interregnum, for example, which shows that the city has remained a continuing focus throughout (post)apartheid literature.[1] This is why, in our interviews, we focused on authors whose work is set in one of South Africa's three major metropolises, Durban, Cape Town and Johannesburg.

With such a spatial focus as one of the driving criteria, it seemed only logical to us to dedicate two of our core questions to the importance of place in the authors' *oeuvres* and aspects of home, belonging and community. Our interviewees' work – while far from being all-encompassing and selected on the basis of certain criteria (such as the texts' general urban focus, a mix of both established and new voices, and a certain literary merit), but still representative – covers the full range from the micro to the macro level of urban life: from the individual characters' interpersonal relationships and their family life, to their 'place' in the neighbourhood, the city, the country and the world at large. Necessarily, some authors' works are more concerned with local aspects while others started locally and then moved beyond the local.

Lauren Beukes, for example, departed from a South African setting in her later works. While her first two novels, *Moxyland* (2008) and *Zoo City* (2010), are set in Cape Town and Johannesburg respectively, *The Shining Girls* (2013), *Broken Monsters* (2014) and *Afterland* (2020) move to the United States. As she mentions in our interview, the decision to move beyond South Africa, while not a conscious strategic move, had a certain liberating effect on her writing and storytelling as it 'freed' her from the South African context and its 'constraints', enabling her to tell a more universal story. It is evident that despite this move away from local settings, there remains a commonality between Beukes' earlier and later work in terms of themes, such as race, racism, gender inequality and hybrid subjectivities.

Imraan Coovadia, in contrast, moves between all three of South Africa's major metropolises. To our knowledge, he is the only writer to have done so. There are other authors, such as Nthikeng Mohlele, Fred Khumalo and Futhi Ntshingila, who write about two of the three cities we focused on in this book. Coovadia says in our interview that 'each city in South Africa has a very different feeling or has a different

---

1. The (post)apartheid city has been prominently researched in South African scholarship. For examples, see Bickford Smith (2016), Kruger (2013), Nuttall and Mbembe (2008) and Pattman and Khan (2007).

dynamic or demographic, and I think it's quite useful to be able to use them as backdrops in different ways'. He moves beyond South Africa to the United States, Europe and Asia as settings, first in *Green-Eyed Thieves* (2006) and *High Low In-Between* (2009) and then again in *A Spy in Time* (2018). With its central theme of time travelling, Coovadia's latest and most experimental novel, besides its further geographical expansion to Marrakesh and Rio de Janeiro, also breaks away from conventional time constraints. *The Wedding* (2001) and *Tales of the Metric System* (2014), with the former telling the story of two so-called 'passenger' Indians and the latter being a fictionalised record of South Africa's history between 1970 and 2010, move between India and South Africa and within South Africa's three major metropolises respectively, but with a distinct historical emphasis. Considering the fact that his novels seem, to some extent, to have a global outlook, it is surprising that Coovadia says of himself that he feels 'unglobal' and that movement seems to be a mere necessity in order to drive the plot forward and create a more compelling story. Nevertheless, or maybe precisely because of this, Coovadia is probably the most eclectic author in the volume with regard to subject matter and geographical scope. We argue that the concern with shifting South African subjectivities in relation to the world at large is a golden thread throughout all his novels. It would be interesting to consider the intersection of movement, globality and subjectivity, particularly in his later work.[2]

Similar to Coovadia's endeavours in *Tales of the Metric System*, Niq Mhlongo's *Way Back Home* (2013) moves outside South Africa for historical purposes. In his retelling of the relatively marginalised history of the anti-apartheid struggle movement's darker side – of corruption, blackmail and violence – the novel's setting shifts between South Africa, Angola and Tanzania. Despite this geographical 'broadening', the novel's story remains on a decidedly local scale. This is not only because Johannesburg is the book's predominant setting, but also because Angola and Tanzania function more as historical backdrops, which, besides being tied to the setting by historical 'veracity', serve the uncovering of repressed (hi)stories that did not fit the grand narrative of resilience and reconciliation during the Truth and Reconciliation

---

2. Coovadia's earlier work has received some critical attention. See, for example, the 2016 *Current Writing* special issue on Coovadia, edited by Ronit Frenkel.

Commission. In this way, the novel 'powerfully and courageously demythologises the grand narrative of the African National Congress' (ANC's) struggle for liberation' (Demir 2019: 199). Despite the moves across international boundaries, *Way Back Home* is a distinctly South African story. Like much of his other writing, this novel makes constant reference to African cultures, one of Mhlongo's predominant intentions, as he emphasises in our interview. In fact, the juxtaposition of Western medicine and traditional ways of healing is one of the central themes in *Way Back Home*, which can be read as serving the (re-)calibration of South African identity after 1994.

Fred Khumalo's *Dancing the Death Drill* (2017) and Nthikeng Mohlele's *Pleasure* (2016) could be considered in a similar vein, with their shifts between South Africa and France, and South Africa and Germany respectively. In contrast to Mhlongo, however, they cannot be considered counter-narratives. While Khumalo's novel demarginalises a lesser-known part of South African history during the First World War, Mohlele's juxtaposition of apartheid South Africa and Nazi Germany serves as a positioning of the South African subject within world history. In doing so, Mohlele intends 'to illuminate the holocausts that happened on the African continent itself, which are less written about, less articulated, less recorded in terms of proper archives of human tragedy'.

We consider the works of Mariam Akabor, Sifiso Mzobe and Futhi Ntshingila to be on the opposite end of the scale from Coovadia in terms of movement and geographical setting. Their works are firmly based in a local setting. While Mariam Akabor, in *Flat 9* (2006), brings a part of the young(er) Indian South African generation to the fore in her stories set in and around Durban's Grey Street area, Sifiso Mzobe, in *Young Blood* (2010), portrays the township of Umlazi and its youth. Futhi Ntshingila, in *Shameless* (2008), is also invested in telling a particular aspect of the country's history, which begins in KwaZulu-Natal. In retelling the conflict between the Inkatha Freedom Party and the ANC in the late eighties and early nineties, however, *Shameless* moves beyond the local to a (more) national level as the story progresses and the characters move to Johannesburg. This is not to critique the locality of the different stories. They rather highlight the continuous necessity to engage with local stories that, as Ntshingila highlights in our conversation, have yet to be told and grappled with.

Fred Strydom's work is, perhaps, the big exception as it seems to be invested in a distinct de-localisation. In *The Raft* (2015), for example, there are only a handful of place markers that allow the reader to position the story within a general South African setting. Beyond that, the novel becomes a *roman à thèse*, to borrow Margaret Lenta's term (2011), which negotiates human subjectivity and our *raison d'être* after the elimination of two of the basic parameters that constitute who we are: memory and history. In our interview, Strydom reiterates this point when he says that South African authors 'aren't constantly providing a state-of-the-nation approach to everything. We can look further, ask more philosophical questions about life in general.'

Despite this wide array of subject matter and geographical scope, we argue that all the authors interviewed in this volume, and many other South African writers too, share a common ground: they all write about the (semi-)periphery of the world-system. As a reminder, the (semi-)periphery is to be understood in relation to the centre of the modern capitalist world-system. According to the WReC, such an understanding does not juxtapose the (semi-)periphery in opposition to 'Europe' and/or 'the West'. They conceive of (semi-)peripheral literature as a recording of modernity and its chronicling of 'combined and uneven' development, with modernity being defined as singular and globally concurrent. This, the collective argues, should allow us to 'challenge our uncritical habit of conflating epistemological and chronological primacy ("modernity happened in Europe first and best, and then in other places", etc.), and get us into the habit of systemic thinking in terms of non-linear conjunctions' (2015: 15). Such a conceptualisation lends itself to the analysis of the above-sketched aspects of setting and movement from a world-literary perspective, thereby placing (post)apartheid literature beyond 2000 within, and analysing its contribution to, the world-literary system with regards to both theme and form.

Having said this, however, we would like to voice some concerns with regard to the WReC's theorisation of world-literature, which are linked to the possibility of opening up further theoretical avenues, and the use of the collective's approach to world-literature within postcolonial studies. While we agree with the WReC's critique of multiple modernities in favour of a singular and coeval modernity instead, as argued above and in our introduction to this book, we take issue with their suggested solution to 'unthinking' Eurocentrism. Their critique of postcolonial studies bemoans the field's conception of multiple modernities and their necessarily being of Western provenance, two basic premises that they find 'both misguided and unnecessary' (WReC 2015: 14). Here, the WReC bases its argument against such a conception on Harry Harootunian (2000), who states that the cost of capitalism and the world-capitalist system's striving for incessant growth

> ... is the production of permanent unevenness, permanent imbalance between various sectors of the social formations, the process by which some areas must be sacrificed for the development of others, such as the countryside for the city . . . the colony for the metropole, or even one city for another (in WReC 2015: 13).

While there is no denying that this description accounts for capitalism's general functioning, the WReC's 'de-linking' of modernity from the West in order to overcome the debate surrounding the 'unthinking' of Eurocentrism is problematic. From a postcolonial point of view, the WReC seems to disregard the fact that their very definition of the modern capitalist world-system, which takes the beginning of the nineteenth century as the starting point, nevertheless inherently puts Europe/the West at the centre of their dialectics of centre and (semi-)periphery. Suffice it to say that at the beginning of the nineteenth century, Europe/the West was at the height of its imperial/colonial power and this power resulted from the continuous exploitation of Europe's/the West's (semi-)peripheries. Imperialism and colonialism were essentially Eurocentric. As a consequence, the WReC's suggestion of putting capitalism at the core of any thinking in connection to world-literature in order to 'de-link' modernity from Europe/the West falls short as it is, in fact, an act of de-historisation. Their suggestion, in our opinion, does not solve the debate of 'unthinking' Eurocentrism that the WReC takes issue with in the first place, and the 'de-linking' of modernity from the West from a postcolonial perspective is not as self-evident as the WReC would have us believe. The WReC's terminology of the world-system and world-literature as consisting of various 'centres' and '(semi-)peripheries' is thus not without its pitfalls as their dialectics reiterates former colonies as (semi-)peripheries within the world-system. The fact that South Africa can be seen as a world-literary centre of the African continent with its own (semi-)peripheries does not eradicate its colonial past. While we do not yet have a comprehensive solution to the issues sketched here, we believe that further expansion of the WReC's conceptualisation of world-literature is needed, particularly with an emphasis on the role of historical contextualisation. In our opinion, to superordinate capitalism as the 'grand narrative' of world history seems to us to want to 'undo' more local historical facets. However, just as the modern capitalist world-system has its (hi)story, so do any (sub-)territories that are analysed from a world-literary perspective.

Furthermore, the WReC mainly draws on Western theories (Franco Moretti, Leon Trotsky, Immanuel Wallerstein and Fredric Jameson, to name but a few) to develop their conceptualisation of world-literature. While we do not question these theoreticians' importance and usefulness for the WReC's argument – after all, we ourselves draw from the same theoretical pool – we see an opportunity to expand and enhance the WReC's conceptualisation within postcolonial studies by incorporating theoretical works from the postcolonial (semi-)periphery. The works of authors such as Achille Mbembe's *On the Postcolony* (2001) and *Critique of Black Reason* (2017), Derek Hook's *(Post)Apartheid Conditions* (2013) and Paul Gilroy's *Postcolonial Melancholia* (2005) come to mind here. All three authors' works would provide valuable insights into aspect of temporality, belatedness and trauma with regard to postcolonial subjectivities and their contribution to, and positioning within, the (literary) world-system.

Returning to our remaining three set questions, we want to use our overview of the authors' answers to these questions to offer further possibilities for research. Asking the authors to comment on possible taboos that have yet to be tackled within literature, as well as emerging voices and genres within the field of (post)apartheid literature beyond 2000, has helped us to sharpen our perception as to further possible fields of study. In line with the WReC, these questions thereby consciously work at the intersection of theme and form and might thus lend themselves to an analysis from a world-literary perspective. Almost all of the authors interviewed in this volume are of the impression that there is no topic that they (still) feel uncomfortable to write about. Through the conversations, however, the authors identify and agree on a number of under-represented topics within (post)apartheid literature beyond 2000. These are queer/transgender subjectivities, a more rigorous tackling of race and racism and a more nuanced representation of gender and gender issues. How important these themes continue to be can be seen when one thinks of Fallism, where precisely these issues were contested and debated from many angles.[3] Interestingly, several authors identified the generation of the Fallists as some of the exciting new voices to appear on the country's literary landscape. This is particularly true if one considers that the Fallists, so far at least, have mainly been working within non-fiction, short fiction and poetry. These voices seem yet to find their way into the field of literary prose. This is also largely the case with the group of young writers that most of our interviewees refer to as the 'born-free generation'. There have been some exciting non-fiction publications, such as Clinton Chauke's *Born in Chains: The Diary of an Angry 'Born-Free'* (2018) and Malaika Wa Azania's *Memoirs of a Born Free: Reflections on the Rainbow Nation* (2014). These two books' titles already show how contested the term 'born free' is. Wa Azania pointedly states:

> I too belong to the category of 'born frees', a problematic definition architected by those who want to keep our people blinded about the real face of the effects of colonialism and apartheid.
>
> Many would have us believe that what transpired in 1994 was a revolution, but this is far from the truth. For a revolution to have occurred, the system would have to have been completely annihilated. The economics and politics of the revolutionised society would have to be an antithesis to the ones that defined the previous regime. But such did not happen in South Africa, where the same system that has given oxygen to the apartheid government continuous to be in existence, to define the face of the republic. That system is capitalism, a brutal system that can only survive through the exploitation of the majority by the elite minority who owns the means of production, primarily, land . . . In South Africa, it is also a system that is anti-black, because while the political breakthrough of 1994 deracialised governance, privilege and poverty continue to have a race: the former is white while the latter is black (2014: 4–5).

3. See, for example, Booysen (2016), Ngcaweni and Ngcaweni (2018), Nyamnjoh (2016), Chantikule, Kwoba and Nkopo (2018) and Chikane (2018).

Like Wa Azania, many authors of the younger generation who write fiction, such as Sindiswa Busuku (2016),[4] Unathi Slasha (2018) and Chwayita Ngamlana (2017), do not necessarily fit the 'born-free' definition, nor, to our knowledge, do they identify with it.

In answer to the question of new genres becoming more prominent within the field of (post)apartheid literature, our interviewees almost unanimously pointed to speculative fiction and crime fiction. The latter has undoubtedly been a booming genre and has become South Africa's biggest 'literary export' – with Margie Orford, Mike Nichol and Deon Meyer's thrillers being published and read across the globe – and would deserve a volume of interviews on its own. The circle of successful authors within the field is constantly growing. Here, names such as Angela Makholwa, H.J. Golakai, Jassy Mackenzie, Charlotte Otter and Andrew Brown come to mind. With regard to speculative fiction, further studies could expand on how black, Indian and Coloured writers take the genre into a new direction. Here, the works of Mohale Mashigo, Fred Strydom, Imraan Coovadia and Masande Ntshanga within the genre offer a starting point. Nthikeng Mohlele also sees the need for more historical fiction, a view Fred Khumalo would probably not disagree with. In May 2018, Khumalo published an article on the return of historical fiction to the (post)apartheid literary scene beyond 2000.[5] In his article, Khumalo mentioned Claire Robertson's *The Spiral House* (2013), Zakes Mda's *Little Suns* (2015) and his own novel, *Dancing the Death Drill* (2017). With the benefit of hindsight, we would add Mphuthumi Ntabeni's *The Broken River Tent* (2018), which won the 2019 University of Johannesburg Literary Prize in the debut category.

We have, of course, barely scratched the surface of what proves to be an enormously thriving and vast literary scene that deserves further critical engagement, both within South Africa and beyond. Staying with the theme of genres, it remains to say that both poetry and drama, which are not represented in this book, would be fruitful fields to be looked at from a world-literary perspective. With this volume of

---

4. Sindiswa Busuku's *Loud and Yellow Laughter* won the 2018 Ingrid Jonker Prize.
5. See https://johannesburgreviewofbooks.com/2018/05/07/historical-fiction-is-back-with-a-fire-in-its-belly-fred-khumalo-reflects-on-how-writing-can-be-a-powerful-tool-for-an-activist/ (accessed 15 May 2020).

interviews, we hope to make a contribution to the ongoing discussion of (post)apartheid literature beyond 2000, the world-literary debate as well as the intersection of world-literature and postcolonial studies.

References

Akabor, Mariam. 2006. *Flat 9*. Durban: umSinsi Press.

Beukes, Lauren. 2008. *Moxyland*. Johannesburg: Jacana Media.

———. 2010. *Zoo City*. Johannesburg: Jacana Media.

———. 2013. *The Shining Girls*. Cape Town: Umuzi.

———. 2014. *Broken Monsters*. Cape Town: Umuzi.

———. 2020. *Afterland*. Cape Town: Umuzi.

Bickford-Smith, Vivian. 2016. *The Emergence of the South African Metropolis: Cities and Identities in the Twentieth Century*. Cambridge: Cambridge University Press.

Booysen, Susan (ed.). 2016. *Fees Must Fall: Student Revolt, Decolonisation and Governance in South Africa*. Johannesburg: Wits University Press.

Busuku, Sindiswa. 2016. *Loud and Yellow Laughter*. Johannesburg: Botsotso.

Chantikule, Roseanne, Brian Kwoba and Athinangamaso Nkopo (eds). 2018. *Rhodes Must Fall: The Struggle to Decolonise the Racist Heart of Empire*. London: Zed Books.

Chauke, Clinton. 2018. *Born in Chains: The Diary of an Angry 'Born-Free'*. Cape Town: Jonathan Ball.

Chikane, Rekgotsofetse. 2018. *Breaking a Rainbow, Building a Nation: The Politics behind #MustFall Movements*. Johannesburg: Picador.

Coovadia, Imraan. 2001. *The Wedding*. Johannesburg: Picador.

———. 2006. *Green-Eyed Thieves*. Cape Town: Umuzi.

———. 2009. *High Low In-Between*. Cape Town: Umuzi.

———. 2014. *Tales of the Metric System*. Cape Town: Umuzi.

———. 2018. *A Spy in Time*. Cape Town: Umuzi.

Demir, Danyela. 2019. *Reading Loss: Post-Apartheid Melancholia in Contemporary South African Novels*. Berlin: Logos Verlag.

Frenkel, Ronit (ed.). 2016. 'Special Issue: Imraan Coovadia'. *Current Writing: Text and Reception in Southern Africa* 28(1): 1–105.

Gilroy, Paul. 2005. *Postcolonial Melancholia*. New York: Columbia University Press.

Harootunian, Harry. 2000. *Overcome by Modernity: History, Culture, and Community in Interwar Japan*. Princeton, NJ: Princeton University Press.

Heywood, Christopher. 2004. *A History of South African Literature*. Cambridge: Cambridge University Press.

Hook, Derek. 2013. *(Post)Apartheid Conditions: Psychoanalysis and Social Formation*. London: Palgrave Macmillan.

Khumalo, Fred. 2017. *Dancing the Death Drill*. Cape Town: Umuzi.

Kruger, Loren. 2013. *Imagining the Edgy City: Writing, Performing, and Building Johannesburg*. Oxford: Oxford University Press.

Lenta, Margaret. 2011. 'Expanding "South Africanness": Debut Novels', in *SA Lit: Beyond 2000*, edited by Michael Chapman and Margaret Lenta, 50–68. Pietermaritzburg: University of KwaZulu-Natal Press.

Mbembe, Achille. 2001. *On the Postcolony*. Oakland, CA: University of California Press.

———. 2017. *Critique of Black Reason*. Durham, NC: Duke University Press.

Mda, Zakes. 2015. *Little Suns*. Cape Town: Umuzi.

Mhlongo, Niq. 2013. *Way Back Home*. Cape Town: Kwela Books.

Mohlele, Nthikeng. 2016. *Pleasure*. Johannesburg: Pan Macmillan.

Mzobe, Sifiso. 2010. *Young Blood*. Cape Town: Kwela Books.

Ngamlana, Chwayita. 2017. *If I Stay Right Here*. Johannesburg: Blackbird Books.

Ngcaweni, Wandile and Busani Ngcaweni (eds). 2018. *We Are No Longer at Ease: The Struggle for #FeesMustFall*. Johannesburg: Jacana Media.

Ntabeni, Mphuthumi. 2018. *The Broken River Tent*. Johannesburg: Blackbird Books.

Ntshingila, Futhi. 2008. *Shameless*. Pietermaritzburg: University of KwaZulu-Natal Press.

Nuttall, Sarah and Achille Mbembe (eds). 2008. *Johannesburg: The Elusive Metropolis*. Durham, NC: Duke University Press.

Nyamnjoh, Francis B. 2016. *#RhodesMustFall: Nibbling at Resilient Colonialism in South Africa*. Oxford: African Books Collective.

Pattman, Rob and Sultan Kahn (eds). 2007. *Undressing Durban*. Durban: Madiba Publishers.

Robertson, Claire. 2013. *The Spiral House*. Cape Town: Umuzi.

Schreiner, Olive. 1883. *The Story of an African Farm*. London: Chapman & Hall.

Slasha, Unathi. 2018. *Jah Hills*. Grahamstown: Black Ghost Books.

Strydom, Fred. 2015. *The Raft*. Cape Town: Umuzi.

Wa Azania, Malaika. 2014. *Memoirs of a Born Free: Reflections on the Rainbow Nation*. Johannesburg: Jacana Media.

WReC (Warwick Research Collective). 2015. *Combined and Uneven Development: Towards a New Theory of World Literature*. Liverpool: Liverpool University Press.

Index

For Product Safety Concerns and Information please contact our EU
representative GPSR@taylorandfrancis.com
Taylor & Francis Verlag GmbH, Kaufingerstraße 24, 80331 München, Germany

www.ingramcontent.com/pod-product-compliance
Lightning Source LLC
Chambersburg PA
CBHW071559110726
47908CB00007B/2161